HANSEN'S
Field Guide to the

BIRDS

OF THE

SIERRA
NEVADA

Keith Hansen

Praise for *Hansen's Field Guide to the Birds of the Sierra Nevada*

"I'm thrilled to see this comprehensive guide from Keith Hansen. Based on a lifetime of careful and thoughtful observation, Keith brings his meticulous clarity and engaging flair to illustrations and text alike. His love of birds shines through on every page as he celebrates the distinctive personality of each species. This is not just a guide to identifying birds, but a guide to *knowing* birds, and with Keith as narrator you can be sure it's both illuminating and entertaining."

—DAVID ALLEN SIBLEY, author of *What It's Like to Be a Bird*

"This isn't a book, it's an experience—a joyful encounter with the treasures of the Sierra Nevada. Through the art and words of the inimitable Keith Hansen, the birds come alive, in all their unique character, on every page. Perusing this work is almost as good as going birding with Keith, and that's saying a lot."

—**KENN KAUFMAN**, author of *Kaufman Field Guide to Birds of North America*

"This is the Sierra field guide I have been waiting for. It is unsurpassed for identification but goes far beyond that. Keith Hansen is my bird illustration mentor. His birds are not only accurate, but alive. The drawings capture the beauty, comic nature, and majesty of birds. The text is carefully refined to highlight need-to-know information that is succinct and rich. You will learn not just how to identify the birds, but how to look with a joyful attention that will open new doors to wonder and nature connection."

—**JOHN MUIR LAWS**, author of *The Laws Field Guide to the Sierra Nevada*

"The term 'a lifetime's work' is often overused, but it applies truly to this book. As a boy Keith started roaming the Sierra Nevada, and this book blesses us with his lifetime of insights, visual and verbal. To paraphrase from his own work, 'If a regular field guide is a utility vehicle, this book is a Ferrari,' and it will speed you on your way to appreciating and truly knowing the birds of the Sierra."

—**STEVE N. G. HOWELL**, senior leader of WINGS Birding Tours

"This is no ordinary field guide. It is, rather, a sumptuous reflection of birds, delivered with both the artist's skillful brush and the writer's imaginative pen. Neither feather nor word is out of place. Keith's exuberance, wealth of field experience, and perfectionism, as displayed in an efficiently pleasing layout, will inspire users not only to correctly identify birds but to fully appreciate their place in the world, while the majestic Sierra Nevada bioregion provides the perfect canvas to showcase his scientific precision and artistic talent. If you really want to comprehend birds, get this book!"

—**PETER PYLE**, author of *Identification Guide to North American Birds*

"If you aspire to cultivate a deep love for birds, you have a soulmate in Keith Hansen and a roadmap in *Hansen's Field Guide to the Birds of the Sierra Nevada*. Long appreciated as a talented bird artist, Keith now takes his place among such interpreters of Sierra bird life as Tracy Storer and David Gaines."

—**DAVID DESANTE**, founder of the Institute for Bird Populations

HANSEN'S
Field Guide to the

BIRDS

OF THE

SIERRA
NEVADA

Keith Hansen
Edward C. Beedy
Adam Donkin

Heyday, Berkeley, California
Sierra College Press, Rocklin, California

Library of Congress Cataloging-in-Publication Data

Names: Hansen, Keith, 1958- author. | Beedy, Edward C., author. | Donkin, Adam, 1974- author.
Title: Hansen's field guide to the birds of the Sierra Nevada / Keith Hansen, Edward C. Beedy, and Adam Donkin.
Other titles: Field guide to the birds of the Sierra Nevada
Description: Berkeley, California : Heyday ; Rocklin, California : Sierra College Press, [2021] | Includes bibliographical references and index.
Identifiers: LCCN 2020052712 (print) | LCCN 2020052713 (ebook) | ISBN 9781597145336 (paperback) | ISBN 9781597145343 (epub)
Subjects: LCSH: Birds--Sierra Nevada (Calif. and Nev.)--Identification.
Classification: LCC QL683.S54 H36 2021 (print) | LCC QL683.S54 (ebook) |
  DDC 598.09794/4--dc23
LC record available at https://lccn.loc.gov/2020052712
LC ebook record available at https://lccn.loc.gov/2020052713

Cover Art: Keith Hansen
Cover Design: Ashley Ingram
Interior Design/Typesetting: Adam Donkin with Ashley Ingram

Published by Heyday in conjunction with Sierra College Press
P.O. Box 9145, Berkeley, California 94709
(510) 549-3564
heydaybooks.com

Printed in East Peoria, Illinois, by Versa Press, Inc.

10 9 8 7 6 5 4 3 2

For her companionship, creativity, insight, and love,
I dedicate this book to my wife, Patricia.

—KH

CONTENTS

WATERBIRDS

SWIMMING WATERBIRDS

FLYING WATERBIRDS

WALKING WATERBIRDS

LANDBIRDS

UPLAND GAMEBIRDS

RAPTORS

OTHER LARGER LANDBIRDS

ACKNOWLEDGMENTS

For me, this book seems a natural outcome of a life of adventuresome travel on one of Earth's great mountain ranges. It's the accumulation of wonderful experiences, careful observations, and profound encounters coupled with treasured relationships. Where does one begin when thanking the individuals who have influenced a twenty-year creation? I would think at the top.

I first met Ted Beedy in 1982 when I illustrated a book he and Steve Granholm wrote, *Discovering Sierra Birds*, for the (then) Yosemite Natural History Association. I was thrilled to illustrate another book, *Birds of the Sierra Nevada: Their Natural History, Status, and Distribution* by Ted Beedy and Ed Pandolfino, published by University of California Press in 2013. The idea of a newer, more complete field guide loomed on my horizon. I wanted to paint and describe every bird species known to occur regularly in the Sierra. I knew I needed the experience and expertise of veteran Sierra birder Ted Beedy. I also needed the designer, Adam Donkin, who knew and shared my passion for the elegance and natural beauty that birds provide us all. We then joined forces with Joe Medeiros of Sierra College Press and Steve Wasserman and Gayle Wattawa of Heyday in Berkeley. Our team was assembled, and off we went—painting, writing, editing, whittling, arguing, and agreeing.

Ted's assistance was instrumental. He thoroughly reviewed the manuscript, and his eagle-eye editing freed me to focus on the paintings and the species accounts. He tackled all status and distribution components for each species and contributed the technical components of our introduction.

An astute naturalist and joy to bird with, Adam Donkin is the foundational designer of this book. He crafted the plate and art layout, creating its look and feel. Figuratively the "bass player" of this band, Adam's steady beat kept me always moving forward. He is a computer whisperer and design virtuoso, and his gifted eye for the principles of arrangement and aesthetics, along with boundless patience for the innumerable tweaks and adjustments, allowed my images to naturally express themselves.

This book has come to fruition because of the steadfast support over the years from our partners. I offer my sincerest gratitude for the patience and encouragement provided us by my wife, Patricia, and by Susan Sanders and Devon Donkin. To all three of you, a personal debt of gratitude.

For his initial vision of creating a comprehensive, entirely new field guide to the birds of the Sierra and his keen ability to get "gears turning," I thank the late Steve Medley of the (then) Yosemite Association.

Although there are many people and supporting organizations to thank, special mention must go to Cole Wilbur and Mark Valentine of the David & Lucille Packard Foundation for a grant funding the creation of the art. This book has been made entirely possible by Heyday and Sierra College Press. With unfailing support for a bird artist with a vision, they generously combined the necessary time needed for the creative process with imagination, trust, and friendship.

There have been many who have given generously of their time, reviewing and commenting on my work. I especially thank my compadre Steve Howell for his careful review of this book's art, layout, and text. He has been generous with sharing his insight, refreshing candor, and notoriously dark chocolate. For his crucial help with editing, book formulation, and guiding me through the labyrinth of this book's production with calm and humor, I thank Joe Medeiros. My thanks go to David Sibley, an inspiration to me and so many bird lovers, for reviewing portions of my art and for turning me on to the all-important color, neutral tint. I thank Peter Pyle, my fellow globe-trotting, Farallon Islands buddy, for always being willing to offer identification tips and for bouncing ideas off each other. For generously sharing a lifetime of pearls regarding birds of the Sierra, I thank two mentors, Dave DeSante and the late Rich Stallcup. A big thanks to bird gurus John Sterling, Scott Terrill, and Ed Pandolfino for reviewing the species list. In addition to offering a wealth of helpful edits, Ted Beedy has helped me navigate this new world of book writing, something for which he should receive the coveted Medal of Valor.

The following organizations have helped in fundamental ways during the creation of this book. I thank the fine folks at Electric Works for their professional scanning of my bird art. To Kelly and

Bartshe Miller, the Mono Lake Committee, numerous friends with the Point Reyes Bird Observatory, as well as David and Sue Yee with the Central Valley Bird Club, I thank you all.

Whether they know it or not, these friends have helped me in supportive and immeasurable ways. They include Josiah Clark, Jon Dunn, Todd Easterla, Burr Heneman, Jack Laws, Dorene and Bob Schiro, Greg Smith, Janet Visick, and Nils and Sarah Warnock. To my family in Yucatan, the Briceños, and to the Villacis here in California, muchas gracias por su apoyo!

For the beautiful studio in which I work, I extend a very special thanks to the late Ewan Macdonald and the amazing staff at the Bolinas Museum. For a safe harbor and the best damned yard for birds, I thank Ann Mitchell, Walker, Rosalie, and the late Hughes Ryan for years of friendship and unfailing support. To the colorful townsfolk of Bolinas, I love and thank you all.

For help and guidance with all things art, I thank my first and greatest art teachers, my mother, Janice, and my ridiculously creative brother Doug. For teaching me about flight and almost everything I know about birds (the metal kinds), my naval aviator father, Bob. To my brother Rob, who showed me my first Cedar Waxwing and started me on this path: I take off my binoculars to you, bro. To a true force of nature, my loving sister, Jennifer, thank you for your wonderful way. To my brother Brad, your gentle spirit, creative mastery through film, and pun-manship inspire, and to my youngest brother, Craig, your creative brilliance and visionary gift throws light farther than you know.

Finally, from my formative years growing up near the base of the Sierra Nevada, my old Fresno buddies and partners in crime, Russell Kokx, Bruce Williford, Kirk Hopkin, and John Silvas.

After twenty-plus years of work on this book, I am finishing it during the early phase of the COVID-19 pandemic. Reflecting deeply on the events of the world, as I shelter in place, my mind and love are with all the people who have been affected.

—Keith Hansen
Bolinas, California

INTRODUCTION

Our goal in creating *Hansen's Field Guide to the Birds of the Sierra Nevada* is to produce an authoritative, comprehensive, and richly illustrated field guide focused on identification of bird species that are known to occur in California's Sierra Nevada region. Although the regional focus of this book is the Sierra Nevada, it also includes most of the species encountered regularly in adjacent regions, including the Central Valley, Cascade Range, Great Basin, and Mojave Desert; it should therefore be a useful reference for birders in those regions as well.

This new book is intended to serve as a companion guide to *Birds of the Sierra Nevada: Their Natural History, Status, and Distribution* by Edward C. (Ted) Beedy and Edward R. Pandolfino and illustrated by Keith Hansen (2013). This reference book provides details on natural history, status, distribution, origins of names, and conservation status of 276 bird species that occur regularly in the Sierra region, as well as brief descriptions of the status and distribution of 166 rare, casual, and accidental species. Although not intended as a field guide, it provided critical information about Sierra birds with an illustration or two of each species.

Hansen's Field Guide to the Birds of the Sierra Nevada is intended to function as a fully illustrated identification manual. Here, each species is portrayed with additional illustrations, indicating important identifying characteristics. This field guide includes full identification accounts and illustrations of 275 regularly occurring species and brief accounts of 52 rare species, for a total of 327 species. We hope that this book will appeal to nearly everyone who found the natural history book useful and to those who desire a guide to help them identify birds accurately in the field. Along with text descriptions, this guide offers accurate images of Sierra Nevada birds in a variety of postures and plumages, both perched and in flight.

The next sections here briefly describe the geographical boundaries, ecological zones, and bird habitats that were defined in the previous book. We include the nomenclature and taxonomy, species abundance categories, seasons of occurrence, other terminology that appears in the species accounts, and bird topography illustrations pointing out feather groups and body parts of a bird, both standing and in flight.

Geographical Boundaries

There are no universally accepted boundaries for the Sierra Nevada region. Using the same geographical borders that we defined in the previous natural history book, we delineate the Sierra Nevada as extending from Highway 36 near Lake Almanor and Honey Lake in the north, to Highway 58 in Kern County in the south. The western border follows the 500-foot elevation contour except for a small portion south of Porterville, where it follows US Forest Service ecological zone boundaries, rising to approximately 1,200 feet at Highway 58. The eastern border is roughly defined by Highways 395 and 14. It includes large lakes, reservoirs, and wetlands adjacent to the region, such as Mono, Topaz, and Honey Lakes; Bridgeport Reservoir; the Carson Valley; and the Owens Valley floor. We define the West Slope as the region west of the Sierra crest and the East Slope as the region east of the crest (figure 1).

Ecological Zones and Bird Habitats

Unequaled in mountain ranges in the lower forty-eight contiguous states, the Sierra Nevada has an elevation gradient spanning almost 14,000 feet. The relatively gradual inclines of the West Slope of the Sierra Nevada change abruptly as the East Slope drops off sharply into the Great Basin. The West Slope of this region offers an extraordinary variety of bird habitats, from the rolling foothill grasslands; through oak-studded savannas and giant conifer forests; up to alpine meadows and chilly, windswept peaks. Lakes, pine forests, pinyon-juniper woodlands, and sagebrush flats dominate the landscapes of the East Slope, as do arid Great Basin scrub and the Joshua tree woodlands of the southeastern desert regions.

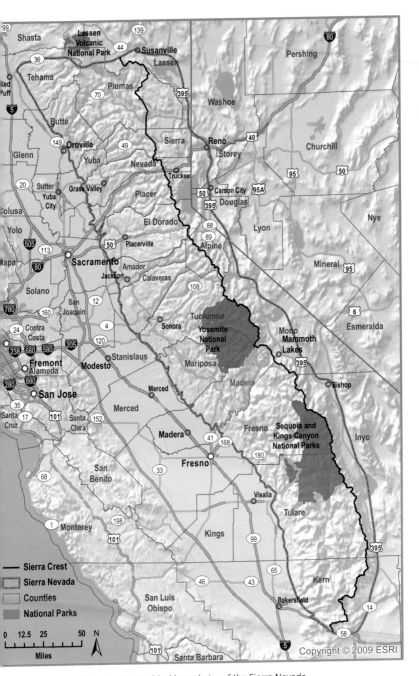

Figure 1. Geographical boundaries of the Sierra Nevada

ECOLOGICAL ZONES

In *Birds of the Sierra Nevada*, we recognized seven major ecological zones that constitute the Sierra Nevada region (table 1, figure 2): Foothill, Lower Conifer, Upper Conifer, Subalpine, Alpine, East (Side) Slope, and Desert. Note that the elevation ranges are approximate and overlap considerably. Local differences in facing slope (aspect), soils, rainfall, and other physical factors alter the exact range of any ecological zone. For more details on each ecological zone and the bird species that occur there, please refer to our previous book.

TABLE 1. APPROXIMATE ELEVATIONS AND TOTAL AREA OF SIERRA NEVADA ECOLOGICAL ZONES

Ecological Zone	Northern Sierra	Southern Sierra	Area (square miles)
Foothill[1]	<500–4,500	<500–5,500	8,337
Lower Conifer[1]	2,000–6,500	2,500–7,000	7,994
Upper Conifer[1]	4,500–8,500	5,000–9,500	1,706
Subalpine[2]	7,500–10,000	8,000–11,500	1,580
Alpine[2]	8,500–10,800	9,500–14,500	2,224
East Slope[3]	3,500–8,500	3,000–9,000	4,397
Desert[2]	–	2,000–7,000	1,515
Total Area			**27,753**

[1] West Slope only
[2] Both slopes
[3] East Slope only

FOOTHILL ZONE includes a diversity of oak and chaparral habitats below the higher conifer-dominated zones. Annual grasslands (less than 10% tree cover) are generally situated in gently rolling terrain, vivid green in late fall through early spring and parched to a golden brown in summer. Oak savannas (10% to 30% tree cover) are a mix of annual grasses and blue oak. Oak woodlands (>30% tree cover) include denser groves dominated by blue and interior live oaks, but can also include valley oak, California black oak, and canyon live oak and foothill pine. Foothill chaparral generally occupies the steeper, more arid exposures dominated by chamise, whiteleaf manzanita, buckbrush, coffeeberry, and shrubby oaks.

LOWER CONIFER ZONE appears in cooler and moister terrain above the Foothill Zone. It includes vast conifer forests dominated by ponderosa pine, sugar pine, incense cedar, Douglas fir, and white fir. Hardwoods such as California black oak, Pacific madrone, and bigleaf maple often intermingle with pines and other conifers. In areas where fire has been prevented for many years, shade-tolerant white fir and incense cedar often outnumber the pines and oaks. This is the largest and most fire-prone ecological zone in the Sierra Nevada region, especially after recent droughts, which left millions of dead conifers that often cover entire hillsides. (Beetles and other insects attack and kill drought-stricken trees.)

UPPER CONIFER ZONE includes mixtures dominated by four or five species of conifers; the most typical species are the Jeffrey pine, incense cedar, Douglas fir, sugar pine, white fir, and some red fir. Black oak reaches this high, but are fewer than farther down. Where the soil is rocky or wet, especially near meadows, lodgepole pine may grow in scattered stands. Giant sequoias, the world's largest known living things, occur naturally only in the western Sierra Nevada, primarily in this zone. Mountain chaparral composed of huckleberry oak, greenleaf manzanita, snowbrush, or chinquapin occupies steep, rocky slopes or forest clearings.

SUBALPINE ZONE is a mix of granite domes, mountain lakes, and meadows intermixed with stands of lodgepole pine, mountain hemlock on north-facing slopes, and occasional western juniper in steep, rocky areas. Whitebark pine grows at the highest elevations on exposed ridges and north-facing slopes up to the tree line. In the southern Sierra, stands of foxtail and limber pine largely replace the whitebarks. At higher elevations, these subalpine tree species are often

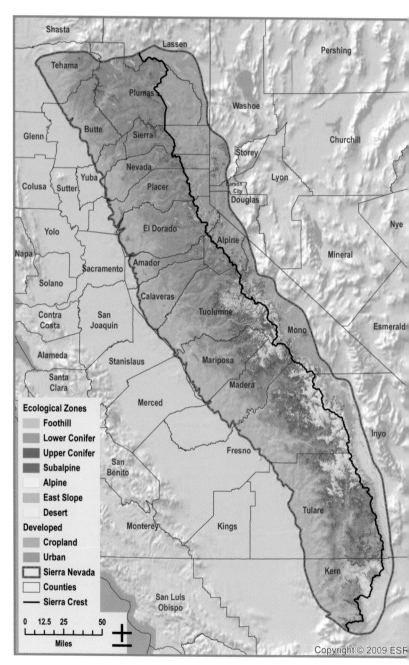

Ecological Zones

- Foothill
- Lower Conifer
- Upper Conifer
- Subalpine
- Alpine
- East Slope
- Desert

Developed

- Cropland
- Urban
- Sierra Nevada
- Counties
- — Sierra Crest

0   12.5   25   50
Miles

Copyright © 2009 ESF

Figure 2. Ecological zones of the Sierra Nevada

much reduced in stature and often *krummholtz* (twisted, gnarled). This zone receives the highest snowfall in the Sierra Nevada region and has a correspondingly short growing season.

ALPINE ZONE is "the land above the trees." Trees cannot exist in this zone due to the extreme climate; shallow, rocky soils; prolonged snow cover; and short growing season. Here, freezing temperatures are possible any day of the year, and herbaceous plants dominate Alpine fell-fields along with stunted willows and other dwarf shrubs. This zone exists northward to Sierra County, but it is far more extensive in the central and southern Sierra Nevada, where rugged cliffs, glacial cirques, rock gardens, and lush flower patches abound.

EAST SLOPE ZONE is in the rain shadow of the Sierra Nevada, and pine and juniper forests here are generally more open and have smaller trees than the similar forests of the West Slope. North of the Mono Basin, forests are dominated by Jeffrey pine, but ponderosa pine is sometimes found as scattered individuals or isolated pockets within larger Jeffrey pine stands, from Tahoe Basin north. Open areas have a diversity of Great Basin shrubs including big sagebrush, bitterbrush, curl-leaf mountain mahogany, and rabbitbrush, along with numerous arid-tolerant grasses and herbs.

DESERT ZONE represents the northern extension of the Mojave Desert and is found only in the extreme southeastern portion of the Sierra Nevada. Joshua trees grow in widely scattered stands interspersed with a variety of evergreen and deciduous shrubs occasionally mixed with single-leaf pinyon pine, Utah juniper, or Mojave yucca. In the eastern Sierra, desert scrub habitats are usually dominated by creosote bushes surrounded by other desert plants such as catclaw acacia, desert agave, burrowbrush, rabbitbrush, teddybear cholla, or beavertail cactus (prickly pear).

SPECIAL HABITATS

The habitats described here are of limited extent in the Sierra Nevada, but provide key resources for birds. Because of their importance and because each occurs across a wide range of ecological zones, they are described separately here.

RIPARIAN FORESTS in the Foothill Zone contain only small fragments of the jungles of sycamores, cottonwoods, and willows that once flourished along rivers of the Sierra foothills. Most were cleared long ago for lumber, firewood, and agriculture, or were inundated by large reservoirs. By far the largest and most impressive remaining lowland riparian forest in the Sierra is along the South Fork Kern River, upstream from Lake Isabella. In the Lower and Upper Conifer Zones, riparian forests are mostly limited to narrow, discontinuous corridors of dogwood, black cottonwood, and aspen, or, more typically, tall willows or alders. In the Subalpine Zone, shrubby willows and alders form a narrow and patchy border along most streams. Aspen commonly form large broadleaved woodlands in the high mountain regions and dominate riparian areas along the entire East Slope, where they are joined by cottonwoods and willows.

MOUNTAIN MEADOWS usually begin as shallow lakes that are gradually filled with sediment from the surrounding uplands and may someday become forests. Grasses, sedges, and rushes share the moist central portions with wild onions, corn lilies, shooting stars, and countless other wildflowers, while young trees attempt to colonize the drier margins. These meadows are most numerous and extensive in the glaciated terrain of the Subalpine Zone, but are also scattered throughout the Lower and Upper Conifer Zones of the Sierra.

FRESHWATER MARSHES are distinguished from deep-water aquatic habitats and wet meadows by the presence of distinctive emergent plants. Rushes, sedges, or other erect, grass-like plants such as tules and cattails are rooted in marsh soils that are permanently or seasonally inundated. Marshes can occur in basins or depressions at all elevations, aspects, and exposures. They are common on level to gently rolling topography below 4,000 feet, but can be found intermittently upward to and even above 8,000 feet in the central to southern Sierra.

RESERVOIRS, LAKES, AND PONDS occur throughout the Sierra Nevada from the low foothills to the Alpine Zone and Great Basin. A great many Sierra "lakes" are actually artificial reservoirs resulting from dams that were created for water supply, fish habitat, or hydroelectric power generation. Most Sierra rivers flow through steep-sided canyons that leave little sediment. Consequently, extensive mudflats are scarce, but they do occur around reservoirs, lakes, and ponds with gentle slopes. Clear natural lakes abound in the Alpine and Subalpine Zones, but offer little food for birds.

ROCKS AND CLIFFS in the northern Sierra Nevada primarily have volcanic origins, while those in the central and southern Sierra have a different geologic history and offer vast expanses of glacier-polished granitic cliffs, domes, and scattered boulders as habitat for birds.

FORAGE CROPS, IRRIGATED PASTURES, AND CROPLANDS nearly always consist of a single species that may be annual or perennial. Most forage crops are planted in the spring and harvested in summer or fall. For the most part, forage crops and irrigated pastures are planted in fertile soils in alluvial valley bottoms or gently rolling terrain in the lower elevations of the Sierra. Along the eastern slope, agriculture is common and varied. Expansive hay and alfalfa fields abound.

ORCHARDS AND VINEYARDS are uniform and relatively barren of breeding birds. In some parts of the Foothill Zone, large-scale conversion of annual grasslands, oak savannas, and oak woodlands to orchards and vineyards has resulted in direct losses of bird habitat.

URBAN AND SUBURBAN habitats offer a patchy mosaic of ornamental plantings, vacant lots, and remnant naturalized habitats that occur between structures. Ornamental plantings in older neighborhoods are often mature, introduced evergreen and winter-deciduous trees that may be as much as a hundred years old. Residential gardens and mature hedges are also characteristic and include many introduced fruiting species that attract a variety of birds.

Organization of This Book

NOMENCLATURE, TAXONOMY, AND SUBSPECIES

Most field guides are arranged to follow some version of the American Ornithological Society's *AOS Checklist of North American Birds*. This taxonomic order is intended to reflect what is known about the evolutionary relationships of birds, based on the most current taxonomic and genetic studies. The intent of this book is to help people identify birds accurately in the field, and not necessarily to address what is currently known about their evolutionary and taxonomic relationships—often based on detailed studies of birds' mitochondrial DNA, which is a tough field mark for most birders! Changing the arrangement of bird species or families is not helpful for most birders when their goal is to locate the bird they are looking at.

We follow the *AOS Checklist* for all common and scientific names and subspecies, where appropriate. However, for this field guide, we have adopted the Howell et al. (2009) system that groups birds according to what they "look like" rather than by strict taxonomic and genetic considerations used in the *AOS Checklist of North American Birds*. The AOS may change the names and order of birds and families with each annual supplement published in the *Auk*. This would mean that the order of all previously published field guides is quickly out of date.

We discuss subspecies occurring in the Sierra when they are identifiable in the field or when current research suggests that a species may be split in the future. We also provide a common name to identify a subspecies when that name is frequently used and widely recognized.

ABUNDANCE CATEGORIES

The approximate abundance of each species is described using the categories listed here. Each category is based on the relative frequency with which an experienced birder might expect to see or hear of a given species in its favored habitat and in the appropriate season during peak birding hours; the species may be more or less numerous at any particular site.

ABUNDANT: Encountered on every day afield, usually many individuals.

COMMON: Encountered on most days afield, sometimes many individuals.

FAIRLY COMMON: One or a few individuals encountered on most days afield.

UNCOMMON: Encountered on relatively few days afield; never in large numbers; often missed unless a special search is made.

RARE: Seldom encountered and often highly localized; at least a few individuals occur in the region in all or most years.

VERY RARE: Not encountered in the region in most years, but a pattern of occurrence may exist over many years or decades.

BIRD SEASONS

The "bird seasons" we have used throughout the book do not follow strict calendar dates but rather capture seasonal changes from a bird's perspective using the standard definitions from *North American Birds*: **WINTER:** December–February; **SPRING:** March–May; **SUMMER:** June–July; **FALL:** August–November.

SPECIES ACCOUNTS

Accounts of all regularly occurring species begin with a **BRIEF COMMENT** or reflection about the first impression of the species, noting distinct features and qualities. The **SIZE** of the bird is then provided in comparison to the next closest species. **DESCRIPTIONS** are also given for each variation in plumage. Much of what a bird is and does revolves around **FLIGHT**, so each species is described "on the wing." An effort to relate the quality, cadence, and sound of each bird's **SONG** and **CALL** comes next. We then provide information on the bird's **RANGE** within the Sierra region. Armed with this knowledge, you should have the tools for knowing when and where to begin a search for any given species. Finally, we provide a list of **SIMILAR SPECIES** in which differing marks and voices are pointed out.

Terminology

As with many things in life, unique subjects often come with their own terminology. Learning a few of these terms will greatly enhance your knowledge and thereby increase your appreciation for the birds you encounter.

Most birds' appearance varies from one to another with subtle to obvious differences between species or subspecies. Variation can also be found between different ages or sexes, or depending on the season or the condition of a bird's plumage. However, for many birds, females and males appear virtually identical—at least to us humans, that is.

CLASSIFICATION

NONPASSERINE: Any species not placed in the order *Passeriformes*. These are usually referred to as the "wet" birds and the "dry" nonpasserines. Dry nonpasserines include gamebirds, hawks, doves, cuckoos, owls, nightjars, swifts, hummingbirds, kingfisher, woodpeckers, and falcons.

PASSERINE: Any species placed in the order *Passeriformes*. These are usually referred to as songbirds or perching birds.

AGE AND SEX

NESTLING or **CHICK:** A bird in or at the nest that is typically incapable of flight.

FLEDGLING: A bird that has left the nest, is typically being tended to by a parent, and is usually not fully experienced at flight. With all pre-cocial species—waterfowl, shorebirds, gulls, and the like—the young depart the nest far earlier than most songbirds.

JUVENILE PLUMAGE/JUVENILE BIRD: A specific term referring to a bird wearing its first coat of nondowny feathers. With most songbirds, this weaker plumage is forced out by rapidly growing and stronger feathers. Frequently this plumage looks much like adult plumage, but is often scaled and cryptic. In larger species such as herons, shorebirds, gulls, and hawks, juvenile plumage is stronger and can be worn for months or a year.

FIRST WINTER: The plumage birds attain after having molted from juvenile plumage.

IMMATURE: Any young plumage that differs from adult plumage, including the juvenile.

SUBADULT: An older immature plumage that resembles that of the adult, as with eagles and gulls. Subadults can appear similar to the adult, but they are simply "not quite there yet."

ADULT: Any bird having reached a stage of maturation where its plumage may change from season to season, but not from year to year.

SEX: May be determined by plumage, size, or voice. When an observer might notice these differences, it is mentioned in the species accounts.

PLUMAGE STAGES AND CONDITIONS OF APPEARANCE

ALTRICIAL: Opposite of precocial. Any species whose chicks hatch naked and helpless. This includes most birds, and all passerines (songbirds). Note, these are not "babies." Mammals give birth to babies; birds hatch from eggs as chicks.

BREEDING PLUMAGE: Appears most often in spring and summer. High plumage typically worn by adults; males appear brighter in color and higher in contrast than females (opposite in phalaropes).

ECLIPSE: A term applied to male ducks, usually in late summer. This briefly held plumage is worn when birds molt from a flightless post-breeding condition into breeding plumage.

HYBRID: Offspring resulting from a genetic pairing between two different species.

INDIVIDUAL VARIATION: Often considerable, even within one species. Like members of our own species, no two birds look identical. Individual variation can confuse and fool even the most astute observer, beginner or advanced.

MOLT: Usually annual, the process whereby birds grow new feathers that force out the old or worn ones. Worn feathers can appear tattered, pale, or frayed at the edges.

MORPH: A color variation, be it light, rufous, or dark. Certain morphs appear in populations specific to a geographical region. Various hawks and other families exhibit such morphs. These colors are kept for the bird's entire lifespan (except in jaegers).

NONBREEDING PLUMAGE: Usually dull or more somber than breeding plumage; most common in fall and winter. This plumage is attained after molting out of breeding plumage.

PARTIAL ALBINISM: Confusing and surprising, appears as patchy, random, or entirely white feathers. Species that frequently exhibit albinism include crows, robins, juncos, and blackbirds.

PRECOCIAL: Opposite of altricial. A species that hatches covered with down and is somewhat to entirely mobile soon after hatching; often accompanies adults away from the nest. Most ground nesters, including waterfowl, gamebirds, and shorebirds, are precocial.

SUBSPECIES/RACE: These terms mean the same thing and refer to geographic variation within a species, usually relating to features such as plumage and size. When subspecies can be identified in the field, we have mentioned them in the species accounts. Subspecies are indicated by a third part added to their scientific name. For example, the Orange-crowned Warbler *Leiothlypis celata* has several subspecies, including *lutescens* (*Leiothlypis celata lutescens*), breeding on the West Slope of the Sierra, and *orestera* (*Leiothlypis celata orestera*), which occurs in the Sierra during migration, mainly on the East Slope.

SEASONAL STATUS

IRRUPTIVE: Species that display mass seasonal movements, usually in the nonbreeding season, and are typically dependent on fluctuating food resources or shifting weather conditions. Examples in the Sierra include Lewis's Woodpecker, Red-breasted Nuthatch, Evening Grosbeak, and Pine Siskin.

MIGRANT/TRANSIENT: Term for species that move seasonally from one place to another. These movements can be altitudinal, somewhat localized, or over great distances globally, as with many song and shorebirds.

NOMADIC: Species that wander from place to place, typically seasonally and most likely in search of food resources.

RESIDENT/SEDENTARY: Nonmigratory species.

BREEDER: Species that breed in the Sierra, typically in spring and summer. These may be birds that either have migrated to the Sierra or are resident.

VAGRANT: Term for species that are found far outside their normal range.

WINTER VISITOR: In the Northern Hemisphere, species that spend winter away from their breeding grounds.

YEAR-ROUND: A species that can be encountered any month of the year, but may be migratory, or not.

VOICE

SONG: A series of complex notes typically communicating to a potential mate or a rival. Given predominately by males, it is most often given in nesting season.

CALL: Typically a single or simple note given to communicate location, intent, or threat. Although calls are short in duration, songs vary greatly and are often more difficult to differentiate than calls. Flight calls, not always given while on the wing, are usually high in frequency and therefore difficult for us to hear.

STATUS

CALIFORNIA BIRD SPECIES OF SPECIAL CONCERN (SEE APPENDIX B): A declining or vulnerable species or subspecies currently at risk. May warrant future listing under the California Endangered Species Act.

ENDANGERED: A species considered to be at risk of becoming extinct.

ENDEMIC: A native species whose distribution is entirely restricted to a defined geographical region.

EXTIRPATED: Locally extinct; a species that no longer occurs in part of its previous range, but is still extant elsewhere within its greater range.

INTRODUCED: A species found outside its natural, historical range, whether because members of the species escaped from captivity or were released into the wild.

THREATENED: A species thought to be at risk of becoming endangered.

PATTERN AND MARKINGS

BAR: A crosswise marking

BARRED: Marked by bars

CRYPTIC: Camouflaged; a pattern that conceals

GHOST PATTERN: A plumage showing traces of a bolder plumage

GLOSSY: Feathers appearing polished or shiny

GRIZZLED: As if tipped with gray hair

IRIDESCENT: A spectrum of shimmering colors

MARBLED: A variegated pattern

MOTTLED: Blotches of different shades

PIED: Contrasting colors, often black and white

STRIPE OR LINE: A lengthwise marking

SUSPENDERS: Two distinct lines up the back

VERMICULATION: Fine wavy barring

BEHAVIOR

CREPUSCULAR: Active primarily at dawn and dusk

DIURNAL: Active primarily by day

MANTLING: Holding wings outspread over captured and downed prey; primarily birds of prey

NOCTURNAL: Active primarily at night

PARASITIC: Describes a bird that deposits its eggs into the nests of other species

ROOSTING: Refers to a bird or birds gathering to rest or sleep; not to be confused with nesting

Anatomy of a Bird

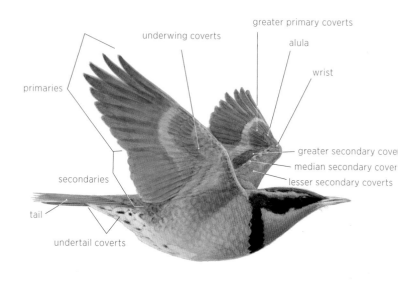

VARIED THRUSH

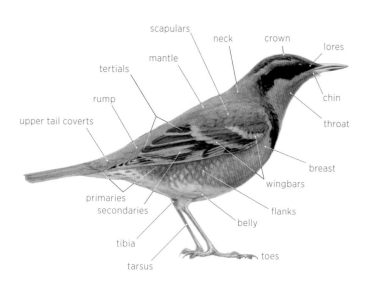

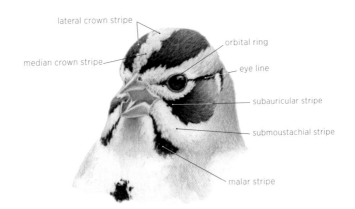

lateral crown stripe

median crown stripe

orbital ring

eye line

subauricular stripe

submoustachial stripe

malar stripe

LARK SPARROW

lores

culmen

upper mandible

gape

lower mandible

chin

throat

malar

eyering

brow/supercilium

cheek/auriculars

nape

BIRDING TIPS AND TOOLS

One great thing about birding is that it is free! You can simply walk outside and usually see birds no matter where you live. Although you really do not need anything other than your eyes and ears for birding, there are some tips, tools, and accessories that will help you locate birds, see them more clearly, and record your observations, all in an effort to enhance your bird encounters.

Power Tools

BINOCULARS. Invest in a good pair and stay with quality brands. Get binoculars that feel comfortable in your hands; are waterproof, clear, and aligned; and focus closely.

TELESCOPE AND TRIPOD. Although more expensive, a good spotting scope and a tripod offer a steady magnified view while also freeing your hands to sketch and take notes.

CAMERA, VIDEO CAMERA. Either is useful for recording, documenting, and sharing your sightings.

SMARTPHONE. Attachments connecting cell phones to spotting scopes greatly increase the quality of your photos. Gather audio recordings of the bird's songs and calls.

NOTE AND SKETCHBOOK. Keep notes or draw sketches of birds to help you remember key marks and the locations you visited. Include the date and a brief account of the day's weather.

In the Field

MOVE SLOWLY—MODERATE THE VOLUME. Birds are attentive to sudden movements and loud noises. A slower pace and calm nature enable you and others to hear and see more.

WHERE TO LOOK. Keep your eyes moving, high and low. Check the tops of trees, poles, ridges, and telephone lines. Focus on areas where two or more habitats meet. Get into the habit of frequently looking at the sky, checking the edges of clouds, and watching for soaring raptors on warm days. In the forest, look for subtle movements in the dark of the underbrush and listen for foraging flocks of insectivores. In open areas, walk through grasslands, scan wetlands and the shores of lakes, and watch for bird interactions.

KEEP YOUR EYES ON THE PRIZE. Although it may sound odd to recommend that you look at the bird when it's still in view, these are often squandered critical moments. Don't waste precious time flipping through your field guide when you could be studying the bird in more detail. If your bird is flying away, stay with it until it vanishes as a speck or into concealment. Watch where it landed; you may have another chance to view it by simply moving closer. Use this time to take mental and written notes of any field marks. Once the bird is gone, that's the time to refer to your guide.

PERFECT YOUR SKILLS OF GETTING OTHERS "ONTO A BIRD." Start with the big picture and work toward the bird. Is the bird flying or perched, moving left or right, above or below the horizon? Be specific. "It's sitting in the oak on a dead branch, sticking out the right side at two o'clock next to a cluster of yellowing leaves."

KEY FEATURES—MARKS AND PATTERNS. If encountering an unknown bird, pay special attention to its face, bill, and behavior. These keys unlock most bird mysteries. Noting bold patterns and unique features, or even a lack of them, can be helpful.

POSITION YOURSELF. Reduce the negative effects of lighting by adjusting your position, often just slightly. Move so that darker objects line up directly behind the bird, and your glaring backlit view will be replaced by one in full illumination.

ATMOSPHERIC EFFECTS AND WEATHER CONDITIONS. Birds seen in foggy conditions often appear larger than they truly are. In full sun, adult gulls appear pale gray; under overcast skies, the same birds appear dark gray. Birds in colder conditions fluff up their feathers and appear larger than normal. Birds in warmer conditions compress their feathers and appear thinner than normal.

PISHING AND SQUEAKING. To attract or invite birds closer, especially songbirds, you can repeatedly utter a dry "pishing" sound like "pish, pish, pish." A high-pitched squeaking sound made by kissing the back of your hand often gets the attention of birds and mammals.

CUPPING YOUR EARS. To hear far better than normal, cup each hand behind each ear.

BLINKING AT BIRDS' FLIGHT. When you are viewing birds in flight, consider repeatedly blinking your eyes. Helpful for discerning shapes and patterns, this technique imparts the impression of momentary "snapshots" that briefly pause in your mind's eye.

BRIEF VIEWS AND FIRST IMPRESSIONS. Although they are frequently correct, first impressions can lead an incautious or overzealous observer down the wrong identification path. Wait to get better views before putting the word out. Everyone makes mistakes. It's a natural part of learning. There is nothing wrong with realizing that you simply do not know the identity of a bird or that you have misidentified it. If you really do not know, then it's usually best not to proclaim.

pink

white

speckled

orange

muted

dingy

ADULT

JUVENILE

Greater White-fronted Goose

Anser albifrons

Geese and ducks migrate great distances, have large clutch sizes and a gregarious nature. Waterfowl vary dramatically in size, structure, and behavior. Swans and geese usually mate for life; sexes are nearly identical. This goose is proportioned like a medium-size Canada with a deeply furrowed neck and large belly. Will graze away from water, where individuals may take up with semi-tame Canadas.

THE BIRD: Adult brownish with snappy white face and flank edges. Belly markings unique. **Juvenile** plain. Lacks white face and belly markings, which develop over the first winter.

FLIGHT: Its annual journey, an iconic spectacle; fulfills the classic image of migration with calling birds in lofty V formations. Flight easygoing, purposeful. Occasionally mixes with others, but usually found in exclusively White-fronted flocks.

VOICE: Highly vocal, often heard at night. An excited two- or three-note call with last note a high-pitched rising *her-wiK! her-WHERE-wiK!*

RANGE: High Arctic breeder. Begins arriving early fall, departs mid-spring. **West Slope:** Rarely landing, flocks fly over en route to Central Valley wetlands. Rare south of Yosemite. **East Slope:** Thousands may congregate in winter and early spring in marsh or agricultural land, mostly Honey Lake or north of Tahoe.

SIMILAR SPECIES: To distinguish among flying geese, note face pattern, throat, neck length, and voice. Domestic barnyard goose often has knob on forehead, no black on low-slung belly.

blue-gray

sloping

sooty

la
bi

blac
"lips

pink

DARK JUVENILE   DARK ADULT   LIGHT JUVENILE   LIGHT ADULT

Snow Goose
Anser caerulescens

Similar in size to the Greater White-fronted, this gregarious and noisy white goose traverses the Sierra, often at night.

THE BIRD: Adult light morph lustrous white. Some birds show rust face staining. Diagnostic black sides to the bill. **Juvenile light morph**, dusted gray on upper parts. Rare dark-morph, also known as **Blue Goose, adult** has a white head, contrasting blackish-brown body, ornate inner-wing feathers. **Juvenile** largely gray with white tail coverts.

FLIGHT: Direct with steady flapping, seldom gliding. A lofty pearl necklace of Snow Geese floating across winter-blue skies offers an opportunity to search for the darker Blue Goose or the smaller Ross's Goose.

VOICE: Vocalizes constantly when disturbed or in flight. Call, a high, sharp, yelping *HRENK! HRENK! HRENK!* Single notes are given in steady, rapid cadence, often with a quick, hollow gulping *hulp, hulp, hulp...*

RANGE: Far northern migrants begin arriving in the Sierra by mid-fall and depart by mid-spring. **West Slope:** Usually observed overhead in flocks, they rarely land at flooded fields, lakes, and reservoirs, mostly north of the Yosemite region. **East Slope:** May gather in large numbers, primarily at marshes and agricultural lands in spring and fall north of the Tahoe region, mostly at Honey Lake.

SIMILAR SPECIES: Ross's Goose, a petite version of Snow Goose, has a small, delicate bill with no black "lipstick."

rounded

blue
base

gray

small
bill

ADULT

JUVENILE

Ross's Goose

Anser rossii

High Arctic and just one of a handful of birds whose entire breeding range lies completely within Canada. Petite, this Mallard-size goose is North America's smallest.

THE BIRD: Adult with a short neck, round head, and dainty pink bill; light-morph adult is an endearing version of a Snow Goose. Diagnostic warty bluish bumps encompass the bill's base. The **juvenile** shows gray on the crown, back of neck, and back, and is overall whiter than the juvenile Snow Goose. The extremely rare **dark-morph** Ross's (not illustrated) is similar to the dark-morph Snow, but **adults** have a dark cap and white wing coverts, secondaries, and rump; **juvenile** shows a dark head.

FLIGHT: When flying with Snows, Ross's Geese are detected by their smaller size and quicker wingbeats. Flying alone or in pure Ross's flock, birds can be identified by their shorter necks.

VOICE: Slightly higher pitched than the Snow's with an evenly paced, bugle-like series of honks: *hrUNK! hurUNK! hrUNK!*

RANGE: In the Sierra, usually observed amid Snow Goose flocks. Arrives mid-fall and depart by mid-spring. **West Slope:** Rare visitor to reservoirs in the low foothills, very rare south of the Yosemite region. **East Slope:** Uncommon north of the Tahoe region, very rare farther south.

SIMILAR SPECIES: Snow Goose is like a larger, longer-necked version of Ross's, but with black "lipstick."

short neck

dark

tiny bill

MINIMA

Cackling Goose

Branta hutchinsii

Like a tiny Canada Goose, the size and shape of a Ross's. Split from Canada Goose in 2004, it is represented by different subspecies, of which *Ridgway's* Cackling Goose *(B. h. minima)* is the one most often encountered in the Sierra. Also known as *Pacific*, typically the darkest subspecies of Cackling. The little bill is only as long as it is deep at its base.

THE BIRD: Adult crown tends to be rounded, and the dark-brown breast frequently contrasts with a white neck ring. Some individuals show a black stripe bisecting the white throat patch. Diagnostic, the wing coverts have thin, pale tips with a contrastingly dark subterminal border. **Juvenile** typically paler breasted than adult, with overall color and contrast subdued.

FLIGHT: Often forming a long "beaded necklace," these vocal birds fly rapidly and directly. Holding their wings slightly bowed, they flap with steady, shallow beats.

VOICE: High-pitched. Reminiscent of a small barking dog: *arNK! arNK! arNK!* sharply accented on each note.

RANGE: Usually found amid flocks of the larger and far more abundant Canada Goose. **West Slope:** Uncommon fall and winter visitor to the low foothills; rare or very rare at higher elevations. **East Slope:** Rare or very rare fall, winter, and spring visitor.

SIMILAR SPECIES: All subspecies of **Canada Goose** are larger, with bigger bills, longer necks, and paler plumage.

Cackling Goose for comparison

white throat

long neck

pale

ADULT

Canada Goose

Branta canadensis

Be it in the iconic southbound V formation that ushers in the shorter, colder days of winter, or the familiar semi-tame residents strolling freshly mown golf courses, this species is represented by more than ten subspecies across North America. Bird forages on aquatic plants, upending from the water's surface, or grazes winter stubble on foot. The large and widely introduced *Great Basin* subspecies *(B. c. moffitti)* is the typical Canada Goose of the Sierra.

THE BIRD: Adult male averages larger than **female. Juvenile** smaller, with color and contrast subdued. Adults with a train of nimble goslings in tow are an endearing sight.

FLIGHT: At great heights, form long horizontal strands that meld into sinewy chevrons. With wings bowed downward, flight is strong and direct with slow, shallow, steady beats. When nearer, wings emit shrill, zipping sound with each stroke: *ziiiP! ziiiP! ziiiP!...*

VOICE: Call, a loud honking toy-trumpet sound with hollow qualities: *hrUNK, hrUNK...* Also utters a gruff and deep *gruH, gruH...* Large numbers create the high-pitched cacophony of a roaring sports event.

RANGE: Both slopes: Common to locally abundant resident at reservoirs and irrigated pastures. Found from Foothill up to Subalpine, especially north of Yosemite. With the addition of wild birds from the north, winter numbers increase.

SIMILAR SPECIES: Cackling Goose about half the size, with steep forehead, short neck, small bill, dark belly.

pink

dusky

black

ADULT

JUVENILE

Tundra Swan

Cygnus columbianus

Often encountered in family groups composed of both adults and two or three full-grown immatures. Sexes identical. California's largest all-white bird feeds at the water's surface, upending and reaching down with its long neck to procure the seeds and tubers of aquatic plants. Also forages in agricultural stubble.

THE BIRD: Feeding, some birds show staining to the face and neck. Otherwise, **adult** is unblemished white with long, sloping bill, usually with yellow spot at base. **Juvenile** sullied grayish tan, darkest on head and neck. Bill transitions from pinkish to black as bird matures and becomes whiter over winter.

FLIGHT: Breaks earthly bonds with labored pumping from great, white wings and loud slapping steps from huge feet. Flocks form leisurely, graceful strands, leaving a lasting impression.

VOICE: Loud and far carrying, with strong trumpet-like notes commingled with pleasing muffled moans and coos. Resonating call is often the first signal of an approaching flock.

RANGE: High Arctic breeder. Arrives early November, departs by mid-March. **West Slope:** Common fall, winter, and spring visitor to Lake Almanor; otherwise rare. Large numbers congregate in Central Valley rice fields. **East Slope:** Uncommon-to-rare migrant and winter visitor to lakes and reservoirs mostly north of Tahoe.

SIMILAR SPECIES: Larger and very rare **Trumpeter Swan** notoriously difficult to separate, with subtle differences in face and bill. **American White Pelican**, black flight feathers.

long tail ♂

♀

colorful

white

BREEDING MALE ECLIPSE MALE FEMALE

Wood Duck

Aix sponsa

All species of male ducks wear bright plumage and usually choose different mates each year. After breeding, males molt into eclipse plumage, becoming flightless for a short period of time. Waterfowl royalty, California's most colorful bird reserves its charm, often perching high deep within trees over water. Nests in tree cavities and artificial nest boxes. Feeds on aquatic plants and organisms, or forages under oaks for acorns and invertebrates. Size between Mallard and teal.

THE BIRD: Adult male with red-hot eyes, a tricolored bill, and odd head shape; appears as if designed by Picasso. **Eclipse male** in late summer–early fall, female-like with ghosts of adult's pattern and subdued eyes and bill colors. **Female** shows a white teardrop around eyes, and her small crest creates a unique shape. A muted version of the adult, **juvenile male** shows a trace of adult's face pattern.

FLIGHT: Shy, eager to flush. Aloft, fast-flying, and curiously lifts and lowers head. All birds have blue speculum, dark underwings, white bellies, and long tails.

VOICE: Male squeals a long, thin, rising and abruptly ending *wizzzzzzzzziP!* Bursting into flight or defending young, the female gives a frantic, haunting, shrill, up-slurred *herrr-RIP!*

RANGE: Denizen of wooded waterways throughout its range in North America. **West Slope:** Foothill and Lower Conifer, especially at waters where nest boxes are placed. **East Slope:** Uncommon to rare.

SIMILAR SPECIES: None.

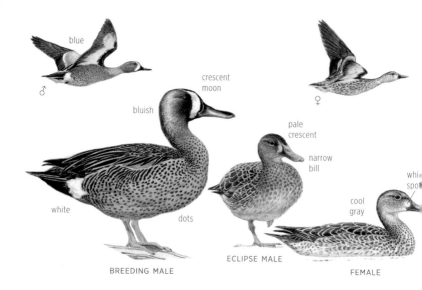

Blue-winged Teal
Spatula discors

Infrequent in status, rare in beauty, and a joy to discover.

THE BIRD: This narrow-billed teal is slightly larger than the Green-winged and just smaller than the wider-billed Cinnamon Teal. **Adult male** is dark, bookended by a white face crescent and flank patch. **Eclipse male** in late summer to early fall looks female-like with ghost of breeding male "crescent moon." **Adult female** and **juvenile** are plain gray, lacking Cinnamon's warmth. Diagnostic marks include a thin, crisp eye crescent, dark eye line, and small white dot at the bill's base.

FLIGHT: Pushing free of the water, leaps into flight; once aloft, proceeds rapidly flashing its blue upper and white underwings while twisting low over the water. Male flaunts sky-blue patch on upper wing; female's is blue-gray. Both show snappy white "wingpits."

VOICE: Rarely heard vocalizing, males give clipped, squeaky, House Sparrow–like chirping. Female utters a gruff, hoarse, and plucking *tuFF! tuFF! tuFF!* reminiscent of male Northern Shoveler.

RANGE: Both slopes: Rare but regular spring and fall visitor, but very rare in winter. Favors marshes, lazy streams, and the shallow shoals of reservoirs, often associating with Cinnamon Teal.

SIMILAR SPECIES: Cinnamon Teal female, warm-colored overall, larger spatulate bill, and blank expression. **Green-winged Teal female** tiny, browner, small billed, lacks blue wing coverts. **Northern Shoveler fall male** may show Blue-wing's white face crescent, but little else to confuse.

baby blue

♂

ruby eye

white

♀

spatulate bill

blank face

warm brown

ECLIPSE MALE

BREEDING MALE

FEMALE

Cinnamon Teal

Spatula cyanoptera

Essentially the western counterpart of Blue-winged Teal.

THE BIRD: Adult male appears dark in low-light conditions, but in full sun this bright chestnut-colored duck spices up any summer wetland. Just larger than Blue-winged Teal, Cinnamon has a more spatulate bill, best seen when facing head-on. Late summer–early fall **eclipse male** has female-like patterning, but a red eye and increased warmth throughout plumage. **Breeding female** and **juvenile** are mottled warm brown and lack bold facial markings, imparting a blank expression.

FLIGHT: Pushing free of the water, leaps into flight; once aloft, proceeds rapidly, flashing blue upper and white underwings while twisting low over water.

VOICE: Male's voice in display nearly coot-like. A dull, grating, ratchet-like *quAH! quAH! quAH!* Female similar to Blue-winged Teal, but a less forceful *tuff, tuff.*

RANGE: Wintering primarily in Mexico, Cinnamon Teal arrive in the lower foothills on both slopes to breed by early March, and most depart by early September. **West Slope:** Uncommon spring visitor to ponds and marshes of the low Foothill Zone. **East Slope:** Common to fairly common breeder at lower-elevation ponds and marshlands.

SIMILAR SPECIES: Blue-winged Teal female, narrower bill, overall cool gray, and patterned face. **Juvenile** can be difficult if not impossible to differentiate. **Green-winged Teal female** petite, small billed, and lacks blue wing patches. **Northern Shoveler female** in flight is larger, similarly patterned, but with an exaggerated bill.

gray

blue

white

white
tail

enormous
bill

pale
crescent

oran

BREEDING MALE

ECLIPSE MALE

FEMALE

Northern Shoveler

Spatula clypeata

Nearly wigeon size with a huge flattened bill, the Northern Shoveler is curiously proportioned. Feeding birds circle en masse to create a slow whirlpool, bringing invertebrates to the surface to be shoveled up into sieve-lined bills.

THE BIRD: Adult male strongly tricolored green, white, and rust with staring, golden eyes. **Adult female**, cryptic in delicate "dry-grass" patterning. Bill orange at base. **Juvenile** similar, bill duller. **Eclipse male** variable with mix of male and female-like plumage. Faint white crescent on face can recall a male Blue-winged Teal, but with glaring golden eyes.

FLIGHT: Strong, direct, and rapid. Flocks race forward in horizontal wingtip-to-wingtip formation, with each bird competing for the lead. This creates an unusually loud *woooOOOOSH!* as they pass overhead. From below, enlarged bill-tip distinctive. Wing pattern *very* Blue-winged Teal–like with blue coverts on male, gray on female.

VOICE: Male gives a flat, plucking *tuK! tuK!...*, often in paired sequence. Descending in volume, female quacks a rapid *Ank-UH, Ank-uh, ank-uh.*

RANGE: Arrives from northern breeding grounds in early September, spends winter, and most depart late April. **West Slope:** Uncommon visitor to lower Foothill ponds, reservoirs, and wetlands. **East Slope:** Common in spring and fall migration, and a few pairs possibly breed in Sierra Valley.

SIMILAR SPECIES: Cinnamon Teal female smaller with reduced, dark bill. **Mallard female** larger with smaller bill.

white

♂

squared
head

♀

plain

orange
sides

lacy

black

BREEDING MALE

ECLIPSE MALE

FEMALE

Gadwall
Mareca strepera

Narrow billed and dark tailed, Gadwall is slightly smaller than Mallard. Usually found in pairs or small groups, unlike most other puddle ducks that gather in larger flocks.

THE BIRD: Adult male handsomely dressed in a gray "herringbone suit" with tan head and brown back. Black tail coverts and orange feet, prominent. **Female** and **juvenile** similar to female Mallard but with a more lacy pattern, simple face, and neat orange sides to the bill. In summer, **eclipse male** resembles female but shows emerging traces of male's finely barred flanks.

FLIGHT: Appears heavy bodied. Typically travels in pairs or small groups. Male has bold white wing patches; females show less white. Underwings and belly are strikingly white.

VOICE: Often overlooked because of somber plumage, but distinct call reveals presence. The highly vocal male delivers a far-carrying, nasal *ANK!* The female utters a coarse and less-defined Mallard-like *quack*.

RANGE: Year-round resident and migrant in California, including both slopes of the Sierra. **West Slope:** Fairly common and widespread winter visitor to lakes, ponds, deltas, and wetlands, but uncommon-to-rare breeder. **East Slope:** Fairly common breeder in spring and summer. Numbers increase in fall and winter when migrants arrive from northern breeding grounds.

SIMILAR SPECIES: Mallard female with white tail, dark line through eye, and blue speculum. **Green-winged Teal female** tiny, dark billed, and lacks white in wings.

white

pointed

♂

♀

green

gray hea

white
patch

BREEDING MALE   ECLIPSE MALE   FEMALE

American Wigeon
Mareca americana

Often found in compact aggregations far from the water, foraging in grazed pastures or on golf courses.

THE BIRD: Between a Mallard and a teal in size. All wigeon show a narrow blue to gray bill, smartly tipped in black. **Adult male** obvious with a green eye swish. **Breeding female** may be overlooked by virtue of her delicate mottling and gray head contrasting with the warm flanks. The female's eye is encompassed by an ill-defined dark area, imparting a nebulous expression. **Eclipse male** appears female-like, but may show subtle green behind the eye and a white wing covert patch.

FLIGHT: When flushed from the water, birds quickly gain altitude, falling into organized lines showing well their contrasting white bellies and pointed tails. Females exhibit pale wing coverts while males are boldly white.

VOICE: The male's voice recalls the *chi-CA-go* call of California Quail but is a higher and squeakier *her HERE! Her*. Female utters a harsh and grating *Grah! Grah! Grah!*

RANGE: Most migrants arrive mid-September, spend the winter, depart by mid-April. **West Slope:** Fairly common to locally abundant at ponds, creeks, and marshlands of the foothills, but rare at higher elevations. **East Slope:** Fairly common in winter, and common in spring and fall migration at marshlands, ponds, and lazy waterways. Rare summer breeder in marshes.

SIMILAR SPECIES: Rare **Eurasian Wigeon female.**

white underwing

white-edged blue

♀

yellow

ring

curlicue

dark eyeline

greenish

♂

white tail

orange

BREEDING MALE

ECLIPSE MALE

FEMALE

Mallard

Anas platyrhynchos

Iconic. Often wiggling an adorned rear end, our largest dabbler is a comical dandy. Children feeding ducks at the park are often introduced to nature with Mallard as envoy.

THE BIRD: Breeding male shows a banana-yellow bill, "Robin Hood Green" head, curlicue tail, and white neck-ring. **Adult female**, camouflaged in "dry-grass" marbling. Her orange bill is crossed by an irregular, black saddle. In early fall, **eclipse male** often looks disheveled or female-like with mottled brown body and gray face. May show varying green behind eyes. **Juvenile** female-like with muted plumage and olive-green bill.

FLIGHT: Explodes vertically from water with powerful strokes. In flight, underwings flash white, a useful mark from great distances. When encountered in pairs, male usually follows the female.

VOICE: Vocalize loudly, frequently when taking flight. Females give loud, familiar *QUACK!* often in series descending in volume: *QUACK! QUACK, Quack, quack, quack...* Foraging in active groups, males utter low, garbled, "conversational" notes: *kwhep, kwhep, kwhep...*

RANGE: Familiar and widespread, the most abundant duck in the region. **Both slopes:** Year-round resident breeding at ponds, marshes, and reservoirs rarely up to Subalpine lakes and meadows.

SIMILAR SPECIES: Northern Shoveler male vaguely similar, shows rust flanks, white breast, and large black bill. **Gadwall female** similar to female, but with small bill, smaller square head, white in wings, and dark-brownish tail.

long neck

blue-gray

stripe

slender neck

ginger

elongated tail

ECLIPSE MALE

FEMALE

BREEDING MALE

Northern Pintail

Anas acuta

Graceful and long-necked, between Gadwall and American Wigeon in size. Known as the "sprig" by some, this bird occurs over most of Earth's land surface.

THE BIRD: The **breeding male** is gray and white with brown head, cradled by thin neck stripe. Greatly elongated central tail feathers form a long "pin-tail." **Adult female** delicately mottled. Relatively pale and cooler toned unless stained cinnamon. Face uncomplicated, bill dusky-gray, neck slender, and tail pointed. **Juvenile** female-like but less warm. **Eclipse male** in early fall, variable, appears female-like with more blue on bill and patches or tracts of breeding plumage emerging.

FLIGHT: Male is svelte with a thin, white neck and a needle-tail, helping accentuate its lithe form. At lofty heights, flies swift and direct, forming long warping strands. Although birds show white trailing edge to the greenish secondaries, all plumages lack bold wing pattern.

VOICE: Male chirps a breezy and *very* cricket-like *kriK, kreK...kriK, kreK*. Female, an agitated, coarse, grating, and clipped *Grek, keK! GreK!...*

RANGE: Migrants arrive mid-October, spend the winter, and depart by mid-April. **West Slope:** Uncommon visitor to low Foothill wetlands. **East Slope:** Fairly common spring and fall migrant. A few pairs breed annually, mostly north of the Yosemite region.

SIMILAR SPECIES: Gadwall female larger with white in secondaries. **American Wigeon female** shares slender neck and slim shape, but white belly contrasts.

with labels: white, short neck, ♂, dark, ♀, small bill, warm, eyeline, white, white, ECLIPSE MALE, BREEDING MALE, FEMALE

Green-winged Teal

Anas crecca

Diminutive, gallinule size, our smallest duck meets in lively "parties" often on mud flats where they feed shorebird-style.

THE BIRD: Adult male combines a warm head, green swath, pink breast, and banana-colored undertail coverts, coalescing into a splendid little duck. Delicately mottled in brown, **breeding female**, eclipse male, and juvenile lack bold markings. A faint "equal sign" across face and thin white line near side of the tail, subtle but diagnostic, separating it from all female ducks. **Eclipse male** has a warm face, **juvenile** like breeding female.

FLIGHT: Sprightly, springs easily to flight. Flocks barrel forward in a twisting ball with no apparent leader and usually fairly low over the water. In flight, the green speculum is less apparent than the white "wingpits."

VOICE: The male gives chirping, cricket-like *krik-KREEK! krik-KREEK!* with emphasis on second note. Female, an agitated, run-together *RANK-ANKH! Ankh, anh, anh anh...* that drops in volume and intensity.

RANGE: Most of the wintering population migrates north and east to breed, but a few remain to breed in the Sierra. **West Slope:** Uncommon fall, winter, and spring visitor, and rare breeder up to the Subalpine. **East Slope:** Fairly common where large flocks may congregate in winter; uncommon breeder at marshes, ponds, lakes, and reservoirs.

SIMILAR SPECIES: Slightly larger **Blue-winged Teal female** and **Cinnamon Teal female** larger billed, bluish wing coverts.

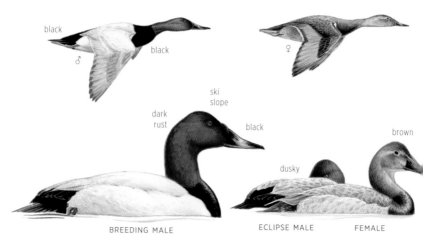

black

black

♂

♀

ski slope

dark rust

black

brown

dusky

BREEDING MALE

ECLIPSE MALE

FEMALE

Canvasback

Aythya valisineria

Ducks fall roughly into equal groups: divers and non-divers, or "puddle ducks." Although all ducks are capable of submerging, divers readily do so when feeding and take wing by running across its surface. Puddle ducks upend when feeding and spring vertically into flight with powerful strokes, exhibiting iridescent secondary wing patches.

THE BIRD: Formidable, larger than the Redhead. **Adult male** boldly rust, black, and ash. This muscular-necked diver floats low in the water. Blackish on face, accentuating ruby eye. **Adult female**, a muted version of male with clouded gray body, blurry facial pattern, and faint eye-ring. **Eclipse male** female-like, with mottling on body and subdued cinnamon head, but red eye.

FLIGHT: Direct and powerful. Shallow wingbeats create an impressively loud whistling. Typically flies low to the water in small, quickly moving squadrons. At higher altitudes, flocks form meandering wingtip-to-wingtip strands.

VOICE: Rarely vocalizes. Groups utter garbled conversational notes, reminiscent of distant goose babble.

RANGE: Uncommon to rare and local at foothill lakes on both slopes. Arrives mid-October, departs by early April. **West Slope:** Flocks often at Lake Almanor, otherwise local west of crest. **East Slope:** Common wintering at Honey Lake and Lake Tahoe. Breeds locally on East Slope. Confirmed nesting in Sierra Valley.

SIMILAR SPECIES: Redhead male, rounded head, blue bill, darker body, golden eye. **Female** browner with little body–head contrast.

pale
gray

gold
eye

round
head

blue

spectacle

smoky
gray

BREEDING MALE

ECLIPSE MALE

FEMALE

Redhead

Aythya americana

This diver, typically of deep lakes and reservoirs, is sturdy, large headed, and slightly smaller than the Canvasback.

THE BIRD: The **adult male** is boldly tricolored smoky gray, black, and cinnamon, with a lightly vermiculated body. The gleaming eye and blue bill contrast with the head. At a distance, the body appears rather dark, and the head is not especially red. **Adult female** largely brownish, face variable, often showing pale "spectacles" and a grayer bill than male. Although this drabness may confuse, the round head is distinct. **Eclipse male** in late summer–early fall, muted with dusky clouding.

FLIGHT: Birds traveling locally move about in weak arrangements, but form cleaner lines at lofty heights with all birds showing contrastingly pale flight feathers and whitish underwings and belly.

VOICE: Rarely vocal in the Sierra, male gives cooing note that begins loudly, then loses volume *whHHEeeeuuuuuuu*. Female, Mallard-like on even pitch with coarse, grating, *graHH! graHH!*

RANGE: Uncommon to rare at foothill ponds and marshes on both slopes of the Sierra. Migrants arrive by mid-October, spend the winter, and depart in mid-April. Small numbers breed on the **East Slope** from Mono Basin north to Sierra Valley.

SIMILAR SPECIES: **Canvasback** has sloping forehead, black bill. Female shows contrast between head and chest. **Adult female** and **young scaup** have dark-brown head, breast, and upper parts, and contrasting white face patches.

round peak

gray
flanks

white
ring

dark
brown

monocle

whi

BREEDING MALE   ECLIPSE MALE   IMMATURE MALE   FEMALE

Ring-necked Duck
Aythya collaris

This well-tailored, scaup-size duck gladly mingles with other winter divers.

THE BIRD: Adult male strikingly bicolored, dressed swimmingly in formal black upperparts, pearl-gray flanks, and burnished purple head. Namesake neck ring vague, two white bill-rings striking. **Adult female** somber in color, but combination of head shape, bill pattern, and pale goggles diagnostic. **Eclipse male** shows dull head, white on face, and browner flanks. **First-winter male** adult-like with dark brownish back and dusky brown flanks. Hybrids with Lesser Scaup known to occur. To identify, note bill, back, and flank color.

FLIGHT: Takes wing with a short, running patter. Once aloft, moves quickly in loose, ill-formed groups on a blur of softly whistling wings. From above, the male appears largely black with contrasting pale-gray flight feathers. From below, the belly is contrastingly pale.

VOICE: Rarely vocalizes away from the breeding ground. Male gives squeaky, garbled, conversational notes, reminiscent of distant, high-pitched geese. Female gives monotonous series of rapid, gruff notes: *queff, queff, queff.*

RANGE: Arrives late September, spends the winter, and departs mid-April. These visitors frequent Foothill lakes, lazy flowing rivers, wooded ponds, and reservoirs. Fairly common on the **West Slope**, but uncommon on the **East Slope**. May breed locally in the northern Sierra, mostly north of the Tahoe region.

SIMILAR SPECIES: Scaup have rounder heads, white secondaries. **Males**, gray backs.

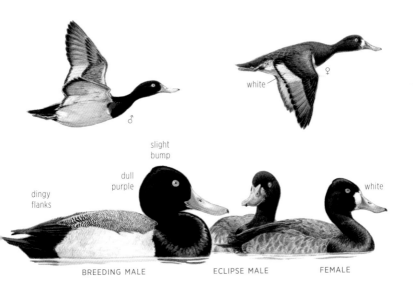

slight bump

dull purple

dingy flanks

white

white

BREEDING MALE   ECLIPSE MALE   FEMALE

Lesser Scaup
Aythya affinis

Slightly smaller and less bulky than the rarer Greater Scaup.

THE BIRD: Adult male head color deceptive, often appearing black, but in favorable lighting, dull purple and rarely greenish, inviting confusion with Greater Scaup. Black breast and tail coverts bookend the medium-gray back and dingy-white flanks. **Adult female** is largely brownish, darkest on head, breast, and vent. The back and flanks are mottled brown and gray. Lacks white ear patch shown by worn female Greater Scaup. **Eclipse male** in late summer and early fall female-like with less white on face and gray emerging on back.

FLIGHT: Runs to take wing, flashing its white secondaries. Belly and underwings strikingly white. Flocks usually form loose assemblages with no apparent leader.

VOICE: Usually silent in the Sierra. A gruff, grating series of notes, often when taking wing: *grrrrRR! grrrrRR! grrrRR!*

RANGE: Arrives mid-October, spends the winter, departs by mid-April. **Both slopes:** Uncommon visitor to large lakes, reservoirs, and slow-moving rivers at low elevations; often associates with Ring-necked Ducks and other wintering divers. No breeding records in the Sierra region.

SIMILAR SPECIES: Greater Scaup rare, bulkier, rounder headed, more black on bill tip. Male shows dull-green sheen on head, paler gray back, white flanks. Female in worn plumage often shows white on cheek. **Ring-necked Duck**, unique bump on the crown, black back, and ornate bill.

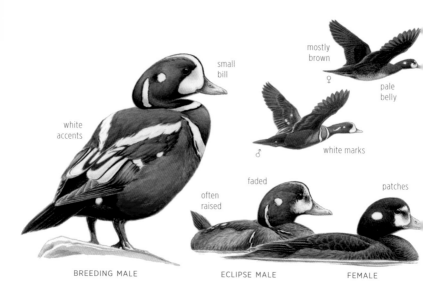

small bill

white accents

mostly brown ♀

pale belly

♂

white marks

faded

often raised

patches

BREEDING MALE   ECLIPSE MALE   FEMALE

Harlequin Duck
Histrionicus histrionicus

Slightly larger than the Ruddy Duck, this small, sturdy diver searches for food either below the surface or while snorkeling with face underwater. Its ability to swim and dive effortlessly against whitewater rapids in summer or the tumultuous surf of the rocky coast in winter is impressive.

THE BIRD: One might not think that the contrasting blue, white, and rust pattern of the **adult male** is a fitting camouflage, but once the drake enters turbulent water splashed by white foam, it all but vanishes. This dazzling plumage is acquired during its second winter. **Adult female** and **juvenile** dark brown with whitish belly and defined white patches on face. With white appointments and the intensity of the flank color subdued, mid-summer to early fall **eclipse male** appears like a muted adult.

FLIGHT: Runs to become airborne. Flies quick and low, virtually always over water. Both sexes appear dark and splashed by white. The male's iridescent secondaries are a feature unique among all Sierra diving ducks.

VOICE: Rarely vocalizes. Male, a high-pitched, nasal squeak. Female gives soft wet-rubber squeak, *ek-ek-ek*, when disturbed or protecting young.

RANGE: Rare, highly localized, and intermittent in the Sierra. **West Slope:** Breeds only on remote reaches of large, swift-flowing rivers, with most records above 4,000 feet from Yosemite north to the Feather River. **East Slope:** No recent or historical records.

SIMILAR SPECIES: None.

white patch ♀

stripes ♂

white cheek

rainbow

IMMATURE MALE

FEMALE

BREEDING MALE

Bufflehead

Bucephala albeola

A diminutive and endearing diving duck, encountered in small parties. Teal size and highly buoyant, this active and seemingly playful duck splashes, runs, and dives with spirited abandon.

THE BIRD: Adult male strikingly white and black, with swollen head burnished green and violet. **Adult female** dark above, light gray below. Cheek punctuated by a bold white spot. **Eclipse male** rarely encountered, appears female-like with whiter face, sides, and wings.

FLIGHT: Takes off with several quick, pattering steps and flies low, twisting on quivering wings. Nimble flocks appear unburdened by orderly formation. Female shows snappy white secondaries and belly. Coming in for a landing, the male splays its bubblegum-pink feet, throws wide his wings, presents four bold stripes, and skis in, chest high, to a stop.

VOICE: Taking wing, may utter a gruff, American Coot–like *greK! greK!*

RANGE: Arriving in mid-October, this fairly common wintering duck visits deep reservoirs, lakes, and rivers. **West Slope:** Fairly common winter visitor to lakes and tree-lined ponds in the Foothill and Lower Conifer Zones. **East Slope:** Fairly common spring and fall migrant and winter visitor to larger lakes and reservoirs. Nearly all depart by mid-April, but there are a few recent breeding records at secluded ponds on both slopes of the Sierra, especially north of the Tahoe region.

SIMILAR SPECIES: Larger **male goldeneyes** show similar wing stripes, but little else to confuse.

large head

extensive white

♂

♀

satiny green

sloping

round

stripes

dull

oran tip

ADULT MALE   IMMATURE MALE   FEMALE

Common Goldeneye
Bucephala clangula

Slightly larger than the Lesser Scaup. Well built and large headed.

THE BIRD: Adult male is the classic winter duck, splendidly dressed in high-contrast arctic-white and ebony-black attire. **Adult female,** storm-cloud gray body, white neck ring, and brown head. Bill dark, usually with an orange ring near tip. **Juvenile** male appears a mix of male and female, showing male's white body, back markings, face spot, and female's brown head and flank mottling.

FLIGHT: Watchful. Often congregates in small, attentive factions anxious to take wing. Exploding from the surface, they charge headlong and flap vigorously to become airborne. Wings of the females create a soft whistle; the males are louder. Once airborne, swift and purposeful as unstructured groups move about low to the water. Rising to greater heights, they configure into orderly formations. When landing, orange feet often visible.

VOICE: Rarely heard. Male gives high *fittzzheeeeew*. Female, a grating *greeH! greeH!* usually when taking wing.

RANGE: Arrives early November, spends the winter, departs by mid-April. **Both slopes:** This visitor from the north is fairly common to cold, slow-moving rivers, large lakes, and reservoirs.

SIMILAR SPECIES: Barrow's Goldeneye, steeper forehead, small triangular bill, less white on wings. **Male**, white crescent on face, row of white squares on back, black spur at breast's side. **Female**, entirely or mostly orange bill and darker-brown head.

large head

♀

steep

satiny purple

crescent

spots

tiny bill

mostly orange bill

ADULT MALE IMMATURE MALE FEMALE

Barrow's Goldeneye

Bucephala islandica

Slightly bulkier than the Common, this arrestingly beautiful diving duck engages in playful games of "tag" with splashing dashes, sudden pivots, and vigorous head bobbing. Vanishing acts of "hide-and-seek" conclude with spirited bird bobbing up cork-like and safely at "home base."

THE BIRD: Adult male boasts a bold pattern and blocky head that changes shape depending on its emotion. Shows a diagnostic row of white spots along the edge of the back, and a black "spur" extending downward from shoulder to the waterline. **Adult female** notoriously difficult to separate from female Common. The dark, squared head; stubby bill; and high forehead impart a cute look. **Juvenile male** in late summer, variable. Appears as a mix of male and female with male's dark bill and facial crescent and female's mottled body and brown head.

FLIGHT: On whistling wings, flaps rapidly and runs to take flight. Powers low to the water with fist-like head jutting forth.

VOICE: Usually silent. Male, a high-pitched, nasal, reedy *gheK! gheK! gheK!* Female, a grating *wrenK! wrenK!*

RANGE: Usually found with Common Goldeneye, this uncommon but regular winter visitor to lakes, reservoirs, and lazy rivers occurs on both slopes of the Sierra north of the Tahoe region, but is very rare farther south. No recent breeding records.

SIMILAR SPECIES: Common Goldeneye female larger with darker, cone-shaped bill blending into its sloping forehead.

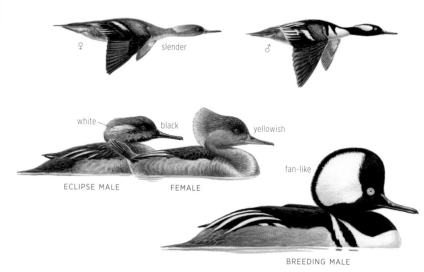

♀ slender

♂

white black yellowish

fan-like

ECLIPSE MALE FEMALE

BREEDING MALE

Hooded Merganser
Lophodytes cucullatus

Depending on mood, this shy Wood Duck–size diving duck fans an expressive crest and holds tail aloft.

THE BIRD: With gleaming eyes, the **adult male** is arresting in pattern. Boldly marked by rich brown flanks edged in black and white. Long, drooping tertials add a touch of flare. The demure **adult female** is the color of winter woodland, with the tip of her crest tawny and the base of her bill yellow. **Eclipse male** variable, appearing female-like but with white in crest, black blotches on face, a black bill, and dark eyes.

FLIGHT: Taking wing, skitters briskly over water. Moves purposefully with stiff, shallow beats. Birds moving about waterway form loose groups without clear leader. At greater heights, forms truer "follow-the-leader" formations.

VOICE: Usually silent. Female utters guttural croaking *grrrEP! grrrEP!* Male gives vibrating, two-part *onK-allllll...*, *onK-allllll...* with a deep, frog-like quality, with second note sustained and descending.

RANGE: Arrives late October, departs mid-April. **West Slope:** Fairly common visitor to wooded lakes and Foothill ponds up to Lower Conifer. A few recent breeding records from foothills south to El Dorado County, mostly in Wood Duck nest boxes. **East Slope:** Common winter visitor to the Tahoe region, where regularly observed at large lakes such as Tahoe and Donner. Otherwise uncommon migrant and rare in winter.

SIMILAR SPECIES: Bufflehead male also exhibits white crest, but little else to confuse.

white

contrasting

rusty

neat
crest

white

ADULT MALE   JUVENILE   FEMALE

Common Merganser
Mergus merganser

About the size of a Cackling Goose, our largest diving duck is at one with its watery world.

THE BIRD: Broad in the beam; floats low in the water. Nape swollen with goose-like neck furrows, the **adult male** is snow white with a narrow black "daypack." **Adult female**, gray body contrasts with rust head, distinct white chin. Her short crest is straight and well kept. **Juvenile** female-like but with white stripe below pale eyes; shorter crest, dull bill. On land, stands atop orange feet that appear like deflated balloons.

FLIGHT: Running hard, covers distance to rise from water. Shaped like a bowling pin with wings, the bird becomes airborne and moves with impressive velocity. Birds at greater heights form winding horizontal strands. Male's gray rump and lower back contrast with white body and inner wings.

VOICE: Usually silent. Male gives a slightly descending and deep frog-like chuckling: *On-ka, On-ka, On-ka...* Female's call, repeated short, gruff *gruh, gruh, gruh.*

RANGE: After the Mallard, the most abundant and widespread breeding duck on both slopes of the Sierra. Resides year-round in large creeks, rivers, and lakes with clear water and plentiful fish. Found from foothills up to the Subalpine. In winter, moves lower than zones heavy with snow.

SIMILAR SPECIES: **Red-breasted Merganser female** rare, smaller, with a wispy double crest, shallow bill; lacks bold head–breast contrast.

white

♂

♀

stiff
tail

white
cheek

blue

cheek
line

NONBREEDING MALE

FEMALE

BREEDING MALE

Ruddy Duck
Oxyura jamaicensis

American Coot size, stocky, and compact. Floating low, this diving duck frequently rafts in tight aggregations. Often sleeps during the day. Some birds hold their tails up at a strong angle.

THE BIRD: Adult male in breeding plumage warmly cloaked in chestnut, with bold white cheeks and radiant blue bill. Understated **adult female** often overlooked, but shows diagnostic dark line crossing her gray cheek. **Nonbreeding male** female-like, with white cheeks. Breeding display original and humorous as male inflates a shiny black chest and raises his tail and small devilish horns. Lifting his head high, he vocalizes and rapidly slaps the bill down to create a brief, generous eruption of bubbles.

FLIGHT: Running with floppy steps, flaps vigorously to take wing. Body twists on its axis; flight appears labored, rarely climbing high.

VOICE: Displaying male utters a rapid "squishy" series of notes that increase in tempo and culminate with an explosive note: *chik...chik...chik. Chik, CHIK-quiBBBBB!* Female, a rough, abbreviated *wah! wah! Wah!*

RANGE: A fairly common fall, winter, and spring visitor to both slopes. **West Slope:** Breeds from Foothill rarely up to Subalpine. **East Slope:** Fairly common breeder from Mono Basin north to Sierra Valley.

SIMILAR SPECIES: Head tucked, breeding male may be confused with **Cinnamon Teal** due to body color. **Bufflehead female** vaguely similar to nonbreeding male but with small white cheek spot.

orange

long

crook

pale

BREEDING

IMMATURE

Double-crested Cormorant

Phalacrocorax auritus

This gregarious waterbird floats low and appears waterlogged. Diving for fish, it holds wings closed and propels itself with feet far back on body. Walking, takes mincing, penguin-like steps. Nests in noisy rookeries, often with herons. Spreads wings to dry. Three species occur regularly in California. Only Double-crested ventures inland. Goose size. Cloaked in "Dracula black," heads tilted on S-curved necks, cormorants appear as a gathering of oblivious ghouls.

THE BIRD: Adult blackish green with scaled coverts. Face and throat orange, eyes opalescent. Bill strongly hooked with dark toothy marks. Early spring, head shows black, or white tufts. **Juvenile** variably pale. Plumage darkens as young bird matures.

FLIGHT: Takes flight slapping water with both feet in unison. At full speed, strong and purposeful. V-shaped flocks form orderly strands. Infrequently soars. Long tail and Adam's-apple neck bulge diagnostic.

VOICE: Usually silent. Vocal when nesting, uttering gruff belches, hollow toad-like croaks, and wooden clacking noises.

RANGE: Resident to lakes and rivers at low and middle elevations. **West Slope:** Fairly common at lower elevations. Uncommon or rare higher. Breeds in northern Sierra at Lake Almanor west of crest. **East Slope:** Uncommon but regular fall, winter, and spring visitor. Rarely breeds east of crest. Intermittent records near Honey Lake.

SIMILAR SPECIES: Loons run to take wing, have dagger-like bills, short tails. **Geese** rise vertically, vocalize, and have straight necks, short tails.

large
feet

JUVENILE

blocky

scaled

jagged

gray
bill

JUVENILE

spangled

NONBREEDING

BREEDING

Common Loon

Gavia immer

Stately. Our largest loon is as heavy as a medium-size goose. When not in flight, it spends virtually its entire life on the water hunting or resting. Snorkeling, it holds its face beneath the surface looking for fish. If prey is spotted, the bird bows slowly forward and slips beneath the surface to pursue quarry, often to great depths. Bill formidable, straight, deep, and blade-like.

THE BIRD: All plumages show the diagnostic neck-notch pattern. **Breeding adult** has a blackish-green head, muscular neck showing a white "picket fence" collar. Back is crossed by white squares blending into tiny dots at water line, creating a starry-night motif. **Nonbreeding adult,** upper parts are unmarked gray-brown. Molting adult in spring shows breeding plumage emerging from body, neck, and head. **Juvenile** like winter adult but with neatly scaled back feathers.

FLIGHT: Takes wing with powerful shallow flaps and runs hard, leaving splashes. Profile unique, torso bulky, head bulbous, feet large paddles.

VOICE: In spring, birds infrequently vocalize with their iconic, drawn-out, haunting yodel.

RANGE: Uncommon to locally common fall, winter, and spring visitor to large lakes and reservoirs, especially on **East Slope**. Rare in summer.

SIMILAR SPECIES: Pacific Loon juvenile and **nonbreeding** rare, medium size, lack white neck notch, and have smaller bills. Very rare **juvenile** and **nonbreeding Red-throated Loons** small, thin necked; have skyward gaze and chisel-shaped bill.

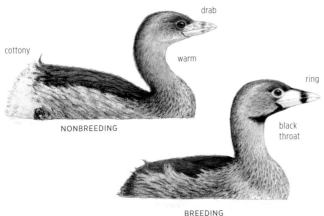

drab

cottony

warm

ring

black
throat

NONBREEDING

BREEDING

Pied-billed Grebe
Podilymbus podiceps

Superficially resembling ducks, grebes spend nearly their entire lives in the water. Bill shapes vary; lobed toes are set far back on body. Pursues fish that are then swallowed headfirst. Vulnerable on land, unable to take wing. Flaps vigorously, runs on the water to become airborne, appearing tail-less and ungainly as toes flop behind. Landing, skis in on belly, wings raised. Chicks hitch rides on parents' backs.

THE BIRD: Our smallest grebe, Green-winged Teal size. Retiring and watchful. Sinks submarine-style, periscope head above the surface. Dark with fluffy flanks and cotton vent. **Breeding adult**, throat black, body brownish buff. Breast feathers recall a wet pelt. Blunt silver bill ringed black. Eye dark. **Nonbreeding adult**, pale throat, dusky bill with faint ring. **Juvenile** like winter adult, but dark lines cross face.

FLIGHT: Flies at an angle, head high, legs splayed. The narrow wings are rather long. Breeding plumage shows white trailing edge to secondaries; nonbreeding lacks it.

VOICE: Long, loud, rapid series of gulping sounds: *COMP! COMP! COMP!* Ends with hiccup, *comp, comp eeeEERP!*, last note sharp, up-slurred. Also, guttural *Cah COW! Cah COW!* and drawn-out mournful, rising *wruuuuK!*

RANGE: Both slopes: Fairly common resident. Doesn't migrate to saltwater in winter like most grebes. Breeds in calm, sheltered ponds and lakes from low to middle elevations.

SIMILAR SPECIES: Eared Grebe paler, thinner bill and neck.

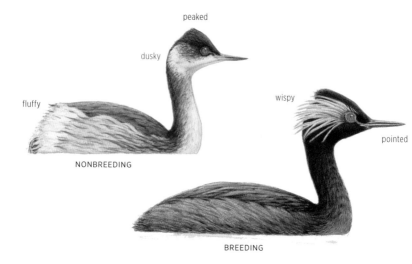

peaked

dusky

wispy

fluffy

pointed

NONBREEDING

BREEDING

Eared Grebe
Podecips nigricollis

Especially buoyant. Daintier than Horned, fluffier than Pied-billed Grebe. Appears as if enveloped in a luxurious fur stole. When active, body feathers flatten and crest swells, rising to a point.

THE BIRD: Bill finely tipped. Breeding **adult** black with rusty flanks and golden veil of filamentous plumes radiating from hypnotic red eyes. **Nonbreeding adult** shows diagnostic blackish crown, face, and back with dusky neck. Fall **immature** like adult nonbreeding, with buff on breast and neck. In early spring, birds molting from gray nonbreeding to the black and rust of breeding appear splotchy.

FLIGHT: Seldom seen flying, but capable of migrating great distances, usually at night. Appears labored taking wing with fervent "on-the-double" running. Nonbreeding birds are black above, whitish below, with secondaries and underwings white.

VOICE: Usually silent, but in large concentrations utter a high-pitched, two-note, up-slurred *Hurreep, Hureep, Hureep* as well as squeaky conversational chatter.

RANGE: Breeds in freshwater habitats, but usually visits highly alkaline and saline waters during migration and on wintering grounds. **West Slope:** Fairly common at Lake Isabella and Lake Almanor, otherwise uncommon west of crest. **East Slope:** Abundant late summer and fall at large alkali lakes, especially Mono Lake. Breeds colonially in wetlands and shallow marshes.

SIMILAR SPECIES: Horned Grebe nonbreeding rare, strikingly black and white, blocky headed, thick necked; suggests miniature Western Grebe. **Breeding**, cinnamon neck, thick golden tufts.

whitish lores

dark face

red eye

thick stripe

pea-green

PALE VARIANT

gray flanks

TYPICAL ADULT

Western Grebe
Aechmophorus occidentalis

Our largest grebes, Western and Clark's, hold their heads aloft, imparting a cobra-like appearance. Body wide at waterline. Waterfowl sleep with bills pointed backward, while grebes sleep with bills pointed forward. Grebes have a curious habit of extending a foot high into the air and waving it.

THE BIRD: Adult upper parts sooty gray to blackish, flanks variably gray. Underparts satin white. Fairly thick neck stripe merges into crown, red eye encompassed in black. The spear-like bill is greenish yellow with a black culmen and undersurface. Spectacular courtships include harmonized head-turning, gifting of plant matter, coordinated running displays. Pairs lift their bodies vertically, contort wings upward, arch necks, point bills skyward, and skitter rapidly across water. Alert or displaying birds spread crown laterally, recalling a matador's hat.

FLIGHT: Taking wing, extends head, flaps vigorously, and runs leaving splashes as green feet flop behind. Wings largely white.

VOICE: A loud, reedy, far-carrying *Kri-KREEK!*, the second note higher in pitch. In courtship interactions, utters creaking conversational chatter.

RANGE: In nonbreeding season, found in significant numbers on most large lakes and reservoirs of the Sierra. **West Slope:** Fairly common breeder at large lakes in the far north and far south, but apparently not in between. **East Slope:** Common breeder from spring through fall in similar habitats to the West Slope, but rare in winter.

SIMILAR SPECIES: See **Clark's Grebe**.

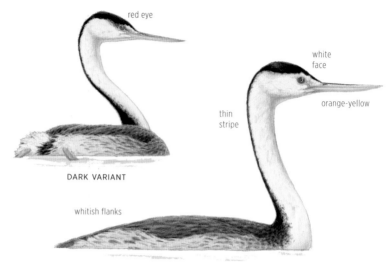

red eye

white face

orange-yellow

thin stripe

DARK VARIANT

whitish flanks

TYPICAL ADULT

Clark's Grebe
Aechmophorus clarkii

Nearly identical in size, structure, and appearance to Western Grebe. With head held high, both impart a noble carriage.

THE BIRD: Viewed with Western, Clark's Grebe is altogether paler. This whiter look is helpful for identification even from a great distance. Typically exhibits a white face, whiter flanks, and, well appreciated on sleeping birds, a thinner black neck stripe. The bright banana-yellow bill "glows" orange in the breeding season. The culmen is crisply ridged black. The undersurface of the bill lacks black shown by Western. While the bill appears somewhat larger on Clark's, this may be an effect of its being brighter and paler. Plumage variation is found in both species with near overlap. Darker-faced Clark's shows dusky feathering extending from the crown to the top of the eye.

FLIGHT: As in Western, the flight is labored and somewhat awkward, but shows more white in wings.

VOICE: Similar to the Western Grebe, the voice is far carrying and reedy. Bird typically gives a single, drawn-out *kreeeK!* with a strong rising inflection. Also gives an extended series of conversational notes: *we-ka, we-ka, we-ka, we-ka...*

RANGE: Range similar to Western Grebe. Clark's are almost always seen with Western Grebes, but are typically less numerous.

SIMILAR SPECIES: Western Grebe has blackish on undersurface of greenish-yellow bill, eyes encompassed in black, a wider black neck stripe, and grayer flanks.

dusky · white eye · casque · ash-colored · pinkish

SUMMER · SPRING · NONBREEDING · JUVENILE

American White Pelican
Pelecanus erythrorhynchos

Gregarious and substantial, pelicans have massive bills and deep throat pouches suited for capturing fish. Two occur in North America. Only the American White Pelican is a regular visitor to the Sierra. A freshwater species, birds hunt cooperatively, capturing prey side by side, shoaling fish forward into shallows with splashing wings, where then scooped up.

THE BIRD: With a wingspan of 9 feet, after California Condor, our heaviest bird. Late winter to early summer, **breeding adult** is white, blushed sulfur on breast and coverts. The nape is adorned with plumes, and on bill, an ornamental horny casque. Casque shed, **late-summer adult** shows dusky peppering on crown. Entirely white, fall, winter, and **nonbreeding adults** lack a crest and casque. Midsummer to early spring, **juvenile** is dusted ash gray.

FLIGHT: Ponderous taking wing with heavy flapping and lead-footed splashes. Airborne, floats on thermals, achieving lofty heights. Leisurely circling in graceful spirals, flocks form glittering cloud that slowly dissolves, sparkles again, then vanishes.

VOICE: Largely silent.

RANGE: Fairly common to locally common at large lakes and reservoirs, primarily on the **East Slope**. Doesn't breed in the Sierra, but flocks pass over in migration between Great Basin breeding grounds and Central Valley wintering areas.

SIMILAR SPECIES: Tundra Swan entirely white, black bill, flies with neck outstretched.

black edge
white
splotchy

MOLTING

black tip

thin eye-arcs

spot

BREEDING

NONBREEDING

pink

brown

FIRST WINTER

Bonaparte's Gull
Chroicocephalus philadelphia

A two-year gull. The smallest regularly occurring gull in the Sierra Nevada.

THE BIRD: From late spring to early fall, **breeding adult** shows black hood and pale medium-gray upper parts contrasting with prominent white primaries. **Nonbreeding adult** appears like a breeding adult, but its head is white with a black ear-spot. **First-winter immature** has a white head, black ear-spot, brown bar on the wing coverts, and black edges to flight feathers. Spring birds transitioning from first winter into first summer grow a splotchy black hood.

FLIGHT: Buoyant and nimble, feeding birds hover butterfly-like, linger momentarily, then gently land. Wings raised, they spin, pivot, flutter up, dangle their legs, then settle. In graceful unison, large flocks rise, drop, cleave to one side, bound forward, then plummet, giving the impression of a slowly bouncing ball.

VOICE: Rarely vocalizes in the Sierra. A harsh, nasal, tern-like *RAaaah! RAaaah! RAaaah!* with a strong emphasis at the start of each note.

RANGE: Both slopes: Usually found at large lakes and reservoirs. Most records are in the fall. In spring, erratic and unpredictable, mostly April. Very rare in winter.

SIMILAR SPECIES: Franklin's Gull rare; breeding adult shows darker upper parts, red bill, bold eye-arcs, and different wing pattern. **Sabine's Gull** rare; breeding adult shows a yellow bill tip, a red eye-ring, and different wing pattern.

yellow eye

BREEDING

black band

freckled

black tip

FIRST YEAR

ring

speckled

pale gray

yellow

NONBREEDING

BREEDING

Ring-billed Gull

Larus delawarensis

A three-year gull. Whether seizing earthworms from a rain-soaked soccer field, flycatching over plowed crops, or extorting cast-off junk food from an asphalt sea, this small regular gull is shrewd, calculating, and streetwise.

THE BIRD: Breeding adult pale gray, shows pale eye ringed in scarlet skin. **Winter adult** like breeding with speckled nape. **Second-winter** birds adult-like with tiny white in wingtip. Tail is tipped black, and the bill and legs are dull pink. **First winter** whitish and well marked with mottled nape and white tail tipped black. Back, coverts, and inner primaries pale gray.

FLIGHT: Wheeling flocks gracefully feed on winged morsels. Quarry spotted, birds break from the spiral with a burst of flaps to deftly snap up insects. When covering territory, lofty birds commute in wide formations with steady, constant flapping.

VOICE: A two-syllable, hollow call that rises, then drops: *aahHHAoww*. Also strained peevish notes, like a sliding finger on squeaky glass.

RANGE: Both slopes: Widespread and fairly common year-round. During fall migration, single birds or small groups congregate at large lakes up to Alpine.

SIMILAR SPECIES: California Gull larger, darker backed. **Adult,** greenish legs, red bill-spot. **Winter adult,** heavily marked shawl on head. **Second winter** recalls Ring-billed, but browner upper parts, longer greenish bill with wide black ring, gray-green legs. **First winter** browner. **Mew Gull** rare, smaller.

BREEDING

dark eye

freckled

red

medium gray

FIRST YEAR

SECOND YEAR

yellow-green

NONBREEDING

JUVENILES

California Gull

Larus californicus

In the Sierra, any gull should be assumed to be a California Gull until proven otherwise. The classic midsize, four-year gull, larger than Ring-billed, smaller than Herring.

THE BIRD: Breeding adult shows white head, blue-gray mantle, wing spots, and yellow bill tipped black and red. **Winter adult**, speckled shawl. **Third year** adult-like, but no red on bill or white wingtips. **Second year** similar to young Ring-billed, but bill and legs dull pink to green. **First year** mottled brown with whitish face. Underparts and tail brown. Bill pink, tip black. Legs flesh. **Juvenile** late summer-fall scaled brown, some blushed cinnamon. Bill black.

FLIGHT: With strange cries cascading from above, wheeling flocks vault the Sierra, some in route to Mono Lake. Descending birds spill altitude. Head earthward, wings held at a 90° angle, they plummet at a frightful velocity, quickly twisting and turning. Agile, they pull out just in time to land safely.

VOICE: Call, a forceful *yALP!* Foraging, gives strong, loud *KaaOW! KaaOW!* Also, strained cries.

RANGE: With California's largest breeding colony at Mono Lake, the most common widespread gull in the Sierra. **Both slopes:** Occurs year-round in flooded agricultural fields, rivers, lakes, and reservoirs, rarely to Alpine.

SIMILAR SPECIES: Ring-billed Gull paler and **Mew Gull** rare, darker; both are smaller, with small bills. **Herring Gull adult** larger, paler mantle, longer bill, white eyes, pink legs.

THIRD YEAR

ring

pale

dark

pale
eye

white

mottled

FIRST YEAR

SECOND YEAR

pale gray

NON-BREEDING

pink

NONBREEDING

Herring Gull

Larus argentatus

When identifying gulls, determine age by eye, bill, leg, and back color. Males average larger than females. Larger species take three to four years to mature; smaller gulls, two to three years. Molting birds change color and pattern each year. Young are browner; adults have white bodies, blue-gray backs, and black wingtips.

THE BIRD: This, our largest four-year gull, associates with Ring-billed and California Gulls. Pink-legged adults show contrast between the pale upper parts and black wings. Staring eyes bestow fierce expression. Note: Birds appear paler on sunny days, darker on overcast. **Winter adult,** mottled neck, yellow bill tipped red and black. **Third winter** adult-like, but bill flesh with black. Wingtips black, scant white. Tail white, marked black. **Second winter** variable, eyes pale, pink bill tipped black, body mottled, rump white, tail dark. **First winter** brownish with pale head and inner primaries. Rump brownish, tail dark, legs pinkish.

FLIGHT: Powerful. Easy on the wing, often soars to great heights. Adults show ink-black wingtips tipped white, pale underwings lacking the dark-based secondaries shown by California.

VOICE: Variable and forceful. A level series of husky *KOW! OW! OW! OW...;* strained, peevish cries; and drawn-out *uheeeeeEE!* with rising inflection.

RANGE: Both slopes: Uncommon late fall, winter, and early spring visitor to large lakes.

SIMILAR SPECIES: California Gull smaller. **Adult,** dark eye, darker mantle, legs green. **Ring-billed** and rare **Mew Gull,** smaller.

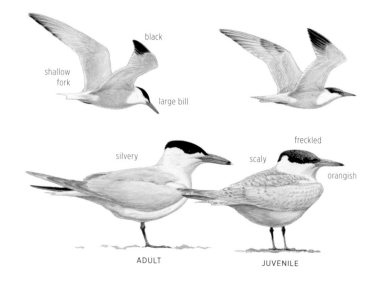

silvery · freckled · scaly · orangish · black · shallow fork · large bill

ADULT JUVENILE

Caspian Tern

Hydroprogne caspia

Great in proportions, California Gull size. Clean in contour, unblemished in plumage, graceful in passage. If a gull is a utility vehicle, then a tern is a Ferrari. Streamlined and stable at high speeds, they corner beautifully and come equipped with internal navigation systems. Set square on thick neck, the blocky head is crowned black with a short-cropped crest. Caspian stands on relatively long legs compared to smaller terns that can appear to be lying down even while standing.

THE BIRD: Breeding adult late winter to fall, black crown encompasses eye. Face, body, and tail white. Upper parts silver gray. Undersurface of outer primaries black. Upper surface grayer, black on trailing edge. Legs black. Adult in late fall to winter, rare. Like **breeding adult**, but forehead freckled white. **Juvenile** back, coverts, and tail have delicate tan chevrons.

FLIGHT: Flies on lithe wings with fluid cadence. Head angled, patrols waterways staring down, scarlet blade hunting for the incautious.

VOICE: Rasping. Conveys impression of being endlessly perturbed. Loudly broadcasting, adults sound like a cat in heat ripping canvas: *EEE-ARRGHHH!* Juvenile follows parent like a lost puppy, crying a high, thin *psseeEEeoh…*

RANGE: Both slopes: Uncommon to fairly common spring and fall at large reservoirs. **East Slope:** Breeds locally at Honey Lake, Bridgeport Reservoir, and Mono Lake. Very rare in winter.

SIMILAR SPECIES: Other **terns** smaller.

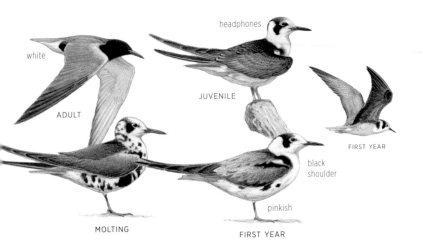

headphones

white

ADULT

JUVENILE

FIRST YEAR

black shoulder

MOLTING

pinkish

FIRST YEAR

Black Tern
Chlidonias niger

Globe-trotters, terns have slender chassis, scimitar wings, forked tails, and pointed cylindrical bills, whereas gulls' are blunt and laterally compressed. Their tiny webbed feet are not well adapted for paddling. On land they stand, walk on mincing steps, or simply sit.

THE BIRD: Dainty, slightly smaller than Killdeer. Breeding adult's shadowy plumage makes it surprisingly difficult to spot in flight. **Adult breeding** head and underparts black, upper parts and wings gray. Bend of wing and vent white. **Adult** late summer to fall molting into winter plumage, upper parts like breeding, head and body splotchy. **Winter**, black "headphones" and distinct scarf. **First winter**, leading and trailing edge of wing darker. **Juvenile** like first winter with faint scales to back and coverts. Legs pinkish.

FLIGHT: Forages by dipping into the water, leaving small splashes. Hovers, momentarily picking up fish and invertebrates. Rarely seems in a hurry. With deep wingbeats, flight is languid and meandering; when covering ground, however, progresses quickly with deep, cleaving strokes.

VOICE: A grating *grrrr, ek, ek, grek, greK! greK!* Also gives a sharp and poignant *chEF! chEF!* In flight, a lisping, anemic, and peevish *tseeeeP! tseeeeP!*

RANGE: West Slope: Uncommon or rare spring, summer, and early fall. Most records from extreme north and south. Breeds locally Lassen County. **East Slope:** Fairly common some years. Breeds sporadically at Honey Lake and Sierra Valley.

SIMILAR SPECIES: None.

freckled

dusky

shallow
fork

MOLTING

black
nape

scaled

tail shorter
than wingtips

black

ADULT

JUVENILE

Common Tern

Sterna hirundo

Not at all common. The classic tern, it's usually found associating with
the more common Forster's, which are slightly smaller, similarly proportioned, and equally elegant.

THE BIRD: Separating **breeding adult** Common from Forster's Tern is
challenging. Darker gray upper parts and ash-gray under, Common shows
slightly smaller bill, and tail-tip falls short of wingtip. **Juvenile** straightforward, showing black "headphones" and orange bill base. Rare **winter
adult** like breeding, but forehead freckled white.

FLIGHT: Hovering with head angled downward, or when hunting, the
flight is graceful and easygoing. Fish spotted, they plunge to seize it. Foray
successful, the wiggler is consumed. When Common is moving greater
distances, wingbeats quicken into rapid, fluid strokes. In flight, adult's
diagnostic dusky outer primaries contrast with the pale inner primaries.
Juvenile has a black shoulder bar.

VOICE: Calls, a forced, nasal *annnnnnngh!*; a grating and quavering *chir-
rrrrr-uh* that drops at the end; or sharp, repeated *chet! chet! chet!* notes.

RANGE: A very rare spring and fall migrant on the **West Slope**. Most
records from **East Slope** lakes and reservoirs. While a few are found in
June, they are slightly more regular in September, notably at Lake Tahoe.

SIMILAR SPECIES: Forster's Tern slightly larger. **Adult** paler above with
silver primaries. Standing, tail streamers extend just beyond wingtips.
Juvenile shows tan blush on upper parts and an isolated black ear patch;
lacks dark shoulder.

silvery

deep fork

dusky

JUVENILE

white

MOLTING

gray nape   black

NONBREEDING

tail past wingtips

BREEDING

JUVENILE

Forster's Tern

Sterna forsteri

Just larger than Common Tern, a beauty of the marshlands. Esthetically refined and supremely graceful. Forked tail closed, it becomes a thin, pinnate train. Pursuing aquatic prey, Forster's plunges headfirst into water with wings folded back. Popping up, it becomes airborne with a few quick flaps. Foray successful, it flips wriggling fish into the air, catches it headfirst, and swallows it whole.

THE BIRD: With satin sheen, breeding **adults** are trimmed with greatly elongated outer tail feathers extending beyond the wingtip. Toward winter, adults develop white forehead, inviting confusion with Common Tern. **Winter adult** is lustrous gray and white, marked by a black bill and ear-spot, and shorter tail. Late-summer **juvenile** shows upper parts edged cinnamon, and primaries dusky.

FLIGHT: Buoyant and graceful with deep, cleaving beats. Hunting, either patrols or hovers in fixed position looking downward for aquatic opportunities, when it either plunges or continues.

VOICE: A descending, irritated, nasal *naaaaaaah!* Gives quick, flat, dry notes like rapidly clinking stones: *tik, tik, tik...* Also, rapid, sharp, distressed notes: *chiT! chiT! chiT!...*

RANGE: West Slope: Uncommon spring, rare fall at low-elevation reservoirs. Very rare winter. **East Slope:** Fairly common near breeding colonies, including Honey Lake, Sierra Valley, Lake Tahoe, and possibly at Bridgeport Reservoir and Crowley Lake. Uncommon in spring and fall migration. Very rare in winter.

SIMILAR SPECIES: See **Common Tern.**

BREEDING

white

black wingpit

large eyes

spangled

short bill

splotchy

JUVENILE   MOLTING   NONBREEDING

Black-bellied Plover

Pluvialis squatarola

The Sierra boasts around twenty-five regularly occurring shorebird species, nine of which breed in the region.

THE BIRD: Plovers run on dry sand or mud, picking invertebrates from its surface. Well over twice the weight of the Killdeer, our largest plover has a robust body and bullet-shaped bill, and exhibits typical start-stop, start-stop plover feeding behavior. **Breeding adult** striking with black velvet underparts framed by a snow-white shawl from brow to neck. Upper parts checkered black and white. Standing, **nonbreeding adult** in winter is overall gray and not boldly marked. **Juvenile** like nonbreeding adult, but upper parts boldly spangled. Fresh bird can show faint golden hue. Breast is delicately streaked, underparts white.

FLIGHT: Transforms in flight, exposing a white rump, bold wing stripe, and black wingpits, marks shown in all plumages. This long-distance migrant is usually encountered in small groups. Flight purposeful and exceedingly rapid.

VOICE: Call, a mournful, loud, far-carrying, three-part *PEE-oh-WHEE!* with second syllable lower, last syllable higher. Also, single rising *WHEE!* or double *oh WHEE!*

RANGE: High Arctic breeder, this spring and fall migrant can be observed in a wide variety of shallow wetland habitats. **West Slope:** Rare. Most at Lake Almanor and South Fork Kern River Valley. **East Slope:** Uncommon in spring and fall with most from Owens Valley, Crowley, and Mono Lakes. Very rare in winter.

SIMILAR SPECIES: None.

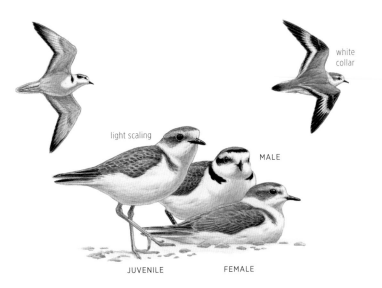

light scaling

white collar

MALE

JUVENILE FEMALE

Snowy Plover
Charadrius nivosus

Smaller than Semipalmated. Tiny black bill, large eyes, rounded head impart gentle look. It's no surprise that with sand-colored plumage, the Snowy blends with its environment. Frequently encountered on alkali mudflats and hesitant to fly, bird tends to run or simply flatten. Dashing on a blur of legs, it stops, quickly tips up, sprints, stops, repeats.

THE BIRD: **Breeding male's** head marked black. **Breeding female** like muted male. **Winter adult** like breeding female. **Juvenile's** upper parts delicately scaled pale.

FLIGHT: Before flying, often lifts wings, reaching high, and flashes silvery underwings across the mudflats. Flies low to the ground. Glides to a stop on running legs, exhibiting pale back, bold wing stripe, and dark tail-tip.

VOICE: Breeding season call, a repeated *toe-wEE! toe-wEE!*, last note rising emphatically. Nonmigrant winter call, a quiet *chert*. Also gives Rough-winged Swallow–like burry, rolling *drrrrrrP!*

RANGE: Winters along coastal California. Arrives inland to breed in early April, returning late September. **West Slope:** Rare, Lakes Almanor and Isabella. **East Slope:** Nests on alkaline mudflats near emerging freshwater seeps at Bridgeport Reservoir and Owens, Mono, and Honey Lakes. Rare, South Lake Tahoe. Because of small breeding population and human disturbance, coastal population federally listed **Threatened**. Interior population adversely affected by habitat disruption.

SIMILAR SPECIES: **Semipalmated Plover** darker brown, complete breast band, orange bill base, legs yellowish orange.

faint
scales

blunt

band

pale

orange

JUVENILE   NONBREEDING   BREEDING

Semipalmated Plover
Charadrius semipalmatus

Known for migrating great distances between northern breeding grounds and southern wintering haunts. A small plover, just larger than Snowy with a breast band that changes thickness with posture, a clown-like face, and a "head-lamp" forehead. Found in small migratory groups where start-stop movements indicate classic plover behavior.

THE BIRD: **Breeding adult** upper parts dark brown, neck ring white. Black-tipped bill and orange legs. **Nonbreeding adult** like breeding, but bill dark, facial markings muted. **Juvenile** like nonbreeding adult, but delicately scaled above.

FLIGHT: The color of wet mud, camouflaged birds can startle when a few underfoot suddenly become many, and an entire mudflat seems to take flight. Vocalizing, they band together, rapidly climbing with cleaving strokes from narrow wings. Dark above, white below, twisting flocks create a flashing impression.

VOICE: Call, far-carrying, emphatic, and up-slurred *chi-weeP!* When foraging, utters garbled conversational notes and short trills.

RANGE: Spring and fall migrant favoring mud, shallows, and drier conditions. Numbers peak in September and diminish by October as southbound juveniles arrive after adults. **West Slope:** Uncommon to rare. **East Slope:** Fairly common, often dozens at Honey and Crowley Lakes during fall migration.

SIMILAR SPECIES: **Snowy Plover** slightly smaller, pale sandy above, breast band incomplete, black bill, gray legs. **Killdeer** much larger, two breast bands, ornate orange rump and tail, different call. Killdeer chick has one breast band but few other similarities.

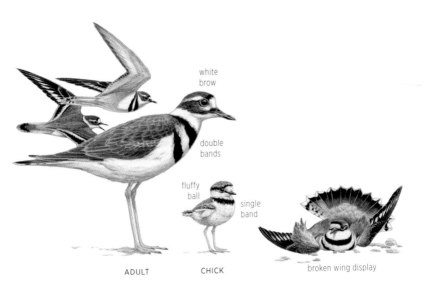

white brow

double bands

fluffy ball

single band

ADULT   CHICK   broken wing display

Killdeer

Charadrius vociferus

Smaller than Black-bellied and larger than Semipalmated Plover. The town crier, Killdeer seem incapable of internalizing a single emotion. If nest is disturbed, teeters dramatically, spreads wings and tail, and falls to its chest. This creates a very convincing broken-wing act to lure intruders from its cluster of precious eggs.

THE BIRD: **Adult** brandishes a well-marked face with scarlet skin around the eye. Orange and brown, the tail is tipped white and scrawled with black. With stubby wings and tail, downy **chick** is a fluff-ball with legs.

FLIGHT: Vocalizing in flight, moves quickly, purposefully, and gracefully on long, slender wings that show well the bold white stripe and flashing white undersurface.

VOICE: Anxious, high, and shrill, includes a crying *tEEEr, tEEEr!* with rising inflection to each note, a rapid trill while running, and a nearly namesake *ti-tearrr, ti-tearrr*. Often vocalizes at night.

RANGE: Widespread resident on both slopes. **West Slope:** Locally common to abundant at lower-elevation habitats with open terrain, lakes, stream edges, irrigated fields, golf courses, even gravel roofs of office buildings. Few breed up to Alpine meadows at the Sierra crest. **East Slope:** Similar to West Slope, but less numerous south of Tahoe region. Departs entirely in snowy conditions.

SIMILAR SPECIES: **Semipalmated Plover** vaguely similar, smaller, one breast band, orange bill and legs. Shape of an **American Kestrel** in flight may confuse.

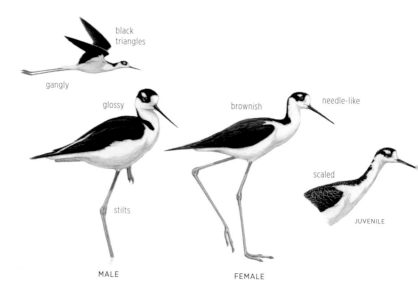

black triangles

gangly

glossy

brownish

needle-like

scaled

stits

JUVENILE

MALE

FEMALE

Black-necked Stilt

Himantopus mexicanus

Stilts often wade in deep water, picking organisms from the surface. While only a little shorter in length than avocets, they are but half their weight. The black, needle-like bill opposite its sharply pointed wings creates an attenuated silhouette. Formally dressed and aptly named stilts take drawn-out strides. Standing aloft on exceptionally thin legs, stilts have comparatively the longest of any Sierra bird.

THE BIRD: Breeding male glossy blue-black above, white below, with a white dot above the dark ruby eye. **Breeding female** like male with brownish upper parts. **Juvenile** like adult with delicate buff scaling on upper parts and paler legs.

FLIGHT: Flocks in flight create choreographed performances of tricolored birds in unison, trailing gangly red legs. Composed of black-and-white triangles, the pattern, body, and wings coalesce into a striking silhouette.

VOICE: Agitated. A sharp, rapid, monotonous *kiT! kiT! kiT! kiT!* Juvenile's call remarkably similar to *KEEK! KEEK!* call of Long-billed Dowitcher.

RANGE: Mostly found in the Sierra from late March through September. **West Slope:** Uncommon in spring and fall at Almanor and Isabella Lakes, very rare west of the crest. **East Slope:** Fairly common breeder at low-elevation wetlands, rare visitor to high-elevation lakes. Very rare anywhere in the region in winter, when some birds move to the Central Valley but most to tropical America.

SIMILAR SPECIES: None.

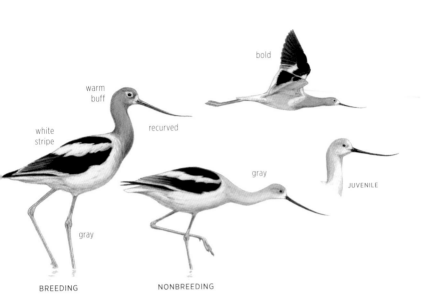

BREEDING   NONBREEDING

American Avocet
Recurvirostra americana

Inherently graceful, avocets are larger than stilts and often wade up to their bellies. Striding on long legs, they feed with a scything movement of their thin, upturned bills to procure organisms at the water's surface.

THE BIRD: Seasonal differences determined by the head color. Sexes differ in degree of bill curvature. **Female** bill is more strongly angled than **male** bill. **Breeding adult** obvious with cinnamon head and neck. Bold upper parts black, with white "racing stripes." **Nonbreeding adult's** head and neck gray. **Juvenile** in late summer briefly shows buff head and neck, then quickly molts to gray nonbreeding plumage.

FLIGHT: On the wing, especially near nests, avocets put on a show. Brazen, eternally clamorous, and boldly bedecked, they hold nothing back. Too close to the clutch? They accelerate, increase the volume, and, frighteningly, pass within a hairsbreadth of liability.

VOICE: A loud, monotonous, strident, clanking *HREEK! HREEK! HREEK!* with rising inflection at end of each note.

RANGE: Typically encountered from spring through fall. **West Slope:** Uncommon visitor to Almanor and Isabella Lakes, very rare elsewhere west of the Sierra crest. **East Slope:** Fairly common breeder and spring and fall migrant at low-elevation wetlands and alkaline marshes at Mono Lake. Small numbers may linger into winter, but most move to the Central Valley.

SIMILAR SPECIES: Unique. No other shorebird has strongly upturned bill.

long tail

lines

eye line

pink

buff
scales

stiff wingbeats

semi-collar

dots

BREEDING

JUVENILE

NONBREEDING

Spotted Sandpiper
Actitis macularius

Sandpipers, typically found in or near water, are built for variations in their environment. Their overall form, leg length, and bill structure give clues to their habits and habitats.

THE BIRD: Just larger than Western Sandpiper, Spotted is typically alone or in pairs. Constantly bobs rear end. Broad collar creates hooded effect. **Breeding adult** shows pink bill tipped black, bold eye line, black scrawling on upper parts, spotted underparts, and pinkish legs. **Nonbreeding adult** brown with delicately barred coverts. Underparts fluffy cotton white. Legs greenish. **Juvenile** like nonbreeding adult, but wing coverts edged buff.

FLIGHT: Diagnostic, moves low to the water with stiff, flicking beats. Covering greater distances, transforms flight style to more typical shorebird cadence, inviting confusion. Upper wing pattern weak, underwings bold.

VOICE: Usually given in flight, voice is loud and clear rising above the water's din. Two-part *to-weeT! to-weeT!* with second note rising. Also, rapid, level notes: *weeT, weeT, weeT...*

RANGE: Both slopes: Resident of turbulent streams and lakeshores at all elevations. Leaves high elevations after breeding. Most birds descend below the snow line in winter. The only shorebird to regularly breed above foothills aside from Killdeer. Fairly common to the Upper Conifer. Uncommon to Subalpine.

SIMILAR SPECIES: Solitary Sandpiper very rare, different flight, thin bill, spectacles, upper parts speckled, dark wings, tail banded black.

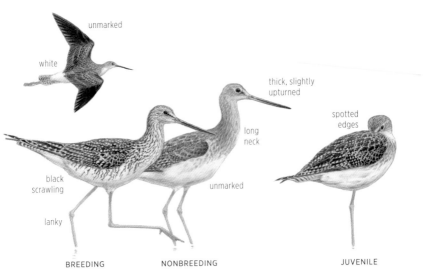

unmarked

white

thick, slightly upturned

spotted edges

long neck

black scrawling

unmarked

lanky

BREEDING   NONBREEDING   JUVENILE

Greater Yellowlegs

Tringa melanoleuca

Slightly smaller than the Black-necked Stilt, Greater Yellowlegs is active, wary, and high strung. With clamorous diatribe and repeated teetering, it gladly notifies all of your arrival. In shallow waters, it sprints, stops, bobs, pivots, and runs, picking up small creatures from the surface.

THE BIRD: Breeding adult gray, extensively marked with delicate black scrawling on neck, upper parts, and flanks. **Nonbreeding adult** like breeding, but lacks black. Appears gray above, white on belly. **Juvenile** like nonbreeding adult, but feathers of upper parts neatly scaled in whitish or buff dots.

FLIGHT: Flies with quick snapping beats on narrow pointed wings. Appears gray and white, with dark primaries. White rump contrasts with the back. White tail barred black, appears gray. Yellow toes project beyond tail. Underwings whitish, flight feathers grayer.

VOICE: A rapid descending, three-note clear and ringing *TEW! Tew, tew*. When agitated utters gruff, monotonous, level notes: *griFF! griFF! griFF!*

RANGE: Widespread migrant to wetlands throughout the lowlands of California. **West Slope:** Fairly common to uncommon March through April and early August through September. Visits Foothill ponds, reservoirs, and lazy streams. Rare or very rare at higher elevations. **East Slope:** Fairly common migrant in Owens Valley, but uncommon elsewhere east of the crest. Rare in winter.

SIMILAR SPECIES: Lesser Yellowlegs rare, nearly identical in all plumages. Soft call; small size; short, straight, thin bill.

black
markings

flashy

BREEDING

straight,
thick bill

pale
scaling

whitish

gray

NONBREEDING

JUVENILE

Willet

Tringa semipalmata

Sturdy and well built. Larger and much heavier than the Greater Yellow-legs, but similar in length. Feeds by running in bursts, prodding the mud and picking at its surface.

THE BIRD: White brow above dark lores creates expressive spectacles. **Breeding adult**, upper parts, head, breast, and flanks randomly penciled in black bars and chevrons. Breast and back veiled tan. **Nonbreeding adult** lacks bold marks. Upper parts mouse gray, throat and belly pale. **Juvenile** like nonbreeding adult, but back and wing coverts edged pale.

FLIGHT: At rest, Willet is "a quiet evening at home," but in flight becomes a wild party! Flies powerfully and directly, showing well the diagnostic black-and-white pattern. If agitated by your presence, nesting birds circle overhead, flapping shallowly and vocalizing.

VOICE: Repeated, loud, ringing *tu will will, will-IT!* with rising, questioning emphasis on last note. If annoyed, gives monotonous, agitated, clanking notes: *kleK! kleK! kleK! kleK!*

RANGE: Localized breeder, but more widespread in spring migration from late March to mid-April, and fall migration from mid-July until end of September. **West Slope:** Rare. Most records at lakes and wetlands, late summer to fall. **East Slope:** In the northeastern Sierra, a common breeder at Sierra Valley and Honey Lake. Fairly common south to Crowley Lake. In migration, fairly common at large wetlands east of crest.

SIMILAR SPECIES: Greater Yellowlegs smaller, more slender body and bill, legs yellow.

coarse markings

exceptionally long bill

barred

cinnamon

shorter bill

ADULT

JUVENILE

Long-billed Curlew
Numenius americanus

Nearly White-faced Ibis size, our largest shorebird. Compared to body length, has the longest bill of any North American bird. Grazing flocks spread out. Striding on long legs, they draw earthworms up from plowed soil or pluck grasshoppers from grass.

THE BIRD: Adult, extremely long bill, pink at base. **Female's** bill averages longer than the male's. Dark crowned, the face sometimes shows a pale eye-ring. **Juvenile's** bill on average is shorter than adults'.

FLIGHT: Profile curious. Underwings and tail cinnamon, outer primaries black. Flight feathers barred. Groups in flight progress in loose formations, in contrast to Whimbrel, which form orderly lines.

VOICE: Loud, ringing, frantic *kur-LEE! kur-LEE!* with emphasis on second note. Also, a series of rapid notes with wavering finish: *kur-kur-kur-kur-LEE! kur-LEE! kur-LEE!* Taking wing, gives strong, sharp, clanking *cha-DEEK! cha-DEEK!* with second note harder, louder.

RANGE: Nests exclusively in the northeast portion of the Sierra. Most widespread in fall migration, late June through August. **West Slope:** Uncommon spring and fall migrant. Some winter in foothill grasslands on both slopes. **East Slope:** Common migrant. Breeds fairly commonly at Honey Lake and Sierra Valley.

SIMILAR SPECIES: Whimbrel very rare, smaller, grayer, lacks warm hues, shorter bill, crown striped, different call. **Marbled Godwit** rare, smaller, straighter pink-based bill. Flight feathers unbarred. Sleeping birds with heads tucked *very* difficult to separate. Godwits have blackish legs; curlews' are gray.

white

rust

pale gray

black spots

JUVENILE

BREEDING

NONBREEDING

Western Sandpiper
Calidris mauri

Frequently referred to as "peep," our smallest sandpipers include Baird's, Least, and Western. Feeds with other peep, rapidly picking organisms from below the mud's surface. Vocalizing, disturbed flocks take wing, land, or depart for calmer haunts.

THE BIRD: Breeding adult, flanks show tiny dots, head and scapulars marked rust. **Nonbreeding adult**, overall pale. Upper parts gray, underparts white. Gray wash on side of breast. **Juvenile** appears a mix between breeding plumage with rust on back, and nonbreeding plumage with gray face and white flanks. Upper parts crisply scaled, some with buff on crown and collar.

FLIGHT: Twisting on their axis, single birds twinkle white then gray. Great numbers form swirling amoebic blobs that condense, darken, rearrange, glitter, and vanish...like a mirage.

VOICE: A sharp *chiT! chiT!* Flocks create a shrill twittering sound reminiscent of a Pine Siskin flock taking wing. Flight call, a flat, burry *jreeet, jreeet...* Also, flat, drawn-out trills.

RANGE: In fall, adults arrive mid-July, followed by juveniles in August, departing by October. Rare in winter. **West Slope:** Rare migrant. Regular at Lake Almanor in fall. **East Slope:** Common spring migrant on mudflats from Mono Basin to Owens Valley.

SIMILAR SPECIES: Least Sandpiper smaller, thinner bill, brown breast, legs greenish. **Sanderling nonbreeding** rare, larger, black primary coverts, lacks hind toe. **Adult breeding**, rust breast and head. **Juvenile** upper parts checkered black and white.

weak stripe

contrast

subtle droop

black spots

rust

drab

streaks

greenish yellow

BREEDING

JUVENILE

NONBREEDING

Least Sandpiper
Calidris minutilla

Our smallest sandpiper is the weight of a Song Sparrow. Mousy by virtue of its minute size, brown plumage, timid head-down posture, and squeaky chatter. Usually found in moderate numbers. Seems to prefer drier mud conditions more than Western.

THE BIRD: Breeding adult drab, appears unkempt with large black centers to back feathers. Breast sides streaked. **Nonbreeding adult**, drab gray-brown with contrasting white belly. **Juveniles** are more colorful than adults and nonbreeding birds. Their upper parts and back feathers are crisply edged rust, white, and buff.

FLIGHT: Bat-like. Shape attenuated with tiny body and short tail. Bird rapidly twists and turns, twinkling light then dark as white underwing contrasts with dark upper. Nervous flocks chatter and change direction frequently. When relaxed, they fly more quietly and directly.

VOICE: A thin, high, shrill, rolling *preeEEP! freeeEEP!* with rising inflection on each note.

RANGE: Arrives before Western Sandpipers in late March, peaking in April. Fall birds arrive in late July and peak in late August. **West Slope:** Uncommon but widespread in spring and fall migration in the foothills. **East Slope:** Common where it is "the peep" of most wetlands. Rare in winter except in Owens Valley and lower foothill areas, where they can be locally common.

SIMILAR SPECIES: Western Sandpiper larger, bigger bill, black legs, whiter overall, especially breast. May resemble nonbreeding **Dunlin** if size and bill length are misjudged.

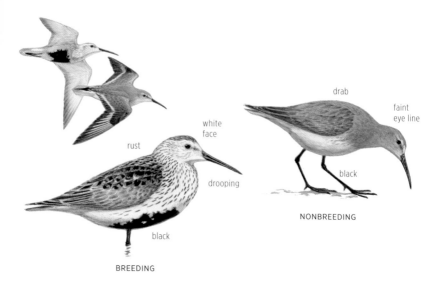

rust

white
face

drooping

black

BREEDING

drab

faint
eye line

black

NONBREEDING

Dunlin

Calidris alpina

Appears like an oversized peep with small head, short neck, and deep chest.

THE BIRD: Breeding adult distinct. Underparts white, streaked black. Upper parts and crown rust, spangled black. Extent of black on belly varies. **Nonbreeding adult**, drab overall with grayish-brown head and upper parts. Brow and throat pale whitish, sides of breast subtly streaked. Unlike almost all other sandpipers, **juvenile** molts into nonbreeding plumage before migration, so is rarely recorded in the Sierra.

FLIGHT: Sturdy, Dunlins fly quickly. While not likely to be encountered in large numbers in the Sierra, immense whirling flocks form mesmerizing illusions. More likely seen coastally, apparitions of glittering confetti that seem to disappear in a mirage. Reforming into an amoebic blob, they again vanish like a phantom, materialize, and on they go.

VOICE: Call, a level, burry, strident *jreeeep! jreeeep! dreeeep!* Feeding, utters contented conversational chattering notes: *jreep, jit, jreep, jit, jit, jreep, jreep...*

RANGE: Winters along coast and in Central Valley. Migrates in spring and fall to the Sierra. **West Slope:** Rare visitor to Foothill wetlands. **East Slope:** Uncommon to fairly common. Peaks April and September. Generally rare in winter, but locally common at Owens Valley and Honey Lake.

SIMILAR SPECIES: Nonbreeding adult Least and **Western Sandpipers** much smaller, with less distinct wing stripe. **Breeding adult** and **juvenile** are scaled above. **Nonbreeding dowitchers** larger, longer bill, white back patch, green legs.

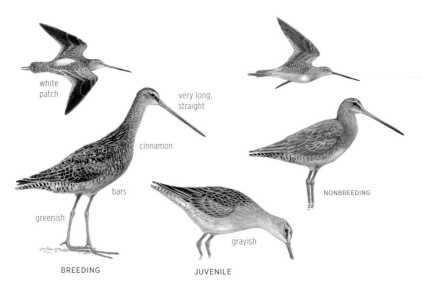

white patch

very long, straight

cinnamon

bars

greenish

BREEDING

grayish

JUVENILE

NONBREEDING

Long-billed Dowitcher
Limnodromus scolopaceus

Larger and longer legged than Wilson's Snipe. Midsize, these gregarious sandpipers forage in tight groups in shallow pools, rapidly pumping their long bills into the mud.

THE BIRD: **Breeding adult** shows bars on sides of breast. Reddish underparts typically extend to vent. **Nonbreeding adult** is almost certainly Long-billed. Famously difficult to separate from Short-billed, it tends to show grayer chest and flanks. On **juvenile**, tertials unmarked dusky with or without pale edge.

FLIGHT: Note long, straight bill, white back patch, toes just past tail. Milling birds form a flock shaped like a rolling ball. Covering greater distances, flocks flatten into a wide, flat plane. Often mixes with Black-bellied Plovers.

VOICE: Diagnostic. A loud, sharp, distinct *KEEK! KEEK! KEEK!* Birds converse constantly while feeding as sharp *keek* notes flow through the flock.

RANGE: Common and widespread wintering in Central Valley. In the Sierra, mostly seen during migration. **West Slope:** Uncommon spring and fall migrant to Foothill mudflats. **East Slope:** Common to locally abundant in similar habitats, especially at Sierra Valley, Honey Lake, and Mono Basin. Generally rare in winter, but fairly common in Owens Valley.

SIMILAR SPECIES: **Short-billed Dowitcher** nearly identical in all plumages. See account for differences. Soft *tew, tew, tew* call is Short-billed's best characteristic. **Wilson's Snipe** less gregarious, furtive, face and back boldly striped, lacks white back patch, has orangey tail and shorter legs.

orange

buff
stripes

barred

short

long,
straight

angled
down

Wilson's Snipe
Gallinago delicata

Effectively employs intricate camouflage, rendering it all but invisible. With crouched appearance, just smaller than a dowitcher. Plunges bill piston-like into quagmire.

THE BIRD: All plumages, be they seasonal, sexual, or age related, appear similar. Buff lines crossing the face continue down the back to create bold "suspenders." Orange tail boldly marked by black and tipped white.

FLIGHT: Bursts from the bog with a hurried flight as bird twists on its axis. Reclusive in winter, outgoing in spring, it performs dramatic roller-coaster displays. From towering heights, it quickly dives earthward. Pulling up at the bottom of the display and spreading the modified tail feathers wide, it produces a deep, rapid, hooting sound that rises in volume: *lu, lu, Lu, Lu, LU, LU! LU!! LU!!!*

VOICE: In flight, Snipes gives a coarse emphatic *jzzzzzek!* From an open perch, the breeding "song" is a monotonous, level, rapid *kret, kret, kret, kret...*

RANGE: Occurs year-round in the Sierra and moves between elevations or across the crest. **West Slope:** Uncommon breeders in the foothills, rarely to Upper Conifer, with fall migrants found as high as 9,000 feet. **East Slope:** Locally common breeder from Owens Valley north to Sierra Valley. Rare north of Reno in winter, uncommon farther south.

SIMILAR SPECIES: Long-billed Dowitcher gregarious, white rump patch, lacks white suspenders, *keek* call notes. **Breeding** rusty, **nonbreeding** overall gray.

MALE

muted

black

FEMALE

WINTER

patternless wings

white

scaled

JUVENILE

Wilson's Phalarope
Phalaropus tricolor

Feeding birds walk, run, or swim. Pecking the surface and paddling with lobed toes, they circle rapidly, creating a vortex to draw organisms to its center for consumption. Sexually, phalarope plumages are opposite of what is typical, with breeding females more colorful and males less.

THE BIRD: A large, long-necked phalarope. **Breeding males** are variable. Although some birds are bright, most are dull, with color and contrast subdued. **Breeding female's** black face, blending into maroon "racing stripes," is one of nature's finest color schemes. **Winter adult** pale gray above, white below. Dark-crowned **juvenile** is whitish below, with upper parts heavily scaled buff.

FLIGHT: White underwings and dark upper create a flashing effect as flocks twist and turn. The rump is boldly white, the tail pale gray, and the toes extend just beyond.

VOICE: A monotonous, level hooting *whe? whe? whe?* with muffled questioning quality.

RANGE: Breeding range barely reaches Sierra's eastern edge. Widespread in the region during migration. **West Slope:** Fairly common spring and fall migrants at Lake Almanor, where they may breed; otherwise, rare fall migrants west of crest. **East Slope:** Fairly common breeder in low-elevation marshes from Honey Lake to Owens Lake. Many thousands stage at Mono Lake in July. Most depart mid-September.

SIMILAR SPECIES: Nonbreeding **Red-necked Phalarope**, shorter neck, black ear patch. **Lesser Yellowlegs**, checkered upper parts; long, yellow legs; rarely swims.

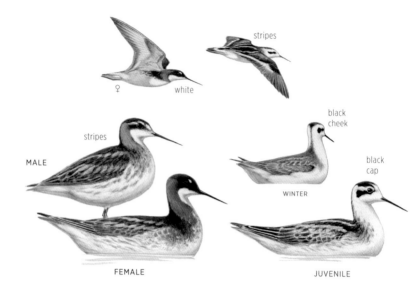

Red-necked Phalarope
Phalaropus lobatus

Smaller than Wilson's Phalarope, larger than Western Sandpiper. Energetic bird hurriedly swims, pivots, and spins, feverishly pecking at the water for food.

THE BIRD: Breeding male face marked white, colors subdued. **Breeding female** lovely with white eye-dot, chestnut neck, striking white throat, and blue-black head and upper parts. Back boldly striped buff. **Nonbreeding adult** plain, crown and cheek dark, upper parts show ghost of back stripes. **Juvenile** crown, nape, cheek, and upper parts black. Back, stripe buff.

FLIGHT: Takes flight effortlessly. While feeding, birds often flutter for short distances. Covering ground, they move quickly and directly. The bold wing stripe and tan back stripes are diagnostic in all plumages. Twisting and turning, flocks create black-and-white glittering effect.

VOICE: Feeding flocks utter squeaky and rapid conversational chatter. Flight call, repeated, sharp, clipped notes in varied cadence: *chit, chit, chiT, chIT! chit, chIT!*

RANGE: Breeds in the Arctic and winters off the coast of South America. Migrates through the Sierra Nevada. **West Slope:** Uncommon to rare at low-elevation ponds, marshes, and lakes. Very rare visitor to Subalpine. **East Slope:** Uncommon except at Mono Lake, where tens of thousands annually stage from late July through September.

SIMILAR SPECIES: Wilson's Phalarope has long, thin neck; white rump; no wing pattern. **Nonbreeding Red Phalarope** very rare and larger, with a blunt-tipped bill and unmarked gray back.

dark

buff

bulge

black whisker

bold streaks

green

ADULT

American Bittern
Botaurus lentiginosus

Herons are statuesque waders with long, dagger-like bills, necks, and legs. They occur in an array of aquatic and terrestrial habitats, consuming finned, furred, and feathered prey.

THE BIRD: Bitterns are solitary and slightly smaller than Night-Herons but longer necked. Lethargic until spearing prey with startling speed. Supremely camouflaged, upper parts intricate brown, rust, gray, and white. Often stretching head high, it points its yellow-and-black bill skyward, revealing coarse stripes, vertical highlights, and cattail patterns to underparts. Displaying bird shape-shifts. Swelling its heads, it exposes white plumes from the sides of its neck.

FLIGHT: Flushed birds typically relieve themselves and utter a gruff, irritated *WROOOCKKK!* Flight feathers are dark, tipped buff. Progresses with deep rowing flaps.

VOICE: "Song" outlandish, far carrying, concussive—like dropping a watermelon into deep water. Produces a liquid gulping with flat first note, a rising second, and emphasis on third: *doop, Ha-GLOOP! doop, Ha-GLOOP!*

RANGE: Both slopes: Uncommon resident and breeder in foothill wetlands. **West Slope:** Breeds in marshes in spring and summer near Lake Isabella. Rare farther north and at higher elevations. **East Slope:** Common in spring and summer at Sierra Valley, where it likely breeds. Uncommon South Lake Tahoe, rare elsewhere. Statewide populations have declined since the 1970s.

SIMILAR SPECIES: First-year Black-crowned Night-Heron gregarious, roosts in trees, upper parts spotted, eyes orange, compact in flight, typically nocturnal.

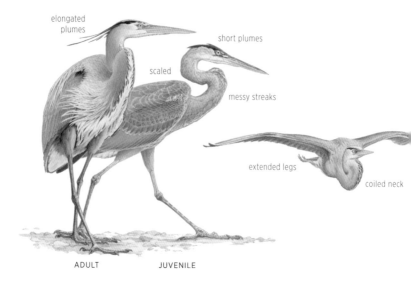

elongated plumes

short plumes

scaled

messy streaks

extended legs

coiled neck

ADULT   JUVENILE

Great Blue Heron
Ardea herodias

Ranging in size from the tiny Least Bittern to the stately Great Blue, herons reach maturity in two to three years. Statuesque; height changes with posture. Roosting, hunkers with neck coiled. Bulky stick nests are built in trees and marshes, usually colonially.

THE BIRD: Feeding, stands over four feet tall. Serenely forages from lake to lawn, relying on glacial pace and somber coloration for anonymity. Prey found, fate sealed, bird springs dagger-tipped serpentine neck into ill-fated fish or gopher. **Breeding adult** bluish gray, neck purplish, bill yellow. **Juvenile** scruffy with ragged crest, scaled upper parts, dusky mandible.

FLIGHT: Flies with slow, deep beats on broad wings. Coiled neck forms graceful curve. Legs trail. Landing, extends neck, appearing momentarily crane-like.

VOICE: A startlingly indelicate gruff, croaking *Aaaaaargh!* Also gives loud quacking *wrenK! wrenK!* Nesting colonies produce wooden clacks and guttural belches, all sounds worthy of a junior high gym class.

RANGE: Both slopes: Widespread, fairly common resident of wetlands. Most numerous heron in the Sierra. **West Slope:** Breeds at Lake Almanor and lower reaches of American, Yuba, Kaweah, and Kern Rivers to about 4,500 feet. **East Slope:** Breeds north and south at widely spaced locations, at least historically. Nonbreeding birds fairly common at lowland wetlands.

SIMILAR SPECIES: Sandhill Crane gregarious, runs taking wing, flies in formation, holds neck outstretched; snapping wingbeats, trumpeting voice. Adult, red forecrown.

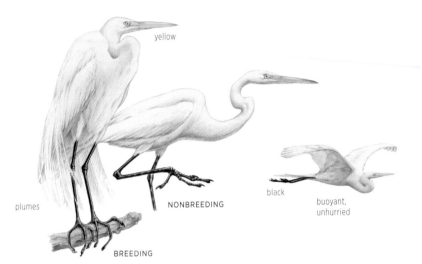

yellow

plumes

NONBREEDING

black

buoyant, unhurried

BREEDING

Great Egret

Ardea alba

Not vocally gifted, herons are fortunately adorned with elongated plumes and partake in exotic courtship displays. All fly with necks coiled and feet extending beyond their tails.

THE BIRD: Visible from great distances. Similar in form to Great Blue Heron, but one-third its weight. Lanky with extremely long, S-curved neck. When roosting, hunkers down. Pursuing small fish, mammals, and amphibians, it stands calmly, stalks slowly, strides fluidly, and strikes instantaneously. Displays with chest high, neck coiled, and golden bill skyward. Lacy plumes burst from back, splaying into a three-foot-wide fan of snow-white "fireworks." When the egret is walking, **adult's** plumes cascade beyond tail, appearing as a bridal train. **Nonbreeding adult** lacks plumes. **Juvenile** nearly identical.

FLIGHT: Flies with wings bowed at the wrist while black legs trail. Flaps with shallow, languid, floating beats.

VOICE: A back-of-the-throat, hollow, strained, and grating *aaaaaaangh* uttered when taking wing. Chicks give a rapid, monotonous pig-like *yink, yink, yink...*

RANGE: West Slope: Common in Foothill wetlands. Rarely to Subalpine in fall. Uncommon resident and irregular breeder at Almanor and Isabella Lakes. **East Slope:** Uncommon migrant to Sierra Valley, Bridgeport Reservoir, Owens River, Tahoe and Mono Lakes. Rare in winter.

SIMILAR SPECIES: Snowy Egret smaller, more active, black bill, yellow lores and toes. Plumes emerge from crown and breast. Flight silhouettes of Snowy and Great Egret can be difficult to differentiate.

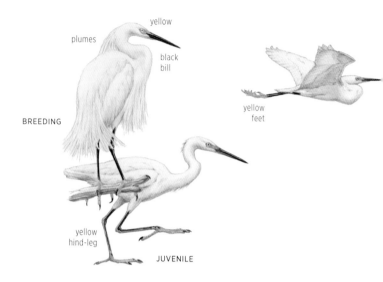

yellow

plumes

black
bill

BREEDING

yellow
feet

yellow
hind-leg

JUVENILE

Snowy Egret
Egretta thula

Less than half the size of the Great Egret and distinctly active. Hunting, Snowy Egret shakes its yellow feet under water, flushing hidden prey into striking range. This hyperactive behavior is diagnostic, allowing for identification, even from great distances, as it dashes, throws open a wing, abruptly changes direction, or stabs at the water's surface.

THE BIRD: **Breeding adult** exudes sheer, lacy, wedding dress–like plumes from the crown, breast, and back. Yellow lores contrast with black bill, as do toes from the black legs, suggesting golden slippers. **Nonbreeding** and **immature** have few if any plumes. Yellow runs up the back of the leg. **Juvenile** nearly identical to nonbreeding, but bill pale at base. Greenish legs darken to black on the front.

FLIGHT: It can be very difficult to separate Snowy from Great Egret if strongly backlit. The bill is more slender, the neck bulge slightly smaller, the rate of flapping quicker.

VOICE: An annoyed, drawn-out, hollow, rasping *aaaaaaaagh* given when the bird is disturbed or flushed.

RANGE: Common resident of the Central Valley, but it rarely ventures into the Sierra. **West Slope:** Individual sightings peppered throughout, mostly below 1,000 feet. **East Slope:** Rare spring and fall migrant to foothill marshlands, where very rare in winter.

SIMILAR SPECIES: **Great Egret** is over twice the size, has a yellow bill, black toes, and an unhurried demeanor.

scaled

streaked

JUVENILE

capped

rusty

ADULT

Green Heron
Butorides virescens

Between the Least Bittern and Black-crowned Night-Heron in size. A furtive loner who prefers the dappled light of leafy streams over sunny exposure. Most of the time, bird holds its head near its body; however, the neck can extend surprisingly far. Flicks tail smartly downward.

THE BIRD: Adult appears dark from afar. When close and well illuminated, beautiful with piercing yellow eyes, colorful maroon-and-white neck, pale-edged coverts, and yellowish legs that become orange in breeding season. **First summer** adult-like, but color and contrast muted, with neck streaked. **Juvenile** neck and breast heavily streaked, all wing coverts edged pale. Bill blackish with pinkish, yellow, or orange base. Legs and feet yellowish green.

FLIGHT: With an arresting call, flushes from cover at water's edge. Appears irritated and eager for privacy. Vanishes upstream, with neck extended and crest fully raised. With deep wingbeats and dangling toes, it covers some distance, retracts neck, and assumes the classic small-heron shape.

VOICE: Flight call a sharp descending *tchRU!* When nesting, utters chicken-like clucking notes and a strange muffled *OW-w-w-ell* with vibrating quality.

RANGE: Both slopes: Resident and breeder at lower elevations. **West Slope:** Uncommon, with most records below about 3,000 feet. **East Slope:** Rare spring and summer migrant to foothill marshlands. Very rare in winter.

SIMILAR SPECIES: Black-crowned Night-Heron juvenile gregarious, larger, browner, heavily spotted on upper parts.

Black-crowned Night-Heron
Nycticorax nycticorax

Gregarious. Daylight reveals a large, football-shaped bird. Larger than Green Heron, stockier than American Bittern. Active all night, but usually seen at dusk and dawn. Hunts patiently, consuming a wide array of creatures, both aquatic and terrestrial.

THE BIRD: Striking **adult** is adorned by long head-plumes. The lores are gray, and legs and feet yellowish. **Second year** like dull version of adult, dusky overall with dark-gray upper parts, blue-green lores, and greenish lower mandible, legs, and feet. Brownish **first-year** bird is darker crowned than juvenile, with less spotting. **Juvenile** eye orange, bill and legs yellowish green, heavily spotted white.

FLIGHT: Commutes between nocturnal feeding and diurnal roosting sites. Appears somewhat owl-like. Progresses with steady, shallow wingbeats in widely spaced flock. From below, adult Night-Heron is pale, inviting confusion with Snowy Egret.

VOICE: Frequently vocal. Flight call, explosive *WROK!* Nesting chicks give quick, clacking *wok, wok, wok...*

RANGE: Roosts and nests in colonies in woodland waterways or cattail marshes. **West Slope:** Uncommon to rare in foothill wetlands mostly below 1,000 feet. Occurs somewhat higher in southern Sierra at Lake Isabella (2,600 feet). Very rare higher. **East Slope:** Locally common March to October in Sierra Valley, Honey Lake. Rare Lake Tahoe. Breeding colonies known from Mono and Inyo Counties.

SIMILAR SPECIES: Compared to Night-Heron juvenile, **American Bittern** larger, solitary, yellow eyed, longer billed, lacks spotting, has contrasting wings.

White-faced Ibis

Plegadis chihi

Three ibis occur in North America, with only the White-faced found in the Sierra. Distinct with long curved bill, a gregarious bird of marsh and pasture. Feeds in compact flocks that are constantly in motion. Pokes, prods, then picks insects from short grass. Up to its belly in water, forages with a scything motion of its bill.

THE BIRD: Long-billed Curlew size, appears black from a distance. **Breeding adult** is a visual delight. Against a maroon backdrop, color dances across the wing coverts as burnished copper plays with iridescent azure, teal, and lilac. **Nonbreeding adult** is a khaki-green version of breeding adult, with iridescent coverts, ruby eyes, gray legs. No white on face. **Juvenile**, gray head speckled.

FLIGHT: Wingbeats are quick, shallow, and snappy, interspersed by long glides. Birds at higher altitudes form orderly strands appearing waterfowl-like. Swale in neck imparts a cormorant-like appearance.

VOICE: Call a forced, gruff, conversational chatter: *hrenK! hrenK!* with emphasis at end of note.

RANGE: Common to locally abundant resident of the Central Valley, but rare visitor to foothill marshes of the Sierra. **West Slope:** Uncommon spring and fall visitor to the South Fork Kern River Valley, rare elsewhere. **East Slope:** Breeds north of Truckee and at times Honey Lake. In wet years only, hundreds of pairs breed in Sierra Valley. Very rare winter.

SIMILAR SPECIES: None.

yellow bill

red

cinnamon

JUVENILE

rust-stained

displaying

straight neck

FRESHLY MOLTED

ADULTS

Sandhill Crane

Grus canadensis

Cranes are tall, long-necked birds of shallow water and open grasslands. Fifteen species occur worldwide, two regularly in North America and one, the Sandhill, in the Sierra.

THE BIRD: Far heavier than Great Blue Heron. Feeding, strides slowly, holds body horizontally, and pecks. Courtship display entertaining. Bird bows, jumps into the air, and, for panache, throws plant matter skyward. Fall **adult** gray. Turns rusty in spring and summer, preening iron oxide–rich soil into plumage. **Juvenile** forehead feathered, bustle small. Upper parts rust colored, not stained. After molting, becomes gray.

FLIGHT: Taking wing, lowers head and takes running strides while flapping. Flight unique, with upward-flicking flaps. Flocks form low, unorganized masses or high, sinewy lines. Coming to Earth, parachutes in, lowers landing gear, and gently puts down.

VOICE: Unmistakable. Can be heard from over a mile. Tosses head back, uttering a rolling, throaty, and bugling *HURK, Kr,rt,rt,rt,t,t,t,t!*

RANGE: Two subspecies winter in California. *Greater* (*G. c. tabida*) breeds south of Canada. Many migrate over Sierra in spring and fall. Great numbers winter in the Central Valley, where joined by smaller *Lesser* (*G. c. canadensis*) arriving from Canada, Alaska, and Siberia. **West Slope:** Often seen and heard, but rarely lands. Most records, Plumas County. **East Slope:** Breeds Sierra Valley with few regular pairs, Bridgeport Reservoir.

SIMILAR SPECIES: Great Blue Heron flies neck coiled, wings bowed; flaps smoothly.

speckled   chestnut   red eye   dull eye   pale

ADULT   JUVENILE

Black Rail
Laterallus jamaicensis

The size of a tailless Fox Sparrow. Utterly covert and well-nigh invisible. So rarely viewed, most naturalists imagine they resemble something between an apparition and a figment. If indeed beheld, a tiny, blackish, mouse-like creature with hypnotic red eyes and a chicken-like bill will gaze back at you.

THE BIRD: Adult's underparts grayish black, upper parts slightly darker. Back, wings, and flanks speckled and barred with salt-like dots. Neck shows a chestnut patch. The eyes, ruby. **Juvenile** adult-like, but throat pale, neck patch less rufous, eyes duller.

FLIGHT: Reluctant to fly, preferring to escape on foot. Forced to take flight, this tiny rail flaps continuously on a blur of wings. Appears entirely black and tailless. Small feet dangle and flop.

VOICE: Often calls spontaneously, and therefore the easiest way to find them. Gives a three- or four-note *kik-kik-kee-doo*, last note descending. Agitated, utters descending series of grinding notes: *Grrr, Grr, Gr, gr, gr, rrr...*

RANGE: First recorded in 1994 in Yuba County foothills. Surveys show they're uncommon local residents of Sierra foothills. **West Slope:** Known breeding populations in Butte, Yuba, Nevada, Placer, and El Dorado Counties. Found in shallow marshes, wetlands, and bogs, often adjacent to porous irrigation ditches. **East Slope:** No records. Due to small population and restricted range, state-listed as **Threatened**.

SIMILAR SPECIES: Newly hatched **Sora** and **Virginia Rail** chicks small, fluffy, entirely black.

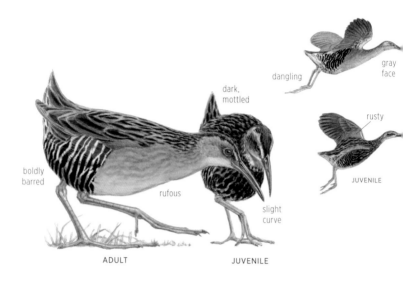

dangling

gray face

dark, mottled

rusty

boldly barred

JUVENILE

rufous

slight curve

ADULT

JUVENILE

Virginia Rail

Rallus limicola

Rails occur over much of the Earth's landmass with over 150 species, 20 of which are extinct. Creeping through marshes and flooded woodlands, they avoid human contact, are typically solitary, and are heard far more often than seen. Appearing aerodynamically dubious in flight, they are, however, capable of migrating great distances.

THE BIRD: Larger than Sora, smaller than Common Gallinule. Rarely posing for inspection, bird works the marshy edge, picks at the mire, and flicks its diminutive tail. Laterally flattened body makes bird appear pot-bellied. Infrequently swims, holding body below surface. With ruby eyes, **adult** shows olive crown and back streaked black. Long legs, pinkish. **Juvenile** is dark, appearing different from adult, with white throat and center of belly.

FLIGHT: Flapping arduously, presents a deep keel-shaped belly and gangly dangling toes. Wing coverts rust in all plumages.

VOICE: Rapid pig-like *oinks* decreasing in strength and running together at the end: *Henk-Henk-Henk, wenk, wenk, wenk...* Gives loud, strident call with emphasis on second note: *Ka-dIK! Ka-diK! Ka-DIK!* Also, reedy, strained, piglet-like squeal, *weeeEEK! kir-teeeeeeEEK!*

RANGE: Both slopes: Local resident of marshes with emergent vegetation. **West Slope:** Fairly common from Foothill to Upper Conifer. Higher-elevation populations probably descend to Lower Conifer for winter. **East Slope:** Fairly common at low elevations, April to September. Most move south for winter.

SIMILAR SPECIES: None.

yellow

black
face

gray

dusky

buff

greenish

JUVENILE

BREEDING

NONBREEDING

Sora

Porzana carolina

Smaller than the Virginia Rail, approximately the weight of a European Starling. Compact and marsh patterned. Chicken-like head-jerking, mirrors flicking tail. Demure behavior conceals its cryptic charm. If not especially timid, can unwittingly materialize foraging the shadows along verge of marsh and bog.

THE BIRD: Breeding adult is striated brownish olive above; flanks delicately barred. **Nonbreeding adult** like breeding, but black confined to lores. **Juvenile** face and underparts pale buff.

FLIGHT: Fairly strong and direct. Appears less ungainly than other rails.

VOICE: Call, a high-pitched two-note *ur-REEP! ur-REEP!* with an emphasis on the rising second note. Gives a mournful series that rises sharply, accelerates, then drops: *tur-REEEE, TUR, TUR, Tur, Tur, tur, tur, tur, tur, turturt.* Also gives a high, strained *eaRK! eaRK! eaRK!* in a long, drawn-out series.

RANGE: Similar to that of other rails, exact distribution is not well known, but considered a resident on both slopes. **West Slope:** Fairly common to uncommon local resident of foothill marshes up to Lower Conifer. Most descend below snow line in winter. **East Slope:** Locally fairly common breeder in marshes in spring and summer. Continues fairly common through fall, but very rare or absent in winter.

SIMILAR SPECIES: Black Rail rare, local, tiny, blacker, speckled white. **Yellow Rail** very rare, similar to juvenile Sora, but shows bold white secondaries in flight, coarse buffy streaks on upper parts.

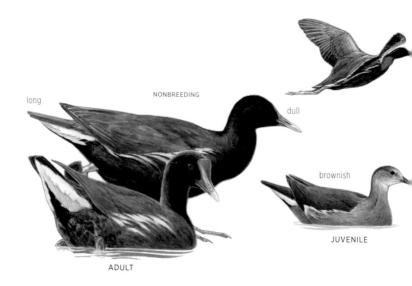

NONBREEDING

long

dull

brownish

JUVENILE

ADULT

Common Gallinule

Gallinula galeata

Swimming across sheltered waterways or clambering among cattails, gallinules usually prefer more cover than coots and less concealment than rails.

THE BIRD: Larger than Virginia Rail, smaller than American Coot. Moves with an exaggerated head-bobbing motion, opposite its flicking tail. Long toes unlobed. **Breeding adult's** fire-engine-red bill with yellow tip is attention getting. Head black, body gray, heel red. **Nonbreeding** very similar to breeding. Bill flesh tipped yellowish. Throat often pale. **Juvenile** like a nonbreeding, but face and underparts pale gray. Bill dark, tipped yellow.

FLIGHT: Prefers to swim. Flapping hard, flies short distances with dangling legs until splash landing. Covering ground, flight is strong and direct as it tucks its toes away to assume a more streamlined shape.

VOICE: A loud, clear, rapid series of coot-like laughing notes that decrease in volume and slow in speed: *ARn! ARn! ARn! ARn, Arn, Arn, arn, arn, arn... arn... arn...* Also, a strained, grating, squeaky wet-balloon *krAKE! KRAKE!*

RANGE: Resident of lowland areas on both slopes of the Sierra. **West Slope:** Uncommon resident or migrant to foothill marshes, especially in central and southern Sierra. **East Slope:** Rare migrant to large marshes with some open water, with most records from Sierra Valley, Mono Basin, and Owens Valley.

SIMILAR SPECIES: **American Coot** larger, white bill, little white under tail, lobed toes, gregarious, comfortable in open spaces.

JUVENILE

lobed

white

short tail

ADULT

American Coot
Fulica americana

Coots congregate openly in unabashed numbers on ponds and lakes. With giant flopping toes and humorous marching gait, they stroll lawns and golf courses, appearing as if wearing scuba flippers.

THE BIRD: Stout, larger than Ruddy Duck. In marshes, feeds on aquatic vegetation by upending, diving, or grazing. Breeding birds engage in splashing fights. **Adult**, ruby eye, maroon blob on frontal shield. Underparts ash, **juvenile** a pale, dark-eyed version of adult. Frosted gold, tiny chicks are blackish with bald pink crown.

FLIGHT: Like a sea plane taking wing, it taxis down liquid runway leaving a widening trail of turbulence in its wake. Fervently flapping, it slowly rises, usually not far above the water. Numbers taking wing create a loud, wet commotion.

VOICE: Wet-balloon squeaks, repeated or in paired sequences: *grreK! grreK, greK!* or *ked-driK, ked-driK...* Gives plaintive *hu-ruHH* with small-goose quality.

RANGE: Both slopes: Resident and breeder at low-elevation wetlands and reservoirs. **West Slope:** Common in Foothill and Lower Conifer. Uncommon to Upper Conifer, rare summer and fall visitor to Subalpine. In winter, most move below snow zone. **East Slope:** Common breeder. Most depart in winter, with great numbers primarily at Lake Tahoe and Bridgeport Reservoir.

SIMILAR SPECIES: Common Gallinule shy, smaller, brown back, longer tail, white flank edge. **Adult** bill red. **Nonbreeding** and **juvenile** bill dark pinkish.

longer than female

olive

white bars

MALE FEMALE JUVENILE CHICK

Mountain Quail

Oreortyx pictus

Larger than California Quail. Shy, cryptic, and a master of denying savory views. Usually found in family tribes adroitly moving through underbrush.

THE BIRD: Adorned by a long, straight topknot, the **adult male** is handsomely marked in a maroon, slate-blue, and khaki combo boldly struck by white, a pattern that breaks up this bird's form. The **female's** plume is slightly shorter than the male's, and her nape is blushed olive. She is otherwise nearly identical. Accompanying parents, **juvenile** at about ten days looks like small, disheveled adult.

FLIGHT: Flies infrequently, preferring to escape on foot. Flushed, it explodes with rapid blur of wings. Glides on bowed wings, rocking on axis.

VOICE: Male gives sharp, slowly repeated, far-carrying *kah-WHARK!* Rock outcrops may yield distant but clear views. Gives querulous *cheK, cheK, cheK, queRANH, queRANH.* If chicks are involved, adults give a peevish whining.

RANGE: Resident mostly at higher elevations on both slopes. **West Slope:** Fairly common from Lower Conifer to Subalpine, favoring mountain chaparral, open forests with dense understories, and rocky slopes and grassy openings. In fall and winter, most descend below snow. **East Slope:** Uncommon resident of scrub and open conifer stands. Winters in sagebrush flats. Breeds locally in desert oases on both slopes of the southern Sierra.

SIMILAR SPECIES: California Quail smaller, topknot curved, scaled underparts. **Chukar** larger, paler, black flank bars, black bridle, red bill.

question mark

apostrophe

scaled

FEMALE

MALE

JUVENILE

CHICK

California Quail
Callipepla californica

Smaller than Mountain Quail, our State Bird is found in large coveys or, when breeding, paired. Precocial, clutches of up to twenty Ping Pong ball–size "dandelions" scuttle behind the adults. Surprisingly, chicks are capable of flight a few days after hatching!

THE BIRD: Adult males wear a harlequin face pattern of black and white with a brown shawl of salt-and-pepper spotting on the hind neck. **Adult females** show a faint, dark earmark, and they tend browner than males. **Juvenile** like a small, cryptic, disheveled adult.

FLIGHT: Takes flight with surprising acceleration. Either continues with another rapid burst or puts to earth and hits the ground running.

VOICE: Given by both sexes, the location call *hur-HERE! hur* has emphasis on second note. Male's song a single *HURRR!* repeated at widely spaced intervals. Contact call *spink, spink, spink...* keeps chicks together, reassembles a flock, or is foraging chatter.

RANGE: Resident both slopes. **West Slope:** Common and widespread in grassland, oak savanna, chaparral, and riparian woodland from Foothill up to Lower Conifer. Avoids dense conifer forests and rare above 3,500 feet. **East Slope:** Uncommon to locally abundant. Range is expanding, with records up to Subalpine. Locally common in desert oases on both slopes of the southern Sierra.

SIMILAR SPECIES: Mountain Quail larger, occurs at higher altitudes; has long, straight head-plume. Throat chestnut, flanks barred.

colorful, naked

muted

long legs

DISPLAY

MALE

FEMALE

Wild Turkey

Meleagris gallopavo

Male turkey is one of the Sierra's largest birds. Female is about half the male's weight. Feeds in groups on seeds, plant matter, insects, and small vertebrates. At night, roosts in trees.

THE BIRD: Boasting colorful wattles, **breeding males** strut for females and each other. Wings lowered and tail fanned, the male's plumage swells, displaying burnished feathers of bronze and copper. Performance is punctuated by a loud "gobble." **Breeding female**, color, plumage, and bare parts subdued. **Juvenile** female-like but smaller, cryptic brown, buff, and whitish.

FLIGHT: Erupts into flight with powerful wingbeats. Moves quickly with deep flaps, interspersed with glides.

VOICE: With a wide vocabulary, birds inform intent and relate their conditions. Hens keep chicks close with calm *alp, alp, alp* or feed with soft conversation. If roosting, gives annoyed clucks: *kak-kaK, KAK! kak-KAK!* or when excited, strident *CHUK! CHUK! CHEK!*

RANGE: First introduced to California in the early 1900s, but did not become fully established until the 1990s. **West Slope:** Now common to locally abundant resident of the foothills, with some birds wandering up to the Lower Conifer, and rarely up to the Subalpine in late summer and fall. **East Slope:** Uncommon and localized with established populations near Honey and Topaz Lakes.

SIMILAR SPECIES: With large size, dark plumage, and bare head, a perched **Turkey Vulture** can briefly fool an observer.

white
intruding

white

NONBREEDING

red

MOLTING

FEMALE   MALE   CHICK

White-tailed Ptarmigan
Lagopus leucura

One-third the weight of the Sooty Grouse and just larger than the Mountain Quail. Molting three times per year, the bird changes its appearance to match the seasonal variations of its seasonally changing environment. As if wearing mittens and scarves, toes and nostrils are enveloped in warm feathering. From winter "snow white" to summer "granite gray" or fall "lichen," an extensive wardrobe provides cryptic security. Whether confident of its camouflaged prowess or oddly unburdened by peril, ptarmigan is easily approached. As with all fowl-like species, its short, sharp bill enables it to procure seed, plant matter, and all manner of insect life.

THE BIRD: Nonbreeding adult entirely snow white. **Breeding male** is cryptic brown, gray, black, and white, with bare red skin above eye. **Breeding female** is heavily barred black, brown, and washed tan. Birds in various stages of molt show white intruding into brown plumage.

FLIGHT: Seldom flies. When airborne, shows striking white wings and tail.

VOICE: A strident screeching and startlingly loud *bek-bek-bek-be-KEK! be-KEK!* with a chicken-like quality.

RANGE: First introduced in 1971 from the Rocky Mountains into Mono County's Alpine Zone, this uncommon resident has now spread 50 miles north along the crest's highest regions to Carson Pass and 70 miles south to Kings Canyon. Winter snows can push bird down to lower elevations on the **East Slope**.

SIMILAR SPECIES: None.

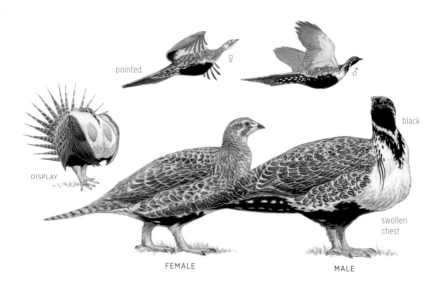

pointed ♀

black ♂

DISPLAY

swollen chest

FEMALE

MALE

Greater Sage-Grouse

Centrocercus urophasianus

These families of terrestrial chicken-like birds include native grouse and quail, and introduced ptarmigan, chukar, pheasant, and turkey. For some, sexes are similar; for others, different. Several have modified plumes and impressive displays. Ground nesters, all produce precocial chicks.

THE BIRD: Conspicuously cryptic. North America's largest grouse. Male nearly twice the weight of female. With extraordinary performances, males gather at prearranged arenas, "leks," to strut for females and each other. With their pinnate tails fanned, the display begins. Enveloped in white "feather boa," large air sacs inflate. Cradled by wings, two yellow "balloons" are quickly thrust outward creating a *poiP!* that carries great distances. **Adult male** wears black beard across swollen breast. With faint face pattern, **adult female** lacks male's pied plumage.

FLIGHT: Erupts with loud *wuP! wuP! wuP!* from large wings. Flight is strong and rapid with long glides.

VOICE: Male, *whutt, whutt* with deep conversational clucks.

RANGE: Resident of the Great Basin. Range extends into eastern Sierra. **West Slope:** No records. **East Slope:** Uncommon to rare. Highly localized resident of sagebrush flats. Leks exist near Honey Lake and areas west of Bridgeport, Mono Basin, and Long Valley. Also east of Sierra, Bodie Hills, White Mountains.

SIMILAR SPECIES: **Ring-necked Pheasant female** smaller, largely tan.

yellow

appears
dark

cryptic

gray
band

DISPLAY

MALE

FEMALE

Sooty Grouse
Dendragapus fuliginosus

Ring-necked Pheasant size, the largest terrestrial bird to occur in the Upper Conifer Zone. Heard far more often than it is seen. At times very tame, at others defies discovery.

THE BIRD: Breeding male overall dark blue-gray, mottled in gray and brown. When displaying, fans its gray-tipped black tail turkey-style. On his brow, a comb swells as neck feathers splay, revealing a warty yellow sac. Supremely camouflaged in coniferous woodlands with intricate brown, gray, and dusky mottling. **Breeding females** vanish when motionless.

FLIGHT: Hard pressed to take wing, but if flushed, Sooty Grouse bursts forth in a flurry of loud, whooshing flaps.

VOICE: In a rather long, drawn-out series of notes, a displaying male's voice is a deep ventriloquial *voooooooP!...voooooooP!* So low in pitch, some find it inaudible. If a search is unsuccessful, try looking straight up into the nearest tree, as the vocal bird may be perched directly overhead. Females give a questioning *wuk? wuk?* or a nervous *w-hoo-hoo* not unlike California Quail's anxious call.

RANGE: Both slopes: Uncommon resident from Upper Conifer to Subalpine. Some birds may wander up to tree line in fall. Rare visitor to the Lower Conifer in winter.

SIMILAR SPECIES: Visually none. Call of the localized **Great Gray Owl** is similarly deep, but with more of a hooting quality: *whooo, whooo, whooo...*

long, pointed

smaller

DISPLAY

FEMALE

MALE

Ring-necked Pheasant

Phasianus colchicus

Often found in small groups. Larger than a chicken, similar in size to Sooty Grouse. Usually first noted when males call or are flushed.

THE BIRD: Adult male, dressed in regal motif, impresses. Appears assembled from the finest textiles of burnished copper and satiny bronze. Embellishments include erectile ear tufts, scarlet face-wattles framing the eyes, and an exceedingly long, tiger-striped tail. **Adult female** the color of winter fields; she vanishes in dry grasslands. Face unmarked. Crown, upper parts, and tail mottled ebony-brown. Underparts sparingly marked by spots and chevrons.

FLIGHT: Takes wing with startling rush of loud flaps and harsh call notes. At full speed, ceases flapping, bows wings, and, as if on rails, glides great distances.

VOICE: Displaying male raises his tail and gives a loud, forced, raspy, two-note *ARH!-arh*, with second note dropping and clipped. In flight utters sharp, choking *KRUH! KRUH! KRUH!*

RANGE: Widely introduced into California from Asia since the 1850s. **West Slope:** Common to locally abundant in agricultural fields in Central Valley. Uncommon and very local in low foothills. Established populations exist in the South Fork Kern River Valley and Placer County. **East Slope:** Uncommon resident of agricultural fields near Honey Lake and Owens Valley.

SIMILAR SPECIES: Female may resemble **Greater Roadrunner** with long tail held at 45° angle, cryptic brown plumage, and ability to run quickly; otherwise unmistakable.

mask, necklace

rusty

black bars

ADULT

JUVENILE

CHICK

Chukar
Alectoris chukar

Robust and noticeably larger than Mountain Quail, this gamebird was introduced from south-central Asia in 1932. This strikingly patterned partridge has a frustratingly successful habit of escaping threats by running uphill, preferably into steep rocky terrain. Summer heat finds birds gathering near remaining water sources.

THE BIRD: Harlequin-like, the plumage seems anything but cryptic; however, once bird stops moving, it blends in surprisingly well with its habitat of rock and brush. The **adult male** is slightly larger than the **female** and possesses a small, blunt spur on the inside surface of its leg. Otherwise, sexes similar. Plumage "airbrushed" powder blue and warm tan with a tawny vent. **Juvenile** appears as a smaller, muted version of an adult.

FLIGHT: Flies infrequently; however, when forced to take wing, large size becomes apparent.

VOICE: Namesake call an accelerating series of frantic notes: *chi-duK... chi-duK, chi-duK, chuK, chuK, CHUK-KAAR! CHUK-KAAR!* Also, a soft tooting call with a questioning inflection: *fwooT? fwooT?* Also gives a distraught, forced, and sharp *arK! arK! arK! arK-arK-arKarKarKARK!*

RANGE: Now established on both slopes of the Sierra; largest populations occur east of the crest. **West Slope:** Uncommon and localized in the foothills from Fresno to Kern Counties. **East Slope:** Locally common in Lassen, Sierra, and Plumas Counties and fairly common to the south in Mono and Inyo Counties.

SIMILAR SPECIES: None.

fingers

dihedral

pink

dusky

silvery

gray

long

JUV

IMMATURE

ADULT

ADULT

Turkey Vulture
Cathartes aura

Four families of raptors constitute diurnal birds of prey, as opposed to primarily nocturnal owls. New World vultures and condors have featherless heads and nonlethal bills and claws.

THE BIRD: Larger than Osprey, smaller than eagles. With keen sense of smell, this gregarious, seemingly courteous "mortician" feeds on carrion with little conflict. Cloaked in undertaker's black, they warm themselves, appearing to welcome fellow mourners with wings held wide. **Adult** head pink, bill tip ivory. **Immature** has some head feathers, bill tip dark. **Juvenile**, gray head, upper parts scaled, shows neat trailing edge to wings. Older molting birds show ragged edge.

FLIGHT: Prefer soaring over flapping. Ascends to great heights searching for carrion. Tipping and rocking, holds wings in shallow V. Has curious and diagnostic habit of bending wings downward at the wrist, flexing like a weightlifter at the mirror.

VOICE: Lacking a voice box, incapable of vocalizing beyond rudimentary retching and airy hissing at nest sites.

RANGE: Fairly common resident, both slopes. **West Slope:** Population reduced when thousands move south in fall, wintering to Central America. Returning in spring, breeds commonly in oak savanna and chaparral of Foothill and Lower Conifer. Fairly common to Upper Conifer. Uncommon in fall to Subalpine. **East Slope:** Uncommon summer resident. Common fall migrant, very rare winter.

SIMILAR SPECIES: Golden Eagle larger, feathered head, stable flight, wings only slightly upturned.

fingers

white

frosting

orange

dingy

gray head

JUVENILE

ADULT

California Condor
Gymnogyps californianus

Enormous, condors are North America's largest flying bird, with a nine-foot wingspan. Condors connect us to prehistoric times when mammoths and saber-toothed cats roamed our ancient landscapes. Feeds on carrion using its sharp bill to open tough carcasses, enabling other predators to partake in the feast. Condors have a feather boa–like ruff insulating the neck.

THE BIRD: **Adult's** upper surface of secondaries edged white. **Juvenile,** plumage brownish black. Dusky underwings reduce stark contrast shown by adult. White on upper wings, reduced.

FLIGHT: Breathtaking. Floats on thermals high above Earth. Great wings culminate with long, finger-like primaries. Covers vast distances in search of food. Circles more slowly than an eagle. Glides more steadily than a Turkey Vulture. Pairs perform choreographed courtship flights.

VOICE: Typically silent. Capable of coarse grunts and angry hisses, often near nest sites.

RANGE: Last wild pair nested in giant sequoia at Sequoia National Park in 1984. All wild condors were removed from the wild by 1987 for captive breeding in the Condor Recovery Program. **West Slope:** Released and some wild-hatched birds fly free in the southern Sierra. Recently documented as far north as Yosemite. **East Slope:** No modern records. On edge of extinction. Due to alarmingly small global population, California Condor is state- and federally listed **Endangered.**

SIMILAR SPECIES: **Bald Eagle juvenile** recalls young Condor. Largely dark with white underwing coverts, but feathered head.

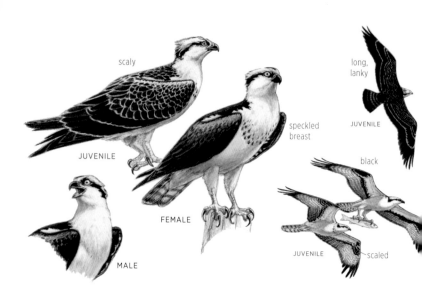

scaly

long,
lanky

JUVENILE

speckled
breast

black

JUVENILE

JUVENILE

scaled

MALE

FEMALE

Osprey
Pandion haliaetus

Highly visible. Larger than Red-tailed Hawk, smaller than Bald Eagle.
Perches on exposed branches over calm lakes and lazy waterways. Feeds
entirely on fish. Builds nests on conifer snags and telephone poles.

THE BIRD: Slender, lanky, slightly crested. Flight feathers barred gray.
Female just larger than male, usually with faint necklace. **Male** breast
typically unmarked white. **Juvenile** breast, nape, and underwings buff.

FLIGHT: Gull-like with shallow M profile. "Hands" hang at the wrist. Hovers
when foraging. When prey is spotted below water, osprey tucks wings
close to body and dives. Swinging feet forward before impact, it forms a
net of talons in front of the face, cushioning impact. Seizing prey, pops to
the surface. Wings outstretched, they push down hard, surging back into
flight. Aloft, points fish forward to carry away for consumption.

VOICE: Very vocal. Call a repeated piercing and far-carrying *PIERP!
PIERP!*

RANGE: Resident. **Both slopes:** Breeds at large lakes, reservoirs, and rivers
with plentiful supplies of fish. **West Slope:** Fairly common from Foothill
to Upper Conifer. Widespread in migration below Subalpine, even far
from water. **East Slope:** Breeds uncommonly at scattered locations at
Lake Tahoe, on tufa towers at Mono Lake, and locally in Alpine and Inyo
Counties.

SIMILAR SPECIES: Immature Bald Eagle never as clean white below, different
flight style. Distant adult gulls in flight appear very similar.

JUVENILE HOVERING

buff

ADULT

scaled

gray

black
shoulder

JUVENILE

JUVENILE

ADULT

ADULT

White-tailed Kite
Elanus leucurus

Delicate, smaller than Northern Harrier. Angelic in poise, a streamlined bird of unblemished tailoring. Captures small rodents, reptiles, and insects with small, yellow toes and bill, both tipped in black.

THE BIRD: Sexes similar. **Adult** strikingly white. Red eyes framed by black "mascara." **Juvenile** adult-like, but plumage marked buff. Grows whiter as it matures. Wings rounder, tail tipped dusky, eyes dull amber.

FLIGHT: Languid, with deep wingbeats. Hunting, hovers buoyantly, tail spread like a ballerina's tutu, legs dangling. Prey spotted, bird brings wingtips overhead into a steep quivering V and descends to Earth. Mated pairs exchange food in flight.

VOICE: Call, a scratchy, agitated *raaahh!* Also gives a *screee-CHUK!* first note rising, second dropping hard. Also gives sweet, nearly Osprey-like *pierP!*

RANGE: Localized resident, both slopes. **West Slope:** Uncommon to meadows, oak savanna, farmland, and hay fields at low-elevation foothills. Often congregates in communal roosts after breeding. Post-breeding individuals rarely wander to Subalpine meadows in fall. **East Slope:** Rare. Very localized to agricultural areas during breeding season. A few may winter near Honey Lake, Mono Basin, and in Sierra and Owens Valleys.

SIMILAR SPECIES: Adult male Northern Harrier pale gray, different flight style, white rump, black wingtips, tail banded; lacks black shoulders. Has **falcon**-like flight silhouette. Moves less purposefully. Recalls **Ring-billed Gull** with long, pointed wings and overall whiteness.

ADULT

flecked

dark head

FIRST YEAR

dark bill

white

whitish face

ragged edge

FOURTH YEAR

ADULT

SECOND YEAR

THIRD YEAR

Bald Eagle
Haliaeetus leucocephalus

Just larger than Turkey Vulture. Body barrel shaped, wings plank-like. Feeds on carrion, steals from Ospreys. Infrequently captures its own fish and waterfowl.

THE BIRD: Adult, five years to mature. Head and tail white, body and wings blackish. **Four-year**, white head and tail, flecked dark, underparts flecked white. **Three-year**, bill yellowish. Osprey-like eye line. Underwings messy. Trailing edge of wings ragged. **Two-year**, trailing edge of wings with bulge, as juvenile feathers extend beyond shorter second-year. **First-year** and **juvenile** wings and tail marked white. Rear edge of wings, neat.

FLIGHT: Flaps with lumbering beats. Soars gracefully, spirals slowly with flat-winged, large-headed profile. Nimble, pursues victims with adroit "piloting." When huge yellow "landing gear" drops, frightening intent becomes fully expressed.

VOICE: Gives gull-like *aronK! ronK! RONK!* that increases in volume, then drops with a *chirT, chiRT, CHIRT, chIRT, chit.* Also, a Peregrine-like *schUK!*

RANGE: Both slopes: Resident, large lakes and reservoirs. **West Slope:** Fairly common breeder south to Tuolumne County. Likely expanding south. **East Slope:** Uncommon breeder with few pairs south to Mono County. Declined during the DDT era. Has made significant recovery. Formally de-listed at federal level due to a range-wide recovery. Both breeding and wintering populations continue as state-listed **Endangered**.

SIMILAR SPECIES: Osprey smaller, white body. **Golden Eagle** browner, smaller head and bill, squared tail. **Immature**, white confined to flight feathers and tail base. Lacks **Bald's** messy appearance.

FEMALE

MALE

JUVENILE

dark
eye

cinnamon

black
tips

white
rump

black

♂

♀

IMMATURE MALE

JUVENILE

Northern Harrier
Circus hudsonius

Generally, between *Accipiter* and *Buteo* size. This lanky generalist hunts near the ground for small mammals, reptiles, and birds.

THE BIRD: Owl-like facial disk diagnostic. Gray **adult male** smudged brown on wing coverts. Whitish underparts sprinkled with rust specks. Dark head imparts hooded appearance. Eyes and legs yellow. **Adult female** upper parts brownish, mottled pale. Lacks warmth of juvenile. Dark face, outlined pale. **Immature male** molts from juvenile into gray adult. **Juvenile** female-like, but underparts warm buff.

FLIGHT: Meanders low with rocking wings held in shallow V. Flight languid, interspersed by quick turns, sudden beats, and brief hovering. Aloft, progresses straighter with measured flapping. Soars infrequently.

VOICE: Calls infrequently. A high, strained, peevish *pseeEEEeeeu*, with begging quality. Like a car's engine not turning over, utters rapid, angry *CHEER! CHUR! CHUr! Chur, chur...*, dropping in power.

RANGE: Lowland habitats, both slopes. **West Slope:** Fairly common breeder in wetlands and pastures, open grasslands, and Foothill oak savannas. Rarely wanders up to Subalpine in fall. **East Slope:** Breeds locally in open sagebrush flats and wet meadows, at times up to 6,000 feet.

SIMILAR SPECIES: Some *Buteos* show white at tail base. None behave like or show white rump of Harrier. If size not fully appreciated, silhouette can appear **vulture**-like.

long, square

rounded

smal head

round

red eye

scaly

pale eye

blue

messy streaks

barred

MALE   FEMALE   JUVENILE

Sharp-shinned Hawk
Accipiter striatus

"True hawks" comprise many groups, including *Accipiters*. This small, high-strung, long-tailed forest hawk is reclusive, seldom perching in the open.

THE BIRD: With browner upper parts, **female** is slightly larger than male, but still smaller than Cooper's. Jay size, **adult male** shows blackish crown and nape, and steel-blue upper parts. **Juvenile** upper parts are brown, scaled buff, and spotted white. Pale underparts are messy with vertical chest streaks and lateral flank bars.

FLIGHT: Frequently encountered in flight, often in migration. Circles tightly, soaring with wings slightly forward. Progresses with quick, snapping flaps and long glides. Small head extends just beyond bend of short, rounded wings. Uses stealth and surprise to pursue small birds with dizzying stoops, explosive bursts of flapping, momentary glides, and abrupt stops.

VOICE: Rarely vocalizes, mainly near nest. Gives thin, American Kestrel–like notes: *sear, sear, sear...*

RANGE: Resident in Sierra. Numbers increase in winter and during migration. Can be observed over any terrain. **West Slope:** Uncommon breeder as far south as Tahoe; rare south. **East Slope:** Uncommon all seasons. Most records in fall near crest.

SIMILAR SPECIES: Cooper's Hawk difficult to separate. Small **males** nearly the size of female Sharp-shinned. **Adult** shows gray cheek, dark-capped appearance. **Juvenile**, golden face, whitish belly, black vertical streaks. In flight, head projects beyond bend of wing. Tail rounded. Slower flapping, less "twinkling" wingbeats. Size misjudged, **Northern Goshawk** can confuse.

cottony

long

rounded

flat

red eye

gray face

golden

large head

steel blue

bold streaks

rounded

MALE

FEMALE

JUVENILE

Cooper's Hawk

Accipiter cooperii

Between Sharp-shinned and Northern Goshawk in size. Fierce hunter of forest and field. Stealthy, Cooper's fixes deep in shadow, biding its time for the incautious or when opportunities are presented on the wing. Victim seized, bird spreads its wings and mantles, covering prey from others, like a muscle-bound trucker hunched over grub at the local diner.

THE BIRD: **Male** smaller than **female**. **Adult**, blackish cap, barred underparts. Orangey-red eyes fearsome. **Female** like male, but upper parts grayer. **Juvenile** upper parts mottled brownish, scaled buff. Scapulars spotted white. Underparts strongly streaked blackish.

FLIGHT: Flaps with deep pumping wingbeats, slower than Sharp-shinned. Head extends beyond bend of wing. Banded tail has white tip. Landing, *Accipiters* shake their tails with wobbly movement.

VOICE: Usually quiet. Call, flicker-like *kenk, enk, enK, eNK, eNK, ENK!* that increases in intensity. Also, peevish sapsucker-like *HEEeeeeuu* that drops in volume. Also gives muffled, "blowing blade of grass" *FRUuuuuu,* beginning explosively and dropping in volume.

RANGE: Resident of forests, both slopes. **West Slope:** Fairly common lower Foothill to Upper Conifer. Uncommon and highly localized March through July. **East Slope:** Rare, widely scattered breeder. Numbers increase during fall migration, all elevations. Widespread at lower elevations in winter. Often visits bird feeders.

SIMILAR SPECIES: **Sharp-shinned Hawk** smaller, large eyes, round crown, square tail. **Northern Goshawk** larger, white brow, broad wings, *Buteo*-like flight. **Juvenile Red-shouldered Hawk** larger, shorter banded tail.

Labels on image: slightly pointed; long; pale brow; gray; barred; barrel-chested; dark streaks; irregular bands; ADULT; JUVENILE

Northern Goshawk
Accipiter gentilis

Hunter of meadow and forest, our largest *Accipiter* is nearly Red-tailed Hawk size. "Berserk assault" describes hunting style. Tough for enduring the elements, muscular for sudden acceleration, and long legged for chases through forest tangle. Body parts of prey litter the ground below the nest, a macabre but characteristic trait.

THE BIRD: **Adult's** reddish eyes impart terrifying gaze. Grayer **male** slighter than browner **female**. **Juvenile**, flanks with spots and chevrons. Undertail coverts streaked.

FLIGHT: Soaring bird appears *Buteo*-like. Hunting Goshawk becomes an entity somewhere between a boxer and a tornado. With a whirlwind's fury it rushes, dodges, and punches through forest clutter with a prize-fighter's agility. With grim indifference, snatches and dispatches quarry, be it grouse, squirrel, or jay.

VOICE: Attention getting. High, thin, strained *tier, tier, tier...* or emphatic *KREH! KREH!*

RANGE: Resident both slopes. **West Slope:** Uncommon breeder in mature conifer forests typically near clearings, from Lower Conifer to Subalpine. **East Slope:** Sparsely distributed in mature conifer forests and aspen groves from lowlands to Subalpine. Most move lower in winter.

SIMILAR SPECIES: Soaring **Red-tailed Hawk**, wings rounded, tail slightly shorter. **Cooper's Hawk**, proportionally large head; tubular body; long, rounded tail; unmarked vent. **Northern Harrier female**, white rump, long tail, different habits.

large head

windows

bands

rust

Accipiter-like

messy

checkered

shortish

long legs

ADULT

JUVENILE

Red-shouldered Hawk

Buteo lineatus

Although *Buteos* are large, robust hawks with expansive wings and short tails, this species is our smallest. Its dark eyes impart a less fearsome gaze than pale-eyed hawks. Often perches on wires, while other *Buteos* prefer sturdier poles. Hunts by sitting not far above the ground, staring down in search of small mammals, reptiles, or insects.

THE BIRD: Midway between a *Buteo* and an *Accipiter* in size, plumage, and flight. **Adult** has warm, orangey head, shoulders, and underparts. Wings and tail with checkerboard pattern. **Juvenile** head and breast heavily marked with rusty streaks, imparting hooded appearance. Underparts messy with bars, chevrons, and anchors.

FLIGHT: Cooper's Hawk–like with brisk, choppy flaps, staggered by long glides. Infrequently soaring, this forest hawk shows translucent windows in primaries. Does not hover.

VOICE: Highly vocal, especially in flight. Gives repetitive, ringing *eAR! eAR! eAR!*, each rapid note down-slurred. Steller's Jay imitates these calls.

RANGE: Resident both slopes. Breeds in oak forests, riparian woodlands, and leafy suburbs from low Foothill to Lower Conifer. **West Slope:** Fairly common, having recently expanded breeding range above 3,000 feet, rarely to Alpine in late summer, fall. **East Slope:** Fairly common, but highly localized in riparian forests and wooded suburbs.

SIMILAR SPECIES: Red-tailed Hawk larger, less vocal; **adult**, rust tail. **Northern Goshawk juvenile**, whiter underparts streaked, favors conifers. **Cooper's Hawk juvenile**, long tail, shorter wings, white underparts streaked.

dark brown

ADULT

JUVENILE

INTERMEDIATE MORPH

Swainson's Hawk

Buteo swainsoni

Slighter than Red-tailed; this hawk's long wings reach the tip of the tail. Delicate bill suited for diet of small rodents and grasshoppers.

THE BIRD: Adult perhaps North America's most variable bird, with light, medium, and dark plumages. **Juvenile**, dark-brown crown, nape, and mutton chops expand at chest and cascade down flanks. Upper parts scaled.

FLIGHT: A graceful shape-shifter. Appears falcon-like with long, pointed wings; Northern Harrier–like coursing low, showing white rump band; or Turkey Vulture–like with wings swept upward, rocking and teetering. Mature bird shows dark rear edge to flight and tail feathers. Juvenile does not. In migration, roosts communally on the ground, often in large numbers. Does not hover.

VOICE: Seldom vocalizes. A drawn-out cry, dropping slightly: *ka-reeeEEEeeer!* Gives short, rapid series with high, thin, strained notes.

RANGE: Both slopes: Visits and breeds in grasslands and irrigated pastures with scattered trees in lowest foothills. Arrives mid-March, breeds and departs in September. Winters from Mexico to Argentina. **West Slope:** Rare; low foothills with few scattered breeders. **East Slope:** Locally fairly common breeder in Sierra and Carson Valleys. Rare south. Some wander to Sierra crest before fall migration. Due to habitat loss, degradation, and exposure to pesticides, state-listed **Threatened**.

SIMILAR SPECIES: Red-tailed Hawk adult larger, bulkier, rounder wings, red tail. **Light birds**, spotted cummerbund. **Dark immature**, pale flight feathers. **Rough-legged Hawk dark morph**, exclusively winter.

pale

buffy

white

white

ADULT

JUVENILE

LIGHT MORPH

reddish

dark
overall

heavily
spotted

ADULT

JUVENILE

DARK MORPH

rusty

ADULT

JUVENILE

RUFOUS MORPH

Red-tailed Hawk
Buteo jamaicensis

Elicits esteem. Familiar and robust with a linebacker's build.

THE BIRD: All **adults**, reddish tail. **Light morph**, the most common morph, shows a faint cummerbund. **Rufous morph**, dark with rust breast. **Dark morph**, overall blackish. **Juvenile** and **young** eyes pale. Tail gray with numerous thin bands. **Light young** paler white. More spotted than adult. **Rufous young** heavily spotted. **Dark young** black, wings flecked white.

FLIGHT: Adult wings and tail shorter than juvenile. Soars on broad wings, hovers infrequently with labored beats or hangs on updraft with wings fixed. Incurs the ire of breeding blackbirds and crows.

VOICE: A loud, piercing, drawn-out, descending *EAAARRrrrrh!* Frequently bestows a "sense of the wild" to macho truck ads. Gives Osprey-like *feaRP!* notes, often near nest. Begging chick gives repeated *fwEEEEEEE!*

RANGE: Our most common, widespread, year-round *Buteo*. **Both slopes:** Common to locally abundant from low grasslands and river canyons to high meadows and Alpine peaks. Migrates in fall at higher elevations. Winter numbers increase as northern and eastern birds move into areas with low snow cover and abundant prey.

SIMILAR SPECIES: Ferruginous Hawks larger, longer pointed wings, white flight feathers. **Light juvenile**, white below, brown above. **Dark adult**, rust wing coverts, dark underwing coverts, head, and body. **Dark juvenile**, little rust, tail darker. **Rough-legged Hawk light**, black belly, black wing spot, white tail base; **dark**, white tail base.

dark

broad,
rounded

orangish

barred

hooded

belly
band

JUVENILE

ADULT

LIGHT MORPH

blackish

pale eyes

barred
tail

ADULT

JUVENILE

DARK MORPH

rust
lips
white
dark
white

ADULT
JUVENILE

LIGHT MORPH

Ferruginous Hawk
Buteo regalis

Very large hawk with white wings, tail. Light and dark color morphs, but latter is rare. Has large head, thick neck, flat crown. Yellow "lips" extend below eyes. Feet feathered to toes. Often perches on ground. Forages for squirrels and rabbits. Often roosts communally.

THE BIRD: Adult eyes dark; young pale. **Light adult** underwings spotted rust. **Light juvenile** shows dark eye line. Dark coverts, flecked white. White flanks and underwings show dark dots. **Dark morph** like light, but underwing coverts dark, white crescent at wrist. **Dark juvenile** adult-like, tail banded gray.

FLIGHT: Soars with wings held in shallow V. Flaps languid, deep, Northern Harrier–like. Hunting, hovers with labored flaps. Silhouette unique with long pointed wings.

VOICE: Calls infrequently. Sturdy, long, descending cry: *AAAaa-rrrrr-rr-rr-h!*

RANGE: Both slopes: Winter visitor to open country, desert edges, and irrigated pastures. **West Slope:** Uncommon fall, winter, and spring, low foothills at edge of Central Valley, rare higher. **East Slope:** Fairly common fall through winter. Especially common, Sierra Valley, Honey Lake, Owens Valley.

SIMILAR SPECIES: Rough-legged Hawk smaller, lacks rust. Small bill and feet. **Light female** and **juvenile**, black belly band and wrist spot. **Adult** flight feathers tipped black, **juvenile** gray. **Dark** uncommon, tail banded. **Red-tailed Hawk** smaller, rounded wings, lacks entirely white tail and wings. **Adult**, orangey tail. **Dark juvenile** tail banded. **Golden Eagle juvenile** large; bold white in wings and tail.

pale

LIGHT MORPH

pale panel

banded

DARK MORPH

dark body

large feet

ADULT

JUVENILE

barred

MALE

black

FEMALE

JUVENILE

LIGHT MORPH

Rough-legged Hawk
Buteo lagopus

About Red-tailed size, but noticeably smaller than the Ferruginous Hawk. A *Buteo* of open winter landscapes, encountered more frequently in light morph than in dark. Unlike other *Buteos*, adult sexes differ in plumage.

THE BIRD: Light morph bird is washed buff and, with cummerbund, appears dressed in formal black and white. Age determined by darkness and contrast to tips of flight feathers and tail; **adult** shows contrasting black, while young show diffuse gray. Eye color is dark in adult, light in **juvenile**. Unlike the Ferruginous, it possesses a very delicate bill and small feet suited for a diet of small mammals.

FLIGHT: Soars with the wings held in a slight dihedral. Flaps with languid, flowing beats. Hunting, hovers by treading air with fluid flaps from long, rounded wings while the head is held motionless as it searches for prey.

VOICE: Rarely vocalizes. The call is a loud, pure, and clear descending scream, *eaaaarrRRRR!*

RANGE: This high-Arctic breeder is irruptive. **Both slopes:** Rare and localized winter visitor to open grasslands. **West Slope:** Uncommon to rare in the low foothills. **East Slope:** Frequent visitor to irrigated pastures and sagebrush steppe. Irruptive numbers are encountered in some winters in Sierra Valley and near Honey Lake.

SIMILAR SPECIES: See **Ferruginous Hawk** and **Red-tailed Hawk** descriptions.

dark
edge

several
bands

black

♀

JUVENILE

LIGHT MORPH

grayish

black
edge

diffuse

JUVENILE

DARK MORPH

black

pale
eye

brown

MALE

FEMALE

JUVENILE

pale

golden

long, broad wings

white

subtle barring

huge feet

JUVENILE

ADULT

Golden Eagle

Aquila chrysaetos

Inspiring. About equal to Bald Eagle in size and weight, but with different proportions and hunting style. Reaches adult plumage at about five years.

THE BIRD: Adult dark brown with golden nape; lacks contrasting markings. Upper wing shows golden coverts. **Juvenile**, bold white patches recede in size as bird matures.

FLIGHT: Soaring on warm thermals, becomes most lofty species in kettle of circling raptors. Flight steady on broad flat or slightly uplifted wings. Concealed in sun's glare, eagle rises to dizzying heights, surveying a sweeping landscape for the vulnerable. Prey spotted, it leans forward, retracts its shoulders, and plummets earthward with astonishing velocity. Lowering "landing gear," it impacts upon quarry to spirit away by sheer strength. Larger game is simply held on to, dispatched by beak and claw.

VOICE: Seldom vocalizes. Gives drawn-out series of notes, each rising in strength: *we-RIP! we-RIP! we-RIP!*

RANGE: Both slopes: A bird of open terrain from valley and desert to Alpine. Winter numbers increase as birds arrive from adjacent regions. Nests in large trees or rugged canyons with cliffs blessed by panoramic views and strong updrafts, allowing ease of access.

SIMILAR SPECIES: Bald Eagle, large head, huge bill, tail wedge shaped. **Young** appear splattered by white paint. **Red-tailed Hawk**, if size misjudged, appears similar. **Adult**, orangey tail, pale underwings. **Turkey Vulture** tiny headed, holds wings in shallow V, teeters while gliding.

dots
hovering
pointed
blue-gray
barred
rusty streaks
spots
streaks
MALE
FEMALE
JUVENILE MALE

American Kestrel
Falco sparverius

Barrel chested and pointy winged, falcons resemble hawks, but are thought more closely related to parrots. Except for kestrels, most feed on birds. Kestrels capture small vertebrates and insects. Landing, kestrel pumps tail and bobs head, appearing off balance. What it lacks in size is made up for in bravery. With lightning reflexes and intricate maneuvering, it aggressively drives off eagles or owls who dare venture within its space.

THE BIRD: Rusty tail is best identification feature. **Male** colorful with blue-gray wings, orangey back. **Female** larger than male, upper parts rust, cryptic, with black barring. **Young male** female-like with blue-gray coverts, heavily spotted underparts.

FLIGHT: Meanders, traipses, dilly-dallies. Hovers with "figure 8" motion, or on breeze. Infrequently soars.

VOICE: Vocal. Flight call, repeated high, thin, frantic *kill-E, kill-E, kill-E...* or *klee, klee, klee.*

RANGE: Widespread but declining. Low-elevation residents, both slopes. Frequents country roads, grasslands, woodland edges, chaparral, even urban areas. Breeds April to September. **West Slope:** Common Foothill breeder, uncommon Lower Conifer. Post-breeding, wanders to crest, late summer, fall. **East Slope:** Fairly common, widespread. Post-breeding, some move to Alpine though may be forced downslope by cold. Non-breeding populations fluctuate, increasing as northern migrants arrive.

SIMILAR SPECIES: Merlin stockier, like small Peregrine, doesn't hover. **Sharp-shinned Hawk**, short, round wings; snappy wingbeat. Birds with kestrel-like silhouette include Killdeer, Mourning Dove, nighthawks, and, if size misjudged, larger falcons.

blackish blue

blackish brown

heavily marked

♀

MALE

FEMALE

PACIFIC

Merlin
Falco columbarius

Just larger than kestrel. Scrappy and antagonistic, with spirit, hunting style, shape, and plumage variations of Peregrine Falcon. Holds dominion over winter skies, antagonizing eagles, boxing hawks, and tormenting vultures.

THE BIRD: Three subspecies occur in the Sierra: *Taiga* (*F. c. columbarius*) from Alaska and Canada's boreal forests, the most frequent visitor; *Pacific* (*F. c. suckleyi*) from the Pacific Northwest; and *Prairie* (*F. c. richardsonii*) from the Great Plains.

FLIGHT: As if late for an engagement, Merlins lean in. They reach frightful speeds flying directly, choosing the shortest course from point to point. Supremely aerodynamic. With fist-like head, and wings cleaving scimitars, this lethal hunter dashes over terrain teeing-up birds for capture, which are often consumed while Merlin is on the wing. Infrequently soars, does not hover.

VOICE: Rarely vocal. A kestrel-like high, peevish series of frantic notes that gain force, then drop: *tee, tEE, TEE! Tee, Tee, tee.*

RANGE: Both slopes: Winter visitor to open grasslands and oak savannas. Arrives mid-September, departs mid-April. **West Slope:** Uncommon in Foothill in winter. Rare individuals are spotted at highest ridgelines during migration. **East Slope:** Rare visitor to agricultural lands and shorelines of large lakes with shorebirds.

SIMILAR SPECIES: American Kestrel smaller, slender, colorful. **Peregrine Falcon** larger, proportions similar, hooded. **Prairie Falcon** larger, tan, black wing pits; often soars. **Rock Pigeon**, very similar flight, wings less pointed, tail shorter.

banded, square

sharp, angular

heavily streaked

whisker

dark brown

medium blue-gray

MALE

FEMALE

TAIGA

faint whisker

powder blue

pale tan

MALE

FEMALE

PRAIRIE

dark gray

dark brown

ADULT

JUVENILE

PACIFIC

Peregrine Falcon
Falco peregrinus

Prairie Falcon size. Female slightly larger than male, otherwise sexes similar with barrel chest, tapered wings, supreme streamlining. Eyes shrouded by "executioner's hood" bestow an intimidating, dispassionate gaze. Long toes form lethal "net" for seining prey from the air, typically small ducks, shorebirds, and songbirds.

THE BIRD: Three subspecies potentially occur in the Sierra: *Tundra* (*F. p. tundrius*), which winters to South America; local *American* (*F. p. anatum*), the most frequently encountered; and the rare visitor *Pacific* (*F. p. pealei*) from the Pacific Northwest.

FLIGHT: Any bird quickly looking skyward can indicate a falcon on high. Soaring on flat wings, it hunts from towering heights. Concealed by the sun's glare, stooping birds attain speeds of over 200 miles per hour! Level flight, powered by stiff, shallow pumping from long, pointed wings.

VOICE: Like a soul in torment, Peregrine utters an unsettling cacophony of otherworldly noises. Vocal, especially near nest. An arresting *skreee-CHUK! skree-CHUK!* With assured misconduct, throws rapid and enraged notes at intruders; *HRENK! HRENK! HRENK!...*

RANGE: Both slopes: Locally uncommon, but increasing. New breeding locations discovered yearly on cliffs or bridges providing views of feeding areas. Might be encountered from lowest valley to loftiest peak. Descends below snow level in winter.

SIMILAR SPECIES: Prairie Falcon, thin whisker, white brow, sandy plumage, whiter below, black wingpits. **Merlin** similar shape, smaller. **Double-crested Cormorant** seen flying directly away, surprisingly similar.

pointed

barred

hooded

blue-gray

brown

streaked

ADULT

JUVENILE

AMERICAN

slender whisker

pale brow

ADULT

JUVENILE

TUNDRA

Prairie Falcon

Falco mexicanus

A nomadic hunter that responds to population shifts of small birds and ground squirrels. When owl or eagle becomes too comfortable in this bird's haunt, an aggressive spirit clears them for departure. Hunts from towering precipice or in the sun's glare.

THE BIRD: Peregrine Falcon size with thinner whisker and white brow, cheek, and underparts. **Female** just larger than **male**. **Adult**, cere yellow, tail banded. **Juvenile**, cere gray, upper parts scaled, underparts buffy, tail unbanded.

FLIGHT: From great heights, dives Peregrine-style and pursues game, hugging ground with level assault, inches above Earth. Reaches dizzying speeds powered by strong, shallow beats. Accelerating down swale, suddenly rises to become lethal before prey can react. Tail held closed in powered flight, fanned when soaring.

VOICE: A two-note Peregrine-like *kri-CHUK!*, first note rising, second dropping hard! Also a quavering, peevish *reeEEE!*

RANGE: Both slopes: Residents of arid regions of grassland. **West Slope:** Uncommon, mostly confined to Foothill, nesting high on sheer cliffs. Forages nomadically. Often seen on highest ridgelines in late summer, fall. Numbers increase in winter as birds arrive from adjacent regions. **East Slope:** Uncommon breeder at low elevations. Post-breeding birds may move to Alpine until forced down by snow.

SIMILAR SPECIES: Peregrine Falcon hooded, wingtips more pointed, no black wingpits. **Adult**, bluish upper parts, **juvenile** dark brown. Except for juvenile *Tundra*, Peregrines lack white brow.

ash-gray, golden buff

dark eyes

floating flight

heart-shaped

hort

long, skinny

loose, fluffy cotton

buffy

MALE

FEMALE

CHICK

Barn Owl

Tyto alba

Of Earth's nearly two hundred owl species, twelve occur in the Sierra. Most hunt nocturnally, some at twilight, a few even midday. Adapted for hunting, owls come equipped with enormous eyes on the front of a swiveling head, a facial disk to focus sound, noise-muffling feathers, and a lethal "net" of talons. Generally, sexes appear similar. Juveniles are smaller, fluffy, and cryptic, and bear little resemblance to adults.

THE BIRD: This medium-size, top-heavy owl possesses black marble-like eyes. White, heart-shaped face is split down the center by vertical wedge. Stands high on "unshaven" legs; the wings extend beyond the tail. **Adult** upper parts a pleasing combination of ash and buff. Encountered in nest with varyingly sized siblings, ungainly **fledgling** is cloaked in cottony white.

FLIGHT: Moth-like. Slow, buoyant, silent, an apparition in white. Primaries banded buff on upper surface, alabaster below. Sometimes forages in daylight.

VOICE: Usually heard vocalizing at night. Call, a "lawn rake on pavement," a harsh *sshhhhhrrreeEEET!* Also, a somewhat unsettling series of dry clicking, insect-like notes *ka-dik, ka-dik, ka-tik, tik, tik, tik, tik, ka-tik.*

RANGE: Both slopes: Fairly common but localized. Roosts in barns, silos, densely foliated trees, or pock-marked cliffs. Occurs from developed Foothill agricultural areas to Lower Conifer.

SIMILAR SPECIES: Short-eared Owl, bounding flight, larger, darker, streaked breast, black wing spot. **Great Horned Owl fledgling** calls from fixed location, strident, drawn-out *eeeEEERRRRRIIP!*

bump-like tufts

dark eyes

rufous spots

delicately barred

ADULT

CHICK

Flammulated Owl

Psiloscops flammeolus

Rarely observed, this tiny, enigmatic bird of the Sierra appears as a living flake of pine bark. Northern Pygmy-Owl size, this predator feeds primarily on insects. As dropping temperatures force six-legged prey beneath ground, this California "dream" winters as far south as the mountains of Mexico.

THE BIRD: With stubby tufts, **adult** is cloaked in "woodsy" vermiculated plumage. Individuals occur in gray and brown. All are anointed by namesake flame-like feathers around eyes, facial disk, and edge of mantle. Dark, marble-like eyes impart hollow, inexpressive stare. With fleshy cere, **fledgling** is fluffy and delicately barred gray. Exhaustingly detailed, bird enjoys anonymity by sidling up to pine bark... and vanishing.

FLIGHT: Proportionally long winged; flight is rapid, direct, silent.

VOICE: Soft, hollow, slightly rising *wHoo!... wHoo!* Notes, sometimes in pairs, are separated by patient pause, and can carry on. Begging chick gives downward, scratchy *chaRR!* or *haRR!*

RANGE: West Slope: Highly localized, locally common in dry pine and oak forests of Lower Conifer between about 2,000 and 5,500 feet. **East Slope:** Uncommon to rare in similar habitats. Found in Plumas County and east edge of Tahoe Basin. Arrives mid-April, departs mid-October.

SIMILAR SPECIES: Western Screech-Owl grayer, lacks rust, longer tufts, yellow eyes. **Northern Pygmy-Owl** tiny, brown and white, "fake eyes" on back of head, yellow ones on front, long tail. **Long-eared Owl**, call notes deeper, slightly longer, similarly slow cadence.

ear tufts

yellow eyes

short tail

gray overall

delicately barred

ADULT

CHICK

Western Screech-Owl
Megascops kennicottii

This fairly small owl is a shape-shifter, transforming from round and adorable to freakishly elongated, from sleepy and disinterested to intently focused and menacing. Coarse markings match rough bark of gnarled snag it nests in or roosts on. Strictly nocturnal; enjoys wide array of prey items from large insects to small mammals, even earthworms!

THE BIRD: Adult overall gray, slightly darker on upper parts with delicate black scrawling throughout. Mantle edged by white spots. Underparts heavily marked with concentrations of black near the chest and framing the facial disk. Large yellow eyes encircled by black orbital ring. **Fledgling**, a wide-eyed, gray-barred fluff-ball with small ear tufts. Likely with siblings at nest cavity.

FLIGHT: On rounded wings, silent, rapid, direct. Appears large headed and short tailed.

VOICE: "Bouncing ball" call, a rapid series of soft *toots* increasing in tempo and volume, then dropping sharply at last note: *toot, Toot, Toot, TOOT! TOOT! Toot, toot.* Also muffled, conversational chortles, or soft trills with downward emphasis. Also, agitated, strident *ha-JEW!* with squirrel-like quality.

RANGE: West Slope: Common widespread resident in Foothill and Lower Conifer. Breeds in valley oak, cottonwood, and sycamore cavities, and Wood Duck boxes. After breeding, may wander to Subalpine. **East Slope:** Uncommon to rare.

SIMILAR SPECIES: Flammulated Owl localized, occurring mid-April to mid-October. Smaller, dark eyes, plumage with rust highlights.

prominent ear tufts

yellow eyes

white

mottled brown

broad, rounded

bulky

grayish tan

CHICK

ADULT

Great Horned Owl
Bubo virginianus

Lord of the night. Roosting in seclusion, deep within shaded forest or sheltered in a cranny high on a cliff face, this sturdy, full-bodied, and fearsome predator possesses the erect ears and focused glare of an enormous cat. Daylight elucidates a large, motionless form the color and pattern of autumn wood. The bane of the songbird world; uproarious commotion and agitated notes erupt upon the disclosure of this ominous carnivore. Face set within a slowly swiveling turret, it stares down through narrow eyes of sleepy indifference. This look of calm and passivity is deceptive, for when dusk settles, this powerful figure moves forth into darkness to seize and spirit away prey, be it the size and gravity of a cat, or the insignificance of an annoying bird who hurls insults by day.

THE BIRD: Adult very large, coarsely marked. **Fledgling** usually near nest.

FLIGHT: Shaped like a wine barrel with bowling ball for head. Flies low on deep beats from broad, rounded wings. Swoops upward to land.

VOICE: Both sexes give loud, level hoots: *hoo...hoo-hoo-hoo...hoo-HOO-hoo.* Emphasis on second-to-last note. Incessantly begging, fledglings give shrill *shreeeeP!*, each note rising.

RANGE: Both slopes: Common in all forests from Foothill to Subalpine, often near ranches where trees provide habitat for day roosts.

SIMILAR SPECIES: Long-eared Owl more slender, appears surprised. See **Barn Owl** call, **Spotted Owl** call.

small facial disk

speckled

rapid flight

pseudo eyes

grayish

streaks

long tail

JUVENILE

ADULT

Northern Pygmy-Owl

Glaucidium gnoma

Outright fearless, blindly ferocious, or simply driven by hunger, this owl, smaller than an American Robin, shows perhaps the greatest size difference between predator and prey. The vast majority of quarry consists of small birds and mammals. Pugnacious, capable of subduing squirrels or quail! Nothing elicits a more powerful protest from the songbird community than this bird. Mercifully, it comes equipped with glaring "eyes" on the back of the head, repelling would-be aggressors from rear assaults.

THE BIRD: Adult upper parts dark brown, speckled white. Facial disk with white brow and whiskers. Underparts white, streaked dark. Curiously flicks tail. **Fledgling** nearly identical to adult. Crown grayer with fewer white speckles. Usually near nest with siblings.

FLIGHT: Tightly wound, this dynamo maneuvers deftly on blur of wings through dense, dark forests.

VOICE: Calls dawn, dusk, or even midday. Gives slow, level, drawn-out series of *toot* notes every two or three seconds. This repetitive cadence can go for several minutes.

RANGE: West Slope: Fairly common resident of all forest types from Foothill to Lower Conifer, uncommon in Upper Conifer. **East Slope:** Uncommon in pine-dominated habitats.

SIMILAR SPECIES: Northern Saw-whet Owl call heard at night. Gives more rapid, level toots than Pygmy's slower cadence. **Townsend's Solitaire** call *very* similar with high, sharp, *toot... toot...* spaced at three-to-five-second intervals. Always good to give pine cones a second glance!

heavily spotted

barred

long legs

bounding flight

unmarked belly

ADULT

JUVENILE

Burrowing Owl
Athene cunicularia

This "down-to-earth" owl nests below, roosts on, and flies low to the ground. Large families of these small owls standing and relaxing about their burrows are a comical affair. Humorously, chick engages in body-pumps, dramatic head-swaying, or exuberant foot chases. Anxious bird swivels its head back and forth, constantly reassessing wide horizons and big skies. Long legs elevate for clear views above low cover. With diverse palate, it garners beetles and mice on foot or, while hovering, small birds in flight.

THE BIRD: Adult expressive with white brow and throat. Tan upper parts, heavily spotted white. White underparts, heavily barred tan, darkest on breast. **Fledgling** typically with numerous siblings at burrow. Simple pattern lacks spotting. Head and upper parts, unmarked tan. Throat strikingly pale, underparts buffy tan, breast dark.

FLIGHT: Moves low to the ground with bounding flight. Hovering motionless in midair on pinwheel-like blur of wings; our only owl species to routinely do so.

VOICE: Calls, a hollow, two-note, far-carrying *phoot-hooooot...* with sustained second note; a shrill, somewhat alarming *skreee-chuk-chuk-chuk-chuk...* with rapid-fire cadence. Fledgling gives shrill, peevish *skree* note with scraping quality, and sprightly *cheP!*

RANGE: West Slope: Uncommon. Highly localized in unplowed grasslands and weedy agricultural fields with ground squirrel burrows. **East Slope:** Rare in similar habitats, Sierra Valley and near Honey Lake. Very rare farther south.

SIMILAR SPECIES: None.

no ear tufts

dark eyes

heavily spotted

dark wrist

strongly marked

huge head

ADULT

CHICK

Spotted Owl
Strix occidentalis

A confiding soul of old-growth forests. Seemingly fearless, this large owl is often easily approached. Cloaked in luxuriant feathers, the full, round body merges into a large domed head, creating classic owl shape. This docile bird's future is uncertain and appears to be declining as strains continue on ever-shrinking habitat. Pressures mount from the Barred Owl, a lethal newcomer; larger, aggressive, and competing for resources, they hybridize with, drive out, or hunt Spotted Owls.

THE BIRD: Adult wood brown, copiously spotted white and tan. Darker head and chest form hooded appearance. Bushy brow and whiskers separate large brown eyes, creating a pale X on face. **Fledgling**, pale tan and dark "cotton ball." Maturing, chick darkens as it loses its fluff.

FLIGHT: Flies silently on heavily patterned wings, marked black at the wrist. Hunts voles, woodrats, flying squirrels, and other small creatures with startling pounce.

VOICE: Loud, deep, far-carrying *Hoo... Hoo-hoo... HOOoooooo*, first three notes level, last sustained, dropping. Also gives dog-like yapping and pure whistled *fwee-uuuuuUUU!* that lilts downward, then climbs dramatically upward. Caterwauling pairs cavort with conversational hoots and whoops.

RANGE: West Slope: Fairly common, mature conifer forests of Lower and Upper Conifer. May descend to Foothill to avoid heavy snow. **East Slope:** Uncommon to rare in pine-dominated forests. Rare south of Tahoe region.

SIMILAR SPECIES: Barred Owl larger, streaked, not spotted.

gigantic head

gray X

marbled gray-brown

flat face

no ear tufts

subtle barring

CHICK

ADULT

Great Gray Owl
Strix nebulosa

With Half Dome–shaped head, perhaps the most charismatic Sierra bird. An "old professor" in a well-worn tweed suit, our distinguished friend is cloaked in granite gray and dusted brown. Face has unambiguous wide-open stare. Outwardly larger than Great Horned, but weighs far less. Considerable size created by long insulating feathers. Feeds night or day. Listens for rodents rustling in ground cover or slipping through snow tunnels.

THE BIRD: Adult very large. Dish-flat face cradled by white jowl marks and crossed by bushy brows and whiskers. **Fledgling** likely encountered in proximity to other siblings; it flexes its wings, comically stretches its neck, and clambers around nest before venturing forth into the world.

FLIGHT: Appears giant headed, with broad brownish wings. Slow, silent flight varied by moments of buoyant hovering and punctuated by nimble pouncing. Covering ground through forest, birds move adroitly and with purpose.

VOICE: "Lazy" stretched-out low notes: *hoo... hoo... Hoo... Hoo... hoo... hoo...*, increasing in volume in the middle and decreasing at the end. Also, a raspy, sharp *eeeEEK!*

RANGE: West Slope: Uncommon. Highly localized in mature forests near large meadows. Breeding pairs known from Yosemite National Park. Scattered records north to Sierra County. **East Slope:** Rare. Possibly breeds in Sierra County. State-listed as **Endangered**.

SIMILAR SPECIES: Spotted Owl and rare **Barred Owl** smaller, browner; heavily spotted, streaked, and barred; dark eyes. **Long-eared Owl** call higher pitch, less regular cadence.

black lines through eyes

orange

rust

black

black and rufous

CHICK

ADULT

Long-eared Owl

Asio otus

When alert, looks alarmed with bug-eyed, wide-open glare. Relaxing, peers through narrow and sleepy 45° angled slits. Superficially resembles Great Horned Owl, but one-fifth its weight. Differs with rufous facial disk, a vertical black line through smaller eyes, and closer-set ear tufts. In winter, bird roosts in dense groves or thickets, sometimes in numbers. Employing superb camouflage, it often perches fairly low to the ground.

THE BIRD: Adult rather slender with long, erect ears, forming expressive V. Body intricately marbled gray, brownish, and rust. White highlights include a V-shaped brow and whiskers. Mantle edged buff. **Fledgling**, marbled gray with dark "mustache."

FLIGHT: Deep beats from rather long, slender wings; flight course direct and less bounding than Short-eared. Rarely flies in daylight unless flushed.

VOICE: Long, level, drawn-out low notes given steadily, every two to five seconds: *wooOH... wooOH... wooOH...* Alarm note, explosive and gruff *HERK!* Also, sharp Sora-like *KREK!* Fledgling gives peevish, slightly downward, "blowing a blade of grass" notes: *pieeer*.

RANGE: West Slope: Found in riparian groves or conifers at meadow edges. Uncommon Foothill resident. Rare higher to Upper Conifer. **East Slope:** Similar habitats. Likely underreported due to secretive habits. Communal winter roosts found in Mono Basin willow thickets.

SIMILAR SPECIES: Great Horned Owl bulkier; widely spaced ears. **Short-eared Owl**, open habitat, unique flight style, pale tan, streaked overall. **Flammulated Owl** voice softer, notes shorter in duration.

buff

dark

streaked
tan

blackish

ADULT

CHICK

Short-eared Owl

Asio flammeus

Staring through alluring "cat eyes" enveloped in "mascara," this owl is slightly larger than the Long-eared. Comparable to female Northern Harrier with its apple-shaped face, habitat preferences, hunting style, general coloration. Although comfortable climbing thermals in the heat of day, this lover of open grassland and marsh is usually chanced on when shadows lengthen and the day reclines into dusk.

THE BIRD: Adult, marsh patterned. Light tan below with crisp, dark streaking over entire upper parts, head, chest. Primaries warm buff. Found in lush grass or low bush, **fledgling** is tan, fluffy. Pale marbling darkens as chick matures.

FLIGHT: Northern Harrier–like. Often forages daylight hours, close to the ground. With deep, languid flaps and curious bobbing movement, gives the impression of a giant nighthawk in slow motion. With a warm, pale panel to the primaries, the long, narrow wings are sparsely marked below. Heavily streaked head and chest contrast with the pale body.

VOICE: Northern Harrier–like with various rasping, scratchy notes, some nasal in quality: *RaaaH! RaaaH!*

RANGE: West Slope: Rare nonbreeding visitor to open grasslands and marshlands of Foothill. Most records, fall through early spring. **East Slope:** Rare to casual, similar habitats. Breeding season records from Honey Lake, Sierra and Bridgeport Valleys.

SIMILAR SPECIES: Long-eared Owl essentially nocturnal. Similar flight shape, darker overall. **Northern Harrier female** color and hunting behavior similar.

whitish face

large head

white spots

boldly marked

unmarked brown

buff

ADULT

CHICK

Northern Saw-whet Owl

Aegolius acadicus

Top-heavy. Perhaps only the Common Poorwill has as large a head in relation to its body size. Smaller than Western Screech-Owl, larger than Northern Pygmy-Owl. An encounter is a staring competition with a bright-faced, cat-eyed "stuffed toy" of an owl. In freezing conditions, it "inflates" to become a round ball with thin slits for eyes. A changing mood transforms its shape. Aroused, aware, or fearful, it flattens its body and squares its circular head.

THE BIRD: Adult face largely white, framed tan. White underparts boldly streaked below with rust. Upper parts brown; smartly spotted white on mantle, wings, and tail. **Fledgling** briefly holds this bicolored buff-and-brown plumage from late spring to early fall.

FLIGHT: On broad, round wings, maneuvers nimbly through dense, forested habitats with moth-like silence.

VOICE: Typically vocalizes at night. At two to three notes per second, the most common call is a monotonous series of rapid notes, given at an even pitch: *toot-toot-toot-toot...* Gives raspy, drawn-out screeches, peevish wails, and feline cries.

RANGE: West Slope: Fairly common spring and summer in conifer forests of Lower and Upper Conifer. Most descend below snow line in winter. **East Slope:** Uncommon resident in pine-juniper woodlands.

SIMILAR SPECIES: Northern Pygmy-Owl call similar, but given more slowly. Call must first be determined to be that of a bird. Some chipmunks give *very* similar tooting notes.

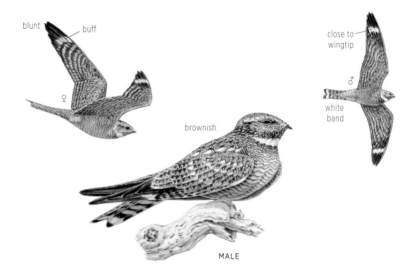

blunt buff ♀ brownish close to wingtip ♂ white band

MALE

Lesser Nighthawk
Chordeiles acutipennis

Primarily nocturnal, nighthawks also hunt in daylight. Tiny billed with gaping mouth, harvests insects from the air. Compared to poorwills, nighthawks have smaller eyes and head, and longer, more pointed wings.

THE BIRD: Blushed buff overall. At rest, largely invisible with intricate vermiculations. American Kestrel–like in length and wingspread, but half its weight. On folded wing, pale primary patch is located beneath tips of longest tertials. **Males** show white wing spot and tail band. **Females** show buff wing spot and lack pale tail band.

FLIGHT: Alone or in small groups, forages fairly close to the earth. Shaped like a small falcon with angled wings. Flight meandering with bounding, sudden turns, and accelerated flutters. Primaries spotted tan, bold wing spot closer to wingtip than in Common.

VOICE: A monotone, soft "purring" trill: *tu tu tu tu tu tu...* like idling motorboat. Gives Pied-billed Grebe–like chatter of less orderly, emphatic nasal notes.

RANGE: West Slope: Uncommon to rare and local, southern Sierra foothills, mid-April to mid-October. Occurs in arid, sparsely vegetated regions. **East Slope:** Fairly common local breeder, Owens Valley. Rare Mono County, largely absent further north.

SIMILAR SPECIES: Common Nighthawk grayer, wingtips more pointed, wing spot further from tip. Dramatic flight display. Voice, loud *PEENT!* Occurs higher elevations. **Common Poorwill** smaller, shorter tail, rufous wings, no white patch. Male, white tail corners. *Poor-will* call.

labels on image: pointed, far from wingtip, ♂, white band, grayish, ♀, MALE

Common Nighthawk
Chordeiles minor

Rollicks at sundown, cavorts high above ridgelines, and swoops low over meadows and sagebrush flats. Nighthawks roost in full view. The cryptic pattern of granitic speckles and spangled shadows enable them to effortlessly vanish. Merlin size by body length and wingspread, but one-third its weight.

THE BIRD: White primary spot, diagnostically midway between wingtip and wrist. Overall grayer than Lesser with no small dotting on primaries. **Male** shows white tail band. **Female** lacks tail band. Her wing spot is white, unlike female Lesser Nighthawk's buff.

FLIGHT: Nighthawks are shaped like a small, dark falcon with a white wing patch. Often in numbers, flies high, performing aerial displays. Male engages in "death-defying" plunges culminating with an explosive *vrrrr-RRUP!* vibration from its wingtips. Mechanically created and startlingly shrill, it sounds as if the air were somehow being ripped.

VOICE: In flight, a forceful *PEEENT!* with "pinched, nasal" quality.

RANGE: West Slope: Fairly common open-country breeder from Foothill to Alpine, mostly north of Fresno County. **East Slope:** Common from low sagebrush to Alpine. Early individuals arrive late May; most, early June. Depart for tropics mid-August.

SIMILAR SPECIES: Lesser Nighthawk difficult to separate when roosting. Arid regions, lower elevations, slightly smaller, buffy. Wing patch closer to blunt tip, different voice. **Common Poorwill**, rufous wings rounded, no wing spot, tends not to fly in the open.

large head

♀

buff

rufous

camouflaged

white tail tip

MALE

Common Poorwill
Phalaenoptilus nuttallii

If you could breathe life into a small pile of leaf litter, bone-dry bark, and fine gravel, your creation just might resemble a Common Poorwill, named for its soothing call. The voice reaches surprisingly far on still spring or summer nights. About the same weight as Lesser Nighthawk, it has shorter tail and round wings. Often detected at roadside. With eyes reflecting orange, a small "burning coal" rising into darkness is likely a poorwill flushing. Nightjars possess an elongated comb-like central toenail, the pectinate claw. This well-formed grooming tool removes moth-dust from plumage after a night's foraging.

THE BIRD: Adult cryptically patterned in gray, black, rust, and white. **Breeding males** show bold white tail corners; females, buff.

FLIGHT: Fluttery and moth-like. Springs from ground or low perch to hawk large flying insects. Rocking side to side, glides holding rufous wings at 90° angle. Poorwills typically then drop, vanishing at the base of a bush.

VOICE: Sings from the ground or a low perch. As its name suggests, utters a soft *poor-WILL* or *furrr-we-ALLL*, with emphasis on the last note.

RANGE: Both slopes: Fairly common in open rocky habitats from low foothills to Subalpine. Arrives mid-May, departs by mid-September.

SIMILAR SPECIES: Far more aerial, **nighthawks** have streamlined body and wings. They exhibit a bold wing spot, and males, a white tail band. Voices differ.

white

black
band

highly
variable

ANCESTRAL PLUMAGE

Rock Pigeon
Columba livia

Familiar, widespread. Around 350 dove species occur worldwide, 4 regularly in the Sierra. When birds take flight, dove wings whistle; most pigeons create clapping sounds. Rock Pigeon claps. With mincing steps, it quickly bobs its bald-looking head. Plumage appears airbrushed. Sexes similar; most adults exhibit neck iridescence. Drinks water without lifting head.

THE BIRD: The classic "pigeon." Nonnative; allows close approach. Midway between larger Band-tailed Pigeon and smaller Eurasian Collared-Dove. Flocks often have variously plumaged individuals. **Adult**, species ancestral appearance dove gray with black wing and tail bands. Head purplish with glittering neck sheen. Eyes reddish, orange, or pale yellow. Feet pinkish. **Juvenile** duller than adult.

FLIGHT: Direct, swift, powerful. When gliding, often holds wings in steep stiff V while rocking back and forth. Gleaming underwings and rump patch white. Flocks form tight, choreographed formations.

VOICE: Balloon-like chest inflates as comforting cooing notes tumble and roll over one another. With a sound that doesn't carry far, it creates the well-known *coo-coo, Ah coo-ca-looooo*.

RANGE: West Slope: Common to abundant in urban, suburban, and agricultural areas with livestock to about 3,000 feet. Localized populations occur to the Sierra crest where freeways cross. **East Slope:** Common resident of towns and ranches.

SIMILAR SPECIES: Band-tailed Pigeon, white collar, dark underwings, tail band. **Eurasian Collared-Dove** pale tan, black collar. **Merlin**, formerly Pigeon Hawk, easily confused for dark Rock Pigeon in a hurry.

white
yellow
green
dark
unmarked
scaly
pale
ADULT
JUVENILE

Band-tailed Pigeon
Patagioenas fasciata

Our largest pigeon, three times the weight of a Mourning Dove. Forms flocks often numbering into the dozens. Searching for acorns, fruit, or grain, this nomadic bird passes quickly above oak woodlands and conifer forests. Acrobatic when feeding, hangs sideways on branches, flapping or repositioning by briefly hovering.

THE BIRD: Sexual differences subtle. Upper parts medium gray, head and breast dusky purple. White collar crosses nape above iridescent green neck. Black-tipped bill and feet yellow. Tail tipped by paler gray band. **Breeding male** eye, bill, head, and breast colors more intense. Differences are nuanced but genuine, and appreciated when pairs are seen together. **Juvenile** like muted adult. Lacks white and iridescent collar.

FLIGHT: Easily startled, loud flocks erupt into flight. Birds appear dark and hold their space within stable and level formations.

VOICE: Mistaken for owls calling during the day. First note questioning, second confirming, gives two-note, hollow moaning *WHO? Woooo.* Also gives raspy *graaaaah, graaaaah.* Wings clap loudly at takeoff.

RANGE: West Slope: Common to abundant but localized in areas with acorn-producing oak trees from Foothill to Upper Conifer; otherwise rare. **East Slope:** Uncommon and very local to Tahoe Basin and Carson Range, where pine nuts and acorns are found.

SIMILAR SPECIES: Rock Pigeon smaller, urban, found in mixed colors, with white rump, silvery underwings. Garbled cooing. **Eurasian Collared-Dove** smaller, paler tan, white tail band.

black

white
band

black

ADULT

Eurasian Collared-Dove
Streptopelia decaocto

Originally from Asia; in few years, it has expanded its range to cover most of Europe. Colonizing North America, arrived in California by the late 1990s. Whether escapees from the Bahamas or a natural expansion from West Africa, they're likely here to stay.

THE BIRD: Between Rock Pigeon and Mourning Dove in size. **Adult** sexes similar. Pale tan, eyes ruby, black collar on hind neck. Vent grayish, underside of white-tipped tail, black. **Juvenile** much like adult. Eyes dark. Collar absent or forming. Upper parts dusky with faint, pale scaling.

FLIGHT: Commutes in small to medium-size squadrons moving in a level, steady, direct flight. High-pitched *toot, toot, toot* wing whistle, similar to Mourning Dove. Displaying, bird launches from perch and beats upward, gaining altitude. At height, it locks wings flat, fans tail, and circles earthward in broad, sweeping arcs, often vocalizing.

VOICE: Like blowing across an empty bottle. Repeatedly gives three hollow cooing notes, middle loudest and drawn out, the last dropping: *whoo, WHOOOOOOO, who*. Shrill flight call approximates blowing a grass blade between thumbs.

RANGE: Both slopes: Shuns wilder terrain frequented by Band-tailed Pigeon; skirts the urban, controlled by Rock Pigeon. Finds fringes of human habitation and farmland its preferred comfort zone, where common to locally abundant.

SIMILAR SPECIES: Mourning Dove smaller, darker tan, black wing spots, pointed tail, different voice. In hurried flight, like **Cooper's Hawk** or **Merlin**.

pointed wings
and tail

♀

spots

scaled

ADULT MALE

reduced
length

JUVENILE

Mourning Dove
Zenaida macroura

Wafting across the landscape on a summer's day, the cooing from this dove soothes the soul. Perched on a wire, this elongated bird with "marble" head and pinnate tail is a familiar roadside attraction. Our smallest dove, slenderer than Eurasian Collared-Dove.

THE BIRD: Adult face and underparts pinkish tan. Spots on wings and beauty mark on cheek, black. Pointed tail, tipped white. Sexes similar, but **male** has longer tail, bluer cap, and brighter neck iridescence than **female**. **Juvenile** like smaller version of adult. Upper parts edged pale, creating scaled appearance. Lacks iridescence.

FLIGHT: Approaches flight in very straightforward manner. Rockets upward, creating sharp whistled notes produced by the wings. Fleet of wing, bird moves directly and briskly, twisting and turning on axis. Upon landing, simultaneously and dramatically pumps head and tail.

VOICE: Iconic and pleasing, the song is breathed out in soft, airy notes. Typically has upward emphasis on the second note: *whoo, WE, whoo, whoo, whoooo*, with the last note sustained and dropping slightly.

RANGE: Both slopes: Common widespread resident of foothill grasslands, open brush lands, ranches, and human habitation of foothills. **West Slope:** Fairly common to Lower Conifer. **East Slope:** Pine forests mid-March to early October. Most move below winter snow where food is available.

SIMILAR SPECIES: Perched or in flight, **American Kestrel** similar. **Eurasian Collared-Dove** larger, grayer, with squared tail.

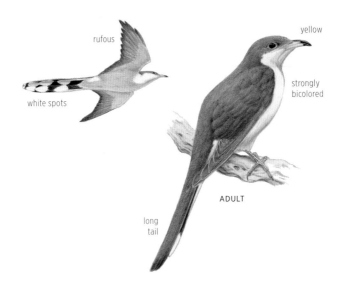

rufous

yellow

white spots

strongly
bicolored

ADULT

long
tail

Yellow-billed Cuckoo
Coccyzus americanus

Cuckoos appear songbird-like but are distinct in several ways. They are "zygodactyl": their two outer toes point backward, the inner two forward. All songbirds have three toes forward, one back. Our two family members, the highly migratory Yellow-billed Cuckoo and the Greater Roadrunner, differ strikingly in appearance and leg length.

THE BIRD: Wingspread and length same as Mourning Dove, but half the weight. Old-world cuckoos are known for nest parasitism; however, Yellow-billed constructs its own flimsy platform to raise its own young. Usually detected by unique voice, this slender bird slinks through canopies of cottonwoods and willows, going unseen. **Adult** sexes similar. Bill yellow, ridged black, slightly curved. Distinctly bicolored olive-brown above, white below. Long, graduated tail has bold white tip to each feather. **Juvenile** adult-like with briefly held dark bill, and duller tail pattern.

FLIGHT: With rufous primaries and long tail, bird has distinct shape and flight style. Flaps with languid rowing beats.

VOICE: Song, a long, rapid series of "wooden clacking" notes. Gradually merges into a hiccupping "back-of-throat" *tik, tik, tak, tok, tok, tik-OP, tik-OP, tik-OP...* Also, slower, mournful, downward "crying puppy" notes: *HMM... HMM... Hm... Hmm... hmmm... hmmmmm...*

RANGE: West Slope: Arrives June, departs by August. Rare and very local, this visitor from the tropics breeds regularly in South Fork Kern River Valley. **East Slope:** Very rare. Resides in tall riparian forests. State-listed as **Endangered** and federally-listed as **Threatened**.

SIMILAR SPECIES: None.

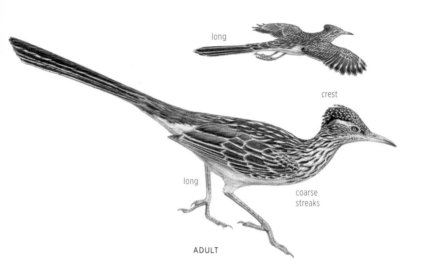

long

crest

long

coarse
streaks

ADULT

Greater Roadrunner
Geococcyx californianus

Appears reptilian. This terrestrial cuckoo comes equipped for life on the ground. Tough feet and powerful legs briskly get it about. Long, rudder-like tail helps balance bird when pursuing dexterous reptiles, insects, arachnids, even birds. Bookended by an expressive crest and tail that it raises or lowers depending on mood. After bitter-cold nights, roadrunner exposes its black rump feathers to soak up the heat of the morning sun.

THE BIRD: Adult sexes similar. Head, neck, and upper parts coarsely marked and glossed bronzy green and copper, outlined in pale buff. Belly and vent whitish. Large, bushy crest mostly blackish, heavily dotted tan. Displays patriotic color scheme on bare facial skin. **Juvenile** similar to adult, but tail and bill slightly shorter. Lacks colorful facial skin.

FLIGHT: Almost exclusively terrestrial, roadrunners prefer escaping on foot. Sometimes takes wing from bush or tree. Labored flight culminates with sliding glide back to Earth. Rounded wings; blackish below, glossed green and neatly spotted above, creating narrow wing band.

VOICE: A mournful cooing. Each "moaning puppy" note lengthens while decreasing in volume: *HOOM, HOOOm, Hoooom, hooooooom.* For close interactions, lure males in by imitating this sound. Also produces dry bill rattle.

RANGE: Both slopes: Fairly common to uncommon resident of desert landscapes and arid brush lands of southern Sierra.

SIMILAR SPECIES: Ring-necked Pheasant female approximates size and general build, but little else similar.

crest

large

bicolored

tricolored

reddish

MALE

FEMALE

JUVENILE

Belted Kingfisher

Megaceryle alcyon

Ranging from sparrow to crow size, Earth's nearly 120 kingfisher species exhibit audacious color combinations; large, often crested heads; and long, straight bills.

THE BIRD: Just smaller than American Crow, this confidently antisocial bird is visible from great distances. **Male** is boldly slate blue and white. One of few species where **females** are more colorful than the males; the female's reddish band effectively subdues her strikingly pied pattern. **Juvenile** appears female-like, but upper breast band is intermingled with rust.

FLIGHT: Notably skittish. Flies directly and powerfully with rowing motion, displaying freckled wing patches. Head motionless, staring down a lethal spear, hovers with body at 45° angle. Prey spotted, folds wings, plunging head-first below the water. If successful, pops up into flight, wriggling quarry in bill.

VOICE: Unreservedly vocal. Translated, kingfisher's clamorous rants would not be appropriate for children under eighteen! Bold, raucous, in-your-face. Bobbing its expressively crested head, it seems to be saying, "You lookin' at me?" With dry rattle, advertises its presence with the cadence and sweet appeal of a rapidly firing machine gun. Tail slowly pumping, kingfisher produces a softer, throaty, annoyed chatter.

RANGE: West Slope: Fairly common resident of streams, lakes, and ponds with abundant fish. Occurs down length of Sierra from Foothill to Upper Conifer. Moves downslope in winter when waters freeze. **East Slope:** Uncommon to rare.

SIMILAR SPECIES: None.

red

grizzled
silver gray

glossed
green

black wings
and tail

dark

mottled

ADULT

JUVENILE

Lewis's Woodpecker

Melanerpes lewis

Woodpeckers boast over two hundred species on Earth, thirteen in the Sierra. Usually solitary, uses curved claws to grip, and stiff tail feathers for support. Chisel-like bill excavates nest cavities, drums to proclaim territory, or chips bark. Barbed tongue procures insects. Some feed terrestrially, others in flight. Some migratory, several irruptive. Flight, usually bounding. Vocalizations include strident notes, rapid rattles, nasal squeals.

THE BIRD: Between Acorn Woodpecker and flicker in size. Breaks the "woodpecker mold": highly social, upper parts glossed green, belly blushed pink, lacks bold patterning. Appearing dark from a distance, prominently perched bird strikes majestic pose. Sexes similar. **Adult**, face dark red, crown and back separated by grizzled collar and breast. **Juvenile**, brown headed, underparts dingy pink. Maturing, pink belly color increases and red face forms.

FLIGHT: Long winged, spends more time in flight than other woodpeckers. Procures flying insects with graceful sallies or by drilling. Flight crow-like, steady, level, nearly lethargic.

VOICE: High-pitched squeaky chatter with Hairy Woodpecker–like *peeek* notes. Male repeats gruff *Churrr*. Drum, a few hard knocks followed by rapid machine-gun culmination.

RANGE: Highly irruptive. Common some years, rare or absent others, depending on food supplies. **West Slope:** Frequents large oaks in open, rolling terrain. Arrives to foothills early November, departs by late March. **East Slope:** Breeds uncommonly, open pine forests. In fall, flocks rarely seen traversing the crest.

SIMILAR SPECIES: None.

white
eye

white

black
forehead

FEMALE

dark
eye

MALE

JUVENILE

Acorn Woodpecker
Melanerpes formicivorus

This cooperatively breeding, socially complex, acorn-caching, phone pole–destroying, foothill-loving woodpecker is a familiar presence in the Sierra. Slightly smaller than Lewis's Woodpecker. In interactions, frequently hitches up bark with wings held outstretched.

THE BIRD: Adult's tricolored face, staring white eyes, and humorous voice impart a clownish appearance. Black upper parts and breast glossed blue-green, flanks heavily streaked. Yellow blush on throat signifies bird's fat content. Sex determined by crown pattern. **Males** show red crown touching white forehead. **Females,** black band bisects red and white. **Juvenile** much like adult, crown less intensely red. Surrounded by gray skin, dark eyes turn bluish, then white as bird matures. Often shows fleshy gape.

FLIGHT: While not as aerial as Lewis's, Acorn Woodpeckers are frequently encountered flycatching or carrying acorns to granaries in oaks, pine snags, or telephone poles. In flight, rump and wings show diagnostic marshmallow-size white spots.

VOICE: A loud, forceful *wen-Ka, wen-Ka, wen-Ka,* with emphasis on second falling note. Also gives rolling *raaaaaanH.* Conversational chatter between birds, a back-and-forth *Rank, rank, RANKa, Wanka, raNKa...* Begging juvenile, a softer rolling *cHUrrr, cHUrrr.* Drumming consists of groups of unorganized knocks, followed by short, rapid drumroll.

RANGE: West Slope: Common to locally abundant resident of oak-dominated woodlands from Foothill to Lower Conifer. **East Slope:** Uncommon and localized in black oak woodlands.

SIMILAR SPECIES: None.

two lines

yellow belly

MALE

tan

barred

FEMALE

white

♂

white

♀

white throat

JUVENILE MALE

Williamson's Sapsucker
Sphyrapicus thyroideus

Between Nuttall's and Hairy Woodpecker in size. All sapsuckers essentially share similar measurements. Unique among our woodpeckers, sexes of Williamson's are strikingly different. Males and females were originally classified as different species! Usually excavating a new nest each year, Williamson's prefers old aspens or lodgepole pines near moist meadows.

THE BIRD: Adult male glossy black and colorfully enhanced with yellow belly and red throat. Shows large wing patches. **Female** flicker-like with tan face, barred and spotted body, black breast spot, and large rump patch. **Juvenile male** similar to adult, but throat white, flanks slightly barred, belly faint yellow.

FLIGHT: Like other sapsuckers, twists and weaves adroitly through forests. Covering greater distances, bounds roller coaster–style.

VOICE: Includes male's rasping two-note call, which rises, then falls: *kwee-aaah.* Also, repeated *chek, chek, chek...* Begging, includes staccato *kra-kra-kra...* and downward nasal *churrrrr.* Drum, rapid series of knocking notes trailing off into shorter series: *ttttttttttttttt-ttt-ttt-ttt-ttt-ttt.*

RANGE: West Slope: Uncommon resident of Upper Conifer and Subalpine forests on boulder-strewn inclines and mountain ridges. **East Slope:** Uncommon to rare, similar habitats. Some resident, others move lower in winter or migrate to mountains of southern California and northern Baja.

SIMILAR SPECIES: Female shares markings with **Northern Flicker female**, which is smaller, barred below, lacking orangey underwings. **Other sapsuckers**, voices more whining; drum more slowly, with shorter pauses.

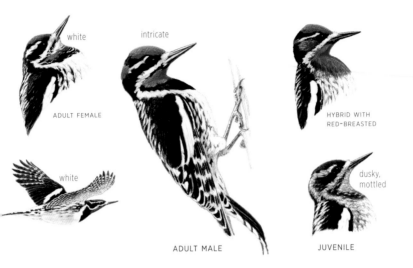

white

intricate

ADULT FEMALE

HYBRID WITH
RED-BREASTED

white

dusky,
mottled

ADULT MALE

JUVENILE

Red-naped Sapsucker

Sphyrapicus nuchalis

Skillful at hide-and-seek, sapsuckers shelter behind trunks and cautiously peer around, giving you the once-over. A bird showing trait of another species should be examined closely for evidence of hybridization. In the Sierra, hybrid Red-naped x Red-breasted Sapsuckers are more likely seen than pure Red-naped.

THE BIRD: Adult boldly pied black and white with crimson crown and nape. Breeding **male** chin and throat red. Breeding **female** chin and upper throat white. **Juvenile** dingy and delicately mottled ashy gray with whitish throat.

FLIGHT: Rapid, with deep, exaggerated bounding. In forests, capable of maneuvering deftly through maze of branches, dexterously weaving and twisting.

VOICE: A strained, peevish Red-shouldered Hawk–like *REAAaaaaa* that drops in pitch. Also gives sharp repeated *cheeer, cheeer, churr, chur, chur...* Chick's begging call, rapid seemingly nonstop *peer-peer-peer-peer-peer-peer-peer...* Drum a "typical sapsucker" staccato. Starts with long roll, followed by decreasing knocks that taper off: *TTtttttt...ttt...ttt...tt...tt...t...t...t.*

RANGE: West Slope: Very rare nonbreeding visitor that winters at seemingly random locations, often in Foothill neighborhoods adorned with ornamental trees or abandoned orchards. **East Slope:** Rare spring or summer visitor to aspen groves in canyons. Limited breeding has been documented.

SIMILAR SPECIES: Red-breasted Sapsucker has red head and breast, lacks black facial appointments. Very rare **Yellow-bellied Sapsucker** lacks red nape; shows black surrounding and isolating red throat spot; has whiter face and frosty appearance to upper parts.

white
whisker

white
spot

white

blushed
yellow

bright
yellow

ADULT *RUBER*

faint
red

dusky

ADULT *DAGGETTI*

JUVENILE

Red-breasted Sapsucker

Sphyrapicus ruber

Locating a sapsucker is like knowing a friend's favorite drinking hole. Go to its "well" and you will likely find it. These shallow holes, weeping with sap, are a focus of winter activity when hummingbirds, kinglets, and warblers come to partake in the sugary entree. Patient, sapsucker spends hours working new wells or feeding from old. Timid, it tends to creep around to the back of tree trunks to elude detection.

THE BIRD: Adult sexes similar. Resident subspecies, *S. r. daggetti*, tends slightly duller red, has longer white whisker, and exhibits "classic" sapsucker back pattern with pale yellow underparts. From the north, *S. r. ruber* is bright ruby on head and breast, shows white spot on nares, yellowish back spots, and lemon belly, resulting in a more colorful bird. Subspecies of some individuals defy classification. **Juvenile's** head, breast, and underparts dusky blackish brown. Crown dirty red. Shows "ghost" pattern of adult.

FLIGHT: In open, bounds dramatically. In dense forest, moves with remarkably adroit zigzagging.

VOICE: Call a lilting, descending Red-shouldered Hawk–like *QUWeeaaah, QUWeeaaah.* Also, strident, repeated "kissing back of hand" sounds. Gives peevish, down-slurred, and quavering *quraaaaa, quraaaaa.* Drum like Red-naped Sapsucker.

RANGE: Both slopes: Fairly common widespread resident from Foothill to Lower Conifer. Uncommon breeder to Subalpine. Hardwood trees and abandoned orchards its preferred habitat. Conifers, less often.

SIMILAR SPECIES: See **Red-naped Sapsucker.**

predominantly
white face

extensive
red crown

black crown

red

FEMALE

MALE

JUVENILE

Ladder-backed Woodpecker
Dryobates scalaris

A Downy-size woodpecker of the arid lands. Appears similar to the oak-loving Nuttall's, but is tinged peachy, with a different voice.

THE BIRD: Delicately marked overall in black and white. Lacks bold white patches. White on face predominates. Underparts often faintly washed tan. The chest shows tiny dots; flanks are lightly barred. **Adult male**, red extends from the nape to forehead; **adult female** crown is black. **Juvenile**, both sexes briefly show red crown after fledging; thus females can appear male-like. Shortly after, female loses the red, becomes entirely black crowned.

FLIGHT: Appears dark above, pale bodied below. Bounds roller coaster–style.

VOICE: Long call, a rapid, strung-out series of notes descending at the end: *CHE, CHE, CHe, CHe, Che, Che, che, che, che, chew, chew, chew, chew...* Call note midway between Hairy Woodpecker's forceful *CHENK* and the Downy Woodpecker's high, sweet *piK*. The drum is a *very* rapid series of knocks in one strand: *ttttttttttttttttttttttttt.*

RANGE: A desert woodpecker whose southern-Sierra range complements that of the Downy and Nuttall's to west and north. Fairly common, but confined to Joshua tree woodlands south of Kern River on West Slope and Inyo and Kern Counties on East Slope.

SIMILAR SPECIES: Nuttall's Woodpecker, oak, foothill, and riparian. Range overlaps only in South Fork Kern River Valley. Black predominates on face. **Male's** red extends only to mid-crown.

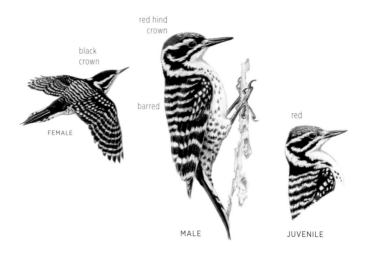

black
crown

red hind
crown

barred

red

FEMALE

MALE

JUVENILE

Nuttall's Woodpecker
Dryobates nuttallii

With global range all but confined to the Golden State, Nuttall's could well be known as the California Woodpecker. Larger than Downy Woodpecker, smaller than a sapsucker, this rather shy resident is often first detected by its distinct call. One of the smaller woodpeckers in the Sierra, it's the only West Slope species with horizontal back bars.

THE BIRD: Delicately marked. Black on face and upper back predominate. Underparts white with black speckles on chest, and bars on flanks. **Adult male** shows red on hind crown. **Adult female** crown entirely black. **Juvenile**, both sexes show red fore-crown. After fledging, female crown and male fore-crown are replaced by black.

FLIGHT: Bounds deeply, often vocalizing loudly.

VOICE: Dry rattle, a somewhat Belted Kingfisher–like *pttRIK pttRIK pRik pTik pTik pTik...* Call note, a soft or dull *chuk*. Also gives series of rapid, excited-sounding notes, similar to Downy: *squenK! squenK! squenK!* Drum, a level, rapid series of knocks: *tttttttttttttttttttttttt.*

RANGE: West Slope: Fairly common resident of live and blue oak–dominated woodlands and riparian from Foothill to Lower Conifer. Rare in black oak woodlands of Upper Conifer. **East Slope:** Rare in similar habitats, mostly Mono and Inyo Counties.

SIMILAR SPECIES: Ladder-backed Woodpecker desert dwelling; range does not overlap except at South Fork Kern River Valley. White predominates on face and back. **Male's** red crown extends to forehead.

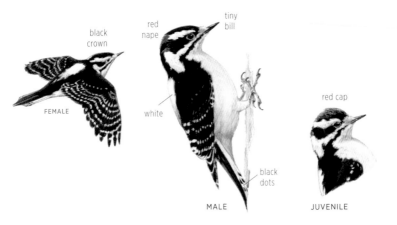

black crown

FEMALE

red nape

white

tiny bill

MALE

black dots

red cap

JUVENILE

Downy Woodpecker
Dryobates pubescens

With good-natured demeanor and cheerful call, a favorite bird for many. Sparrow size, our smallest woodpecker appears as a tiny Hairy. Neighborly, mixes comfortably with any gathering of forest songbirds to enhance forest health by consuming all manner of insect. Western Downy shows fewer wing spots than its eastern counterparts.

THE BIRD: Tiny bill barely extends beyond nasal tufts. Upper parts black with white spot. Wings with limited spotting. Sometimes washed buff, white underparts are unmarked. Outer tail feathers show diagnostic black dots. If size misjudged, nonvocal Downy and Hairy Woodpeckers can be notoriously difficult to separate. **Adult male** shows red nape; **female** does not. **Juvenile**, both sexes show extensive red crown, but color less intense than adult.

FLIGHT: When on the move, spirited with dramatic bounding. Shows large back spot and white outer tail feathers.

VOICE: A bright *piK* or *piNK!*, often repeated. Gives squeaky laughter-like series of *pik* notes starting explosively and descending into bouncing-ball cadence. Drum, a long, loud, forceful staccato given in level "roll," sometimes in shorter bursts.

RANGE: West Slope: Fairly common, riparian forests, neighborhood ornamentals, and orchards from Foothill to Lower Conifer. **East Slope:** Rare resident of aspen groves and ranches with deciduous trees.

SIMILAR SPECIES: Hairy Woodpecker larger, bigger bill, stronger call, no black tail spots. **Nuttall's Woodpecker** barred upper parts, barred flanks. **Ladder-backed Woodpecker** range barely overlaps; heavily barred.

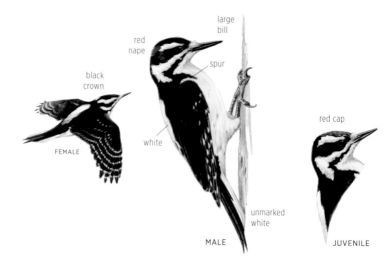

large
bill

red
nape

spur

black
crown

white

FEMALE

red cap

unmarked
white

MALE

JUVENILE

Hairy Woodpecker

Dryobates villosus

A loner. Smaller than White-headed, larger than Black-backed Wood-peckers, this hardworking wood chipper is Downy's husky twin. Detected by forceful call or loud concussive hammering. Chipping and whacking on trees, the Hairy seems on an unending quest for wood-boring insects.

THE BIRD: Bill large and clearly visible. Note black chest spur. Limited spotting on wings. Underparts whitish, sometimes washed tan. Outer tail feathers unmarked. **Adult male**, red nape patch. **Adult female** lacks red. **Juvenile**, both sexes red crown less saturated than adult, flecked black and white. After fledging, female crown and male fore-crown replaced by black.

FLIGHT: Rapidly covers ground in powerful bounds, often with strident call note, or rolling version of it. Bird moves through forest twisting and turning with effortless dexterity.

VOICE: An explosive, distinct *SPINK!* "Laughter" call, vaguely kingfisher-like series of sharp, run-together *SPINK* or *PINK* notes with cadence of machine gun set on automatic. Broadcasts with loud drumming.

RANGE: West Slope: Fairly common resident from Lower Conifer to older Subalpine forests with tall snags. Many descend to Foothill, consequently rare higher in winter. **East Slope:** Uncommon, pine and juniper forests to tree line. In winter, favors aspen groves and trees near ranches.

SIMILAR SPECIES: Downy Woodpecker small, tiny bill. Black dots on outer tail feathers. Calls and drums similar, less forceful. **White-headed Woodpecker's** "rolling" call similar in shorter bursts.

red nape

white

FEMALE

red cap

MALE

JUVENILE

White-headed Woodpecker
Dryobates albolarvatus

With a hauntingly ghost-like face, this medium-size, simply patterned woodpecker is noticeably larger than a sapsucker and just smaller than a Hairy. Nonmigratory, it is strictly western in distribution.

THE BIRD: Besides the white crown, face, throat, and wing patch, **adult's** plumage is black. **Male** shows a bright-red nape patch; **female's** crown is entirely white with a black nape. **Juvenile**, both sexes show an extensively red crown, far forward of where the adult male's red nape is located. This red is molted out soon after fledging.

FLIGHT: Similar to the Hairy, White-headed makes rapid progress in long, bounding "leaps." As with other woodpeckers, bird vocalizes in flight, and if exuberant on landing, exhibits an exaggerated head-pumping, body-pivoting movement.

VOICE: The call note is nearly identical to the Hairy, but usually given twice or in short bursts. Connects bursts into drawn-out rattle for its "laughter" call. Gives a rapid, galloping, repeated *chur-tek! chur-tek! chur-tek!* Begging chick utters sharp, repeated, peevish, and slightly squeaky *squeeet! squeeet! squeeet!* approximating the sound of a small rodent in distress.

RANGE: West Slope: Fairly common resident of Lower and Upper Conifer. Breeds and forages in the dead snags and gnarled stumps of pines, firs, and cedars. **East Slope:** Uncommon in similar habitats south to Mono County.

SIMILAR SPECIES: Visually none, but **Hairy Woodpecker's** call note and "laughter" call very similar.

yellow

white stripe

black cap

FEMALE

reduced yellow

MALE

JUVENILE

Black-backed Woodpecker

Picoides arcticus

Nonmigratory. Ranges along narrow finger from Canada's boreal forests to the central Sierra. Crowned gold, California's sole three-toed woodpecker. Frequents open, mature forest and recently burned areas rich in wood-boring insects. At risk; its numbers decrease with fire suppression, increase with burns. Chooses large snags for nesting. Focuses on a single portion of a tree; chipping and chiseling create telltale piles of bark flakes at the tree's base, helpful for focusing search. This species often allows close approach.

THE BIRD: Slightly larger than Hairy Woodpecker, **adult** is black backed, glossed blue with heavily barred flanks, delicately spotted wings, and white outer tail feathers. **Adult female** crown dark. **Adult male** crown golden. **Juvenile**, both sexes adult male–like, shorter billed with smaller, yellow crown.

FLIGHT: Dark from above, aside from white tail feathers. Birds move tree to tree with typical woodpecker undulating flight.

VOICE: Ongoing, seemingly unending Brewer's Blackbird–like *cheK! cheK! cheK!* Gives Hairy Woodpecker-like roll, *hrdddddddddr*, which rises and falls in volume. Drum, a loud, level, resonating machine-gun cadence. Juvenile, monotonous chattering.

RANGE: West Slope: Uncommon resident 5,000–10,000 feet to mature pine and fir forests of Upper Conifer and Subalpine. **East Slope:** Rare, similar habitats. Regular, Tahoe Basin.

SIMILAR SPECIES: Hairy Woodpecker brow, back, and flanks white. **Williamson's Sapsucker male**, eye line, wing patch, white rump. Throat red, breast black, belly yellow.

red

gray

RED-SHAFTED FEMALE

tan

YELLOW-SHAFTED FEMALE

red — black

YELLOW-SHAFTED MALE

RED-SHAFTED

YELLOW-SHAFTED

MALE

Northern Flicker
Colaptes auratus

After Pileated, our largest woodpecker. Occurs in two subspecies that interbreed: western North America's *Red-shafted* Flicker and the *Yellow-shafted* of the East. Feeds on trees for various insects and fruit, or curiously on the ground consuming ants. Nesting in oak or sycamore, often in conflict with European Starlings for nesting space.

THE BIRD: Barred above, spotted below, and punctuated by a black breast and bold, white rump. *Red-shafted* shows orangey salmon underwings. "Pure" bird shows gray head, tan forehead and underparts. **Adult male** shows a red whisker. **Adult females** lack it. *Yellow-shafted* shows yellow underwings. Face and underparts tan, crown and nape gray. **Male** whisker black. Both sexes show red nape. Many birds intermediate in pattern.

FLIGHT: Powerful rowing roller-coaster flight with shallow bounds. Bright underwings and white rump especially visible. Infrequently catches insects on the wing.

VOICE: Long call, a sustained series of rapid angry notes: *kenk, Kenk, KENK, KENK!* Also *WEEK-UH, WEEK-uh, week-uh, week-uh...*, gradually descending in volume. Call, a loud, far-carrying, piercing *KEW!* Proficient drummers, flickers favor highly resonating branches for broadcasting to potential mates.

RANGE: West Slope: *Red-shafted* common to locally abundant resident of diverse habitats. Foothill oak savanna to Upper Conifer. **East Slope:** Common, open conifer forests, aspen groves, or lawns with ornamental trees. Uncommon Subalpine. *Yellow-shafted* and intermediate types are uncommon migrants or spend winter.

SIMILAR SPECIES: None.

crest

red whisker

stripe

black forehead

black whisker

white patches

FEMALE

MALE

Pileated Woodpecker
Dryocopus pileatus

A great black-and-white bird, America's largest woodpecker. The force and volume created by the concussive blows from this crimson-crested lumberjack attest to its strength. Searching for beetles, grubs, and ants, it hammers and hacks, cleaving chunks of bark and leaving fist-size holes. Sweeping crest opposite chisel-shaped bill imparts Pterodactyl-like silhouette.

THE BIRD: Black with long, curved crimson crest. Face, throat, and eyes white. Neck stripe merges with underwing. White wing spots materialize into "loud" flashing patches once this crow-size bird takes flight. Tail long, stiff, and distinctly wedge shaped. **Adult male** shows a red forehead and whisker; **adult female's**, black. **Juvenile** adult-like but bill shorter, eyes darker, sometimes reddish. Male's red crest and whisker muted.

FLIGHT: Accompanied by call, flight is powerful and gently rolling, with wingtips nearly touching on bottom of each downstroke.

VOICE: Resounding, far-carrying, and briefly echoing *henk, henk, Henk, Henk, HENK, HENK, HENK!* Flight call slower, paced with irregular cadence: *henk, henk...henk, henk...henk...henk.* Drum, an explosive, rapid-fire machine-gun staccato with resonating quality; quickens in speed while dropping in volume.

RANGE: West Slope: Uncommon to locally fairly common resident of large stands of mature forest, mostly Lower and Upper Conifer. **East Slope:** Uncommon Tahoe Basin, rare in pine forests elsewhere.

SIMILAR SPECIES: Northern Flicker's *kenk, kenk, kenk...* reminiscent of distant Pileated, but remember, flicker is quicker.

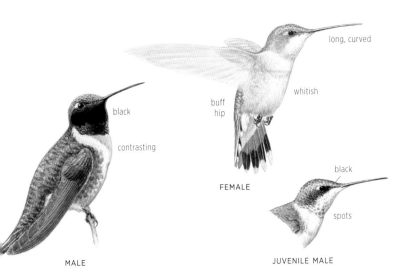

long, curved

whitish

buff
hip

black

contrasting

FEMALE

black

spots

JUVENILE MALE

MALE

Black-chinned Hummingbird

Archilochus alexandri

A New World family, hummingbirds boast over 350 species, with 5 found regularly in the Sierra. Ranging from Alaska to Chile, they reach their greatest diversity in South America. Earth's smallest birds, with the fastest wingbeats. Sexes appear strikingly different.

THE BIRD: Medium size, slender, "marble headed." Smaller than Anna's, larger than Calliope Hummingbird. **Adult male** identified by black-velvet throat and violet neck band. Alabaster chest and belly create a white Y. Black tail, extremely pointed. With green, black, and white tail, **female** and **young male** are nuanced. White underparts and buffy gray flanks impart a clean look. **Female** shows dusky throat flecks. Female-like, **juvenile male** shows dark lores and cheeks, spotted throat, and scaled crown. Longest four wing feathers show broad tips; inner six narrow.

FLIGHT: Hovering, continuously pumps spread tail, making identification straightforward. Pumping lessens when bill enters flower.

VOICE: Sweeter and squeakier than Anna's. Gives trills and rapid double *ti-tik* notes. Wings give slight, shrill hum.

RANGE: Arrives from south-central Mexico to breed in April. Departs early September. More common in southern Sierra. **West Slope:** Fairly common, Foothill riparian and chaparral. Some move to Upper Conifer late summer, fall. **East Slope:** Uncommon to rare spring and summer visitor. Visits feeders and gardens.

SIMILAR SPECIES: **Anna's Hummingbird female** larger, spotted flanks, flicks tail less, louder call. **Costa's Hummingbird female** desert, smaller, rounder, no buff flanks, shorter tail.

straight

spot

magenta hood

heavily scaled

FEMALE

splotchy

MALE

JUVENILE MALE

Anna's Hummingbird
Calypte anna

Our most common hummingbird and only resident, benefits from flower gardens and hummingbird feeders. For problematic identifications, note overall structure, primary shape, and tail pattern.

THE BIRD: California's largest regular hummingbird species. Iridescent colors vary under different lighting conditions. Whether feathers are fresh or worn can affect colors. Anna's appear apple or dull gray-green with strongly spotted flanks. Aggressive, **male** is barrel chested with iridescent red, lavender, and shimmering green helmet. Variable, **female** is grayish, green, pale, or dark, with red central throat spot. Tail greenish black with white tips. **Juvenile male** female-like, with irregular red head splotches. **Juvenile female** drab, delicately scaled above.

FLIGHT: Display dramatic. Head high, bill down, male ascends above perched female or anything serving as the focus of his active libido. At zenith, he plummets toward her. Before impact, throat feathers splayed, he executes 180° j-hook, creating a shrill *CHIRP!* from modified tail feathers. Hovering, spasmodically flicks tail.

VOICE: Nonmusical, similar to cicada insects. Male, thin, lisping *fizzzih-fizzzih-fizzzih...* In interactions, utters rapid squeaking.

RANGE: West Slope: Oak woodland and chaparral, Foothill to Lower Conifer. Breeds March through September. Some to Upper Conifer and Subalpine meadows. **East Slope:** Uncommon in towns. Breeds north of Tahoe, rarely Mono County, Owens Valley. Post-breeding may move to Subalpine in fall.

SIMILAR SPECIES: Black-chinned and **Costa's Hummingbirds** smaller, clean flanks. **Rufous, Calliope,** and **Broad-tailed Hummingbirds,** rufous flanks and tails.

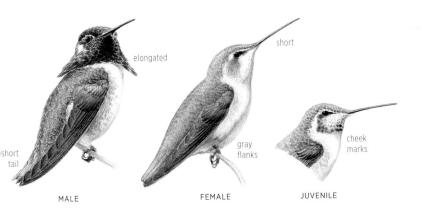

elongated

short

short
tail

gray
flanks

cheek
marks

MALE   FEMALE   JUVENILE

Costa's Hummingbird
Calypte costae

From its home in the natural furnaces of California's hottest regions comes a minute being. Demanding attention, male perches prominently to defend territory. Female actively builds nest, broods eggs, or tends chicks.

THE BIRD: Smaller than Anna's, **adult male** displays elongated gorgets of glittering violet and ultramarine blue. White breast and cheeks contrast with throat and flanks. Short, slightly curved bill opposite stubby tail imparts roly-poly shape. The pinnacle of subtlety, **adult female** boasts sundrenched gray cheeks and whitish collar. Delicately scaled **juvenile** molts late summer, early fall. Individuals with random purple on head are usually males; however, adult females can also show purple.

FLIGHT: Display astonishing! Maximizing the effect from flared gorgets, male positions female's back to the sun. In series of sweeping movements, he hovers inches from her, embellishing his presentation with strident notes from modified tail feathers. Hovering, rhythmically pumps tail.

VOICE: A long, level, shrill note. Calls include strident *psiT! psiT!*, rapid "moist" cowbird-like trill, dry Bushtit-like chatter.

RANGE: Uncommon breeder, desert scrub, rocky slopes, March through April. Northernmost range barely extends into southern Sierra. **West Slope:** Most records, South Fork Kern River and Piute Mountains. Rare north. **East Slope:** Uncommon early spring, eastern Kern and Inyo Counties. Rare, May to June north to Mono Basin.

SIMILAR SPECIES: **Anna's Hummingbird female**, spotted flanks. **Black-chinned Hummingbird female** slender, longest primaries broad. Others, rufous flanks, tails.

green crown

spiky

short tail

MALE

short, straight

buffy

FEMALE

green spots

JUVENILE

Calliope Hummingbird
Selasphorus calliope

North America's smallest bird. Earth's tiniest long-distance avian migrant. A diminutive denizen of high meadows rich in wildflowers. Hyperactive, can be mistaken for a bumblebee.

THE BIRD: Emphasizing minuscule size, short tail falls shy of or at wing-tips when perched. Bill base encompassed in white feathering. **Adult male** opens or closes pinkish-purple gorgets, creating different appearances. Closed, it elongates into Costa's-like shape. Flared, becomes spiky array hemmed in white. Dark outer tail feathers, rufous based and modified with club-shaped tips. **Adult female** shows faint throat flecks, buff flanks, and white-tipped tail feathers. **Juvenile** female-like with more spotted throat and ginger flanks.

FLIGHT: Feeding, floats flower to flower. Display a slow, measured "stair step" toward predominantly perched female. Hovering inches from her face, male's wings and tail create rhythmic buzzing. Display reaches climax with male's throat flared.

VOICE: Like the old wood-and-metal bird squeaker. Call, high, thin, sweet, clipped *tsip, tsip...* or *tseeeP! tseeeP!*

RANGE: Arrives in April from southern Mexico to breed. Males depart July; female and young, September. **West Slope:** Fairly common breeder Upper Conifer to Subalpine. Uncommon spring migrant to Foothill. May move to Alpine meadows before migrating. **East Slope:** Fairly common breeder, meadows, aspen thickets, brushy canyons to Alpine.

SIMILAR SPECIES: Broad-tailed Hummingbird East Slope, **male** solid rose throat. **Female** larger, eye ring, longer tail. **Rufous Hummingbird female** larger, bill longer, tail more rufous.

orange

black

MALE

spot

rufous

white

FEMALE

dots

JUVENILE

Rufous Hummingbird
Selasphorus rufus

Migrates from as far as Alaska to southern Mexico. Does not breed in California. The most numerous hummingbird in migration. Large numbers at feeders are impressive. Arriving birds sweep into region like an "impassioned" red wave. Jousting, they capitalize on food sources, out-aggressing local species with high-speed bill-to-tail pursuits.

THE BIRD: Smaller than Anna's, Rufous are medium size. **Adult male** a "red-hot coal" with white breast. Spiky tail is orange, tipped black. Male can show green on back, inviting confusion with very rare Allen's. **Adult female** shows orange spot on freckled throat. **Juvenile** clearly freckled. White-tipped tail feathers show orange base, except central two. **Juvenile** in first migration appears female-like with heavily spotted throat.

FLIGHT: Wings create a shrill whine, making it possible to tease out Rufous from adjacent species. Rarely partakes in display, but creates sounds by aggressive diving.

VOICE: In feeding disputes, gives thin trills, buzzes, shrill squeaks. Gives soft repeated *tsup*.

RANGE: Flowery meadows, rocky slopes, brushy areas. **Both slopes:** Locally fairly common to abundant migrant Foothill to Alpine mid-March through April. Males move south in June; females and juveniles, mid-July through September.

SIMILAR SPECIES: **Calliope Hummingbird female** smaller, short bill and tail. **Broad-tailed Hummingbird female** East Slope, rare, larger. **Allen's Hummingbird female** very rare, identified in hand only, narrower outer tail feathers. **Anna's Hummingbird** in light mist appears copper, inviting confusion.

white
brow

soars

Black Swift

Cypseloides niger

There are just over one hundred swift species worldwide; three occur in the Sierra. Sexes similar. Descend into Yosemite from on high, and Half Dome's polished face rises to meet you. From dizzying heights, Black Swifts rocket across Bridalveil Falls or a hairsbreadth off the brow of El Capitan. Acceleration and maneuverability as playthings, velocity and momentum matters of law, these are creatures of great prowess.

THE BIRD: Nearly Purple Martin size. Sooty with white brow. **Female** and **juvenile** belly and vent scaled white. **Male** has more forked tail.

FLIGHT: Built for life on scythe-like wings. Employing languid flapping and soaring glides, climbs high above Earth, covering hundreds of miles in search of insects. Capable of flying continuously for months, annually vaults several countries each migration. From the sanctuary of slate-gray clouds, it shifts into an unconstrained projectile, reaching stupefying speeds.

VOICE: Near roosts or chasing, rapid Pygmy Nuthatch–like squeaky chips, otherwise rarely heard.

RANGE: Widespread, uncommon, localized. Arrives to breed mid-May, departs late August or later. **West Slope:** Breeds behind waterfalls in isolated river gorges from Lower to Upper Conifer, Tulare to Butte County. Population limited by wet, inaccessible nesting requirements. Yosemite Valley hosts largest breeding population. **East Slope:** Rare breeder, Madera and Alpine Counties. Rare in migration.

SIMILAR SPECIES: **Purple Martin male,** shorter, thicker wings. **White-throated Swift**, bold pattern, longer tail.

stiff wingbeats

ash throat

stubby tail

Vaux's Swift

Chaetura vauxi

Our smallest swift often mingles in large numbers with similar-size Violet-green Swallows.

THE BIRD: With blunt head and tail, this smoky-brown swift is unicolored, with slightly paler throat and rump. **Adult** virtually identical to **juvenile**. Each tail feather is tipped with a tiny, pin-like spine for roosting birds to put their weight on as they cling to vertical surfaces.

FLIGHT: Scan the sky through binoculars or look at lofty raptors against clouds to detect these minute specks at foolish heights. Twinkling bird holds wings out stiffly and slightly bowed, gliding rapidly as if on rails. In migration, tornado-shaped masses descend from sky and flow downward, entering roosts with coordinated movements. Peeling off, bird enters snag or chimney while others take another pass, until all birds are safely "tucked in" for the night.

VOICE: Call extremely high, thin, and strident. Also louder, repeated *tsip, tsip, tsip*... chips, as well as twitters.

RANGE: Uncommon migrant. Forages at all elevations over forest, ridge, chaparral, or meadow. Arrives mid-April, early May. Departs September, October. Winters mainly Mexico and Guatemala. **West Slope:** Breeds middle elevations, Lower and Upper Conifer south to Tulare County. Conifer snags in steep terrain make nesting abundance difficult to determine. **East Slope:** Rarely breeds. Likely nests Tahoe Basin, and Placer, Nevada, and Sierra Counties.

SIMILAR SPECIES: **Swallows**, flapping less stiff, longer tails, more vocal.

White-throated Swift
Aeronautes saxatalis

Often detected by drawn-out, piercing calls. Can be encountered at any location and most seasons.

THE BIRD: Intermediate in size between Vaux's and Black Swift. Strikingly cloaked in black-and-white "Orca" pattern. From below appears white headed. White brow, lores, throat, belly, tips of secondaries, and flank patches. Crown and face paler.

FLIGHT: A true aerialist. Nimble, this sky pilot is adroit on the wing. Tight formations swirl near breeding cliffs. Cruising rapidly, birds cover immense distances in quest of insects. With powered flaps, scythe-like wings appear slender, with tail held closed. Soaring, holds wings and tail spread. White secondaries wash out against sky, creating pinched-in look. Unless observed near breeding areas, sightings often brief. On sunny days, bird tends to stay higher, often out of sight. In dreary weather, it descends, allowing closer views.

VOICE: Highly vocal. Call alarming when close. A loud, shrill, drawn-out series of descending notes with maniacal laughter-like quality.

RANGE: Uncommon in winter away from South Fork Kern River. Some depart for warmer regions. Arrives to foothills mid-March, and higher April and May. Birds move downslope September. **West Slope:** Fairly common local breeder on cliffs, canyons, and bridges, Foothill to Subalpine. **East Slope:** Fairly common breeder, Mono County, Owens Valley. Very rare north.

SIMILAR SPECIES: **Black** and **Vaux's Swift** entirely dark. **Violet-green Swallow** smaller, short winged, white vent.

satin purple

forked tail

♀

gray collar

brown

subtle streaks

MALE FEMALE JUVENILE

Purple Martin
Progne subis

Harbingers of spring. Of ninety worldwide swallow species, seven occur in the Sierra. Social. They spend more time on the wing than other songbirds. Some winter in South America. Sexes similar in some species; others not. Some exhibit glossy plumage. Possess short secondaries and disproportionately long primaries. Bills are short and broad, feet small.

THE BIRD: Usually in small groups; unabashedly vocal. Our largest swallow, slightly bigger than European Starling; sometimes mistaken for European Starling in flight. **Male**, long wings and forked tail, black. **Female**, back glossed bluish. Eyes encompassed in black, face and underparts dingy gray. **Juvenile** similar to female, lacks purple. Crown dark brown.

FLIGHT: Something to behold. Gracefully cleaves the air, soaring on sickle-shaped wings. Wingbeats appear languid, rowing, and focused down and back. One of few passerines capable of soaring. Rises to considerable heights on thermals, harvesting insects carried aloft.

VOICE: Chortles. Tumbling loud, rich, liquid, gurgling notes with electronic buzzes and rubber-band twangs.

RANGE: Uncommon and local. Breeds in large trees with cavities, frequently hillsides with expansive views. Arrives from South America to northern Sierra by April. Breeds early May and June, departs by August. **West Slope:** Rare. Breeding colonies sparsely distributed, Foothill to Lower Conifer. **East Slope:** Very rare. Mostly low-elevations transients, April and August.

SIMILAR SPECIES: Black Swift silent, slender, stiff wingbeats, longer wings, shorter tail.

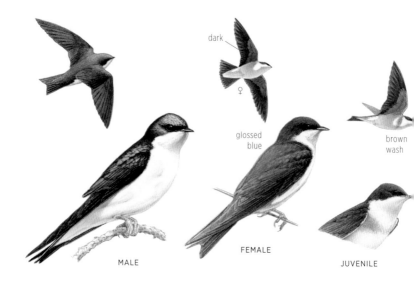

dark

♀

glossed
blue

brown
wash

MALE

FEMALE

JUVENILE

Tree Swallow
Tachycineta bicolor

Usually near water, enlivens any environment with its natural beauty. Breeds in abandoned woodpecker holes, nest boxes. Glittering-blue "vacuum cleaner," snaps up insects above ponds or flowery meadows.

THE BIRD: Fairly large, Cliff Swallow size. When perched, wing extends to tip of tail. From gape to tail, glossy **adult male** strongly bicolored bottle blue and white. White breasted, **adult female** is variable. Some similar to glossy male; most, dark brown blushed bluish. Lacking blue, **juvenile** like dull female. Brown upper parts with breast wash invites confusion with Bank Swallow.

FLIGHT: Twinkles. In warm weather, bird soars, wings fully spread. Primaries dark, compared to wax-paper translucency of Violet-green Swallow. Cold bird fluffs up white flanks, imparting Violet-green appearance. In courtship and play, or when gathering nesting material, bird captures floating feathers.

VOICE: Vocal in flight. Gives sweet, liquid, tumbling notes; dry, reedy calls; martin-like chortles. Perched, converses with monotonous House Sparrow–like chirping.

RANGE: Winters to Central America. Arrives February, breeds, departs September. **Both slopes:** Fairly common or local to wetland, spring and fall. **West Slope:** Breeds Foothill to Upper Conifer. Uncommon to meadows in Subalpine, late summer, fall. Uncommon low-elevation winter visitor. **East Slope:** Breeds in aspen, cottonwood groves south to Mono County. Uncommon south.

SIMILAR SPECIES: Violet-green Swallow small; short tail, long wings; brow, flanks white. **Bank Swallow** small, breast band. **Northern Rough-winged Swallow**, brown breast, no throat–face contrast.

short

white

translucent

white brow

white

gray

long wings

♀

MALE   FEMALE   JUVENILE

Violet-green Swallow
Tachycineta thalassina

Pattern and color of the male's plumage rivals that of any tropical exotic. Beholding this beauty in optimal lighting can be difficult, but is well worth the effort. To appreciate true colors, position yourself above the bird with the sun at your back.

THE BIRD: Bank Swallow size, small, stocky. When perched, long wings extend beyond short tail. White "saddlebags" envelop rump sides. **Adult male** lovely. White encompasses eye. Shows moss crown, grass back, violet rump. Colors and contrast subdued, **female** and **juvenile** in late summer, early fall are somber versions of male. Female, Tree Swallow–like, dull greenish-brown back, dusky face, less white above eye. Note short tail, white flanks.

FLIGHT: Long-winged white body twinkles. Primaries have wax-paper transparency, adding to bird's paleness. Tail short, dark, slightly forked. Forms flocks in fall, often with Vaux's Swifts.

VOICE: Less liquid than Tree Swallow. Dry, rapid chips, recalls striking high-tension wire. Gives conversational trills, electronic buzzes, "House Finch babble." Juvenile gives high, American Pipit–like *sip-it.*

RANGE: A fairly common breeder, arrives late February, departs late August; few linger through September. **West Slope:** Breeds in meadows and riparian woodlands, Foothill to Subalpine. **East Slope:** Breeds in cottonwood and aspen groves south to Mono Basin, rarely to Subalpine.

SIMILAR SPECIES: Tree Swallow larger, blue, longer tail, eye area dark, rump dark. **Bank Swallow**, upper parts brown, tail longer, breast band.

square

brown

white

cinnamon
edges

rich
buff

ADULT

JUVENILE

Northern Rough-winged Swallow
Stelgidopteryx serripennis

The "dirt swallow." A subtle bird of earthy beauty. This subterranean-nesting swallow bores holes into dirt and is the color of dirt, and its call is quite literally...*dirrrrrt!*

THE BIRD: This fairly large swallow lacks bold contrast or striking features. Pale, tan throat, and clay-colored chest softens contrast shown by other white-bellied swallows. Sexes similar. Wings dark brown, **adult** shows a frosty sheen to upper parts. Belly and vent strikingly white. **Juvenile** adult-like, but throat and flanks blushed pinkish buff. Wing feathers neatly edged cinnamon.

FLIGHT: Frequently encountered in small flocks or pairs. Languid flaps sweep sideways. Deep wings, front to back, give broad appearance. Brown upper parts trend pale toward rump. From below, base of flight feathers translucent. Swollen cottony undertail coverts envelop sides of tail.

VOICE: In flight often gives distinct rolling, burry, repeated *dirrrrt!*

RANGE: Local in distribution. After wintering in Mexico and Central America, arrives to foothills in late March, departs September. **West Slope:** Fairly common to rivers and lakes, Foothill to Lower Conifer. Breeds in small colonies in steep banks along streams. Post-breeding, move as high as Alpine. **East Slope:** Uncommon breeders. Rare to Subalpine meadows.

SIMILAR SPECIES: Bank Swallow local, small, white throat, breast band. **Tree Swallow female**, white throat, darker upper parts, liquid call. **Western Wood-Pewee** not gregarious, rests after each foray.

white
brow

band

white
edges

ADULT

JUVENILE

Bank Swallow

Riparia riparia

If you note a distinct breast band on a little swallow, you are beholding one of California's most geographically restricted species. Cloaked in browns and white, it bequeaths a well-dressed look with its snappy "necktie." Like Northern Rough-winged Swallow, this earth-toned, dirt-loving soil excavator hollows out nest chambers from stream banks.

THE BIRD: Diminutive. Sexes similar. **Adult** dark chocolate brown above with crisp brown breast band, thin white brow. Like Tree Swallow, white throated, with wings extending to tail-tip. Collar frames dark cheek. **Juvenile** shows crisp white tertial edges.

FLIGHT: Small. Impressively maneuverable. Thin, dark breast band difficult to discern. Pale rump appears frosted. Strikingly bicolored; gleaming white underparts contrast with dark underwings. From below, dark forked tail extends just beyond white vent.

VOICE: Call, a rapid buzzy chatter. Gives conversational electronic notes.

RANGE: Winters in South America. Rare in migration. Arrives mid-April, early May. Extremely local colonial breeder within steep cuts along stream and river banks. Departs by September. **West Slope:** Breeds locally in eastern Plumas County. **East Slope:** Breeds near Honey Lake, south of Reno, Mono County, and northern Owens Valley. Largest colonies near Crowley Lake and Bridgeport Reservoir; otherwise rare migrant. Due to its limited breeding range and threats to existing colonies, state-listed **Threatened.**

SIMILAR SPECIES: Tree Swallow juvenile larger, breast band diffuse, no pale collar. **Northern Rough-winged Swallow** larger, throat and breast brown.

buff

square

white

chestnut

hood

splotches

pale edges

ADULT

JUVENILE

Cliff Swallow

Petrochelidon pyrrhonota

If the Barn Swallow is a sports car, then the Cliff is a pickup. As if wearing a backward "baseball cap," this no-frills construction worker means business. From the moment it arrives, this colonially nesting day laborer busies itself with masonry and upkeep to its adobe home. Scoops of wet "cement" are carried in the crop of this mud-dauber who spits them up, forming strong, grapefruit-size globes. Lasting several years, they're designed with "downspouts" for quick getaways. After Tricolored Blackbird, our most gregarious nesting songbird.

THE BIRD: Smaller than Purple Martin, larger than all other Sierra swallows. Sexes similar. Buffy rump diagnostic. **Adult** crown and back glossed bluish. Forehead marked by pale "miner's lamp." Colors subdued, **juvenile** shows little resemblance to adult, with white forehead scrawling and swollen lips. Upperparts and tail dark brownish, secondaries edged white.

FLIGHT: Highly gregarious and communicative. Choreographed flocks effortlessly enter congested suites in unison. Higher, with unlimited space, flock integrity diminishes.

VOICE: Unique, if not bizarre. Gives conversational babble, electronic buzzes, static clicks, and synthesized feedback loops. If colony is disturbed, irked birds circle in mass, uttering annoyed, whiny, downward *seeu! seeu!*

RANGE: Winters in South America. Arrives to breed March, most depart late August, rare later. **Both slopes:** Expect anywhere in migration. Uncommon above Lower Conifer. Greatest breeding concentrations on dams and bridges spanning rivers.

SIMILAR SPECIES: None.

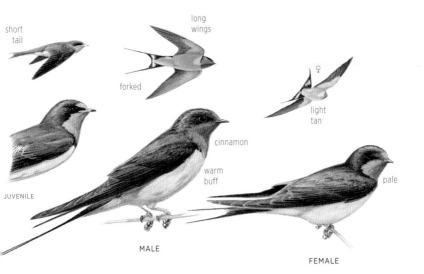

short tail

long wings

forked

♀

light tan

cinnamon

warm buff

pale

JUVENILE

MALE

FEMALE

Barn Swallow
Hirundo rustica

Shaped for speed. With a nearly worldwide distribution, this aerialist looks fast even when sitting still. Perched or in flight, this long-distance migrant likely possesses the longest wings in relation to its body of all Sierra passerines.

THE BIRD: Tree Swallow size, but more rangy with elongated wings and tail. Cinnamon throat demarcated by blue collar. **Adult male** midnight blue above, warm below, tail streamers long. **Female** male-like, underparts less warm. **Juvenile** more diffused than female, shorter tail and wings.

FLIGHT: Smartly tailored, a bird of sleek design, graceful lines, and polished exterior. Flashy tail band comes standard along with internal navigation system and automatic braking. Expect tremendous performance from this bird on the wing. Nimble in crowded situations, enjoys rapid acceleration, corners beautifully, and, with natural cruise control, built for the long haul.

VOICE: Perched or in flight, chatters excessively with sweet, cheerful, tinny, scratchy, static "computerized" notes strung together. Driving away predators or escorting troublemakers to calmer skies, alarmed birds give a rising, strident *tzeeeEET!*

RANGE: After wintering as far as South America, arrives in March to breed, departs by October. Large numbers in fall. Very rare winter visitor. Found near ranches or farms. **West Slope:** Common to locally abundant in Foothill. Fairly common to uncommon to Upper Conifer. **East Slope:** Fairly common, low elevations to Subalpine.

SIMILAR SPECIES: Aside from other swallows, none.

white
patches

thick

orange
bill base

streaky
vest

ADULT   JUVENILE

Olive-sided Flycatcher
Contopus cooperi

Earth's largest bird family, New World flycatchers, insectivores, boast about 425 species. Nearly all thirteen Sierra species are migratory; sexes similar. All have large, rounded crests, dark eyes, small feet; several have flat bills. Colored in soft earth tones. Calls include simple notes. Stereotypical flycatcher songs include thin, strident, burry phrases.

THE BIRD: Perched upright atop tall trees, this large-headed, full-chested flycatcher is noted by its calls. Twice the weight of Western Wood-Pewee. Brownish **adult** shows white vertical area separating flanks. Sometimes exposes white spots on back. Flanks and whisker area streaked. Wingbars subtle, primary extension long. **Juvenile** adult-like, wingbars buff, belly pale yellow.

FLIGHT: Body motionless, head constantly scans for passing insects. Prey spotted, pursues with purpose, rapidly ascending. Hawking skills impressive. On long primaries, twists and swoops, imparting martin-like appearance.

VOICE: An iconic three-note song of mature forests: *Wot! peeves you?* First note hard, second questioning, third drawn-out, descending. Also, three-note *pip, Pip, PIP!* often in migration.

RANGE: From as far as South America, arrives late April, breeds, departs by mid-August. **West Slope:** Fairly common breeder from Lower Conifer to Subalpine. **East Slope:** Uncommon breeder, mature pine forests. Migrants possible any habitat.

SIMILAR SPECIES: **Western Wood-Pewee** smaller, proportionately longer tailed, smaller bill, different call.

gray wingbars

pale bill base

no eye-ring

buff wingbars

long

ADULT

JUVENILE

Western Wood-Pewee

Contopus sordidulus

Common and noticeable with an "out in the open" feeding style. Perches more prominently than *Empidonax* flycatchers and typically not quite as conspicuously as the Olive-sided Flycatcher. Frequently vocalizes, adding a sad refrain to the forest's avian concert. Hunting, sits with the body still but head moving nearly continuously, often at oblique angles.

THE BIRD: Larger than *Empidonax* flycatchers, smaller than phoebes. **Adult** is slightly crested, smoky faced, long winged, and wide shouldered. Overall olive-brown and gray with whitish wingbars and tertial edgings. Lacks eye-ring, shows gray lores. Dark bill has fleshy base to lower mandible. **Juvenile** adult-like, but wingbars edged buff.

FLIGHT: Perched, pewees might appear *Empidonax*-like, but in flight they hunt with faster, farther forays. Usually returns to its preferred perch, where it aligns wingtips and tail with a quick shuffle. Rarely flicks tail. Long primary extension is testament to its annual migration to South America.

VOICE: Familiar throughout Sierra. Gives forlorn, descending *BReeeeeeee-aaaar*. Also singsong phrases with sweet whistles or rising and falling burry notes.

RANGE: Common in foothills, spring migration. **Both slopes:** Arrives May, breeds commonly in pine, aspen, and riparian forests. Shuns dense forest and burned areas lacking tall snags or trees. Departs September.

SIMILAR SPECIES: **Olive-sided Flycatcher** bigger, larger bill, contrasting belly, white flank spot, different voice. **Willow Flycatcher** smaller, flicks tail, back olive-brownish, pale lower mandible, different call.

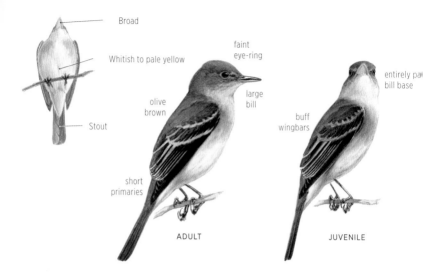

Broad

Whitish to pale yellow

Stout

faint eye-ring

olive brown

large bill

short primaries

buff wingbars

entirely pal bill base

ADULT

JUVENILE

Willow Flycatcher

Empidonax traillii

Empidonax flycatchers can be identified by their size, eye-ring shape, bill size, wing length, and voice. Best indicators are breeding range and habitat.

THE BIRD: To find Willow Flycatchers, go where mosquitoes are! Thrives in insect-rich willow-dominated riparian meadows. Smaller than Western Wood-Pewee, our largest *Empidonax*. **Adult** is brownish olive, with whitish throat and brownish breast. Eye-ring the least distinct of all *Empidonax*. Wide lower mandible is orangey. Wingbars are distinct when fresh, dull when worn. **Juvenile** adult-like, but wingbars buffy, belly yellowish.

FLIGHT: Often forages lower than other flycatchers without single-perch fidelity others favor. In migration, found in various habitats.

VOICE: Song, first part rising, second part level then descending *buuRIP! Fitz-BEEEUU!* Call, soft, airy *whiT!*

RANGE: Fairly common migrant, both slopes. Arrives mid-May, breeds, departs mid-August. Three identical subspecies are *Little* (*E. t brewsteri*), *Southwestern* (*E. t. extimus*), and *Mountain* (*E. t. adastus*). *Little* breeds wet meadows, Lower and Upper Conifer, both slopes most of Sierra's length. *Southwestern*, few dozen breed, black willow forests, South Fork Kern River. *Mountain* migrates through **East Slope**. Few may breed western edge of Great Basin and Owens Valley. Because of small populations and degradation of required habitats, all are state-listed **Endangered**. *Southwestern* federally listed **Endangered**.

SIMILAR SPECIES: **Western Wood-Pewee** larger, longer primaries, different call. **Other** *Empidonax* smaller, greener, dusky or grayish, eye-rings, smaller bills, different voices.

Mostly dark

Breast wash

large head

tiny bill

long primaries

short tail

ADULT

gray head

vest

yellow

JUVENILE

Hammond's Flycatcher

Empidonax hammondii

Appears top-heavy with large head, small bill, and short tail. Usually forages higher than Dusky Flycatcher, enjoying canopy shade. Kinglet-like with tiny bill, nervous wing-flicking, and eyes bookended in white.

THE BIRD: Smaller than other *Empidonax*, nearly Hutton's Vireo size. Bill is dark, short, and narrow with pale, orangey base. Dark breast wash creates vested look. Primary extension long, tail slightly forked. Worn breeding **adult** is fairly drab, greenish gray above, belly whitish. However, freshly molted in fall, appears more like **juvenile**, being brighter, more colorful with bolder wing markings and yellower belly.

FLIGHT: Frequently flicks wings and tail, especially on landing. Sallies for insects, usually returning to the same perch time and again.

VOICE: Difficult to separate from Dusky Flycatcher. Song, first notes, a quick up-down *Fee-sip!* followed by rising, burry *buurrriP!* Call note forceful *PIP!* or *PIT!*

RANGE: Arrives April, breeds, departs mid-September. To complete molt, leaves later than Dusky. **West Slope:** Fairly common to Foothill in migration. Breeds in mature forests, Lower to Upper Conifer. Post-breeding uncommon to Subalpine. **East Slope:** Uncommon spring migration, rare fall. Does not breed east of crest.

SIMILAR SPECIES: *Empidonax* can be compared at migratory stopping points or where breeding ranges overlap. **Dusky Flycatcher**, shorter primaries, longer tail. **Gray Flycatcher** pumps tail downward. **Pacific-slope Flycatcher** greenish yellow, bold eye-ring, pale lower mandible. **Willow Flycatcher** browner, faint eye-ring, pale lower mandible.

Distinct tip

Fairly long and pale

long
bill

Pale edges

slightly
olive

b
tip

Fairly long

yellowish
wingbars

short
primaries

white
edge

ADULT

sulphur

JUVENILE

Gray Flycatcher
Empidonax wrightii

Typically encountered in arid pine forests, pinyon-juniper woodlands, and sagebrush on East Slope. Appears as a washed-out grayish *Empidonax*.

THE BIRD: Lanky with long tail and bill. Our longest *Empidonax*, not as heavy as Willow Flycatcher. Curiously pumps tail downward; all other *Empidonax* pump upward. Yellowish lower mandible, smartly tipped black. Lores pale whitish. Worn **adult** largely pale gray with thin, anemic wingbars and little to no yellow on belly. Freshly molted adult and **juvenile**, slightly brighter with stronger contrast. Overall gray, wings and tail blackish. Back and rump blushed olive, belly sulfur. Wingbars blushed yellowish, tertials edged white. Outer web of outer tail feather whitish.

FLIGHT: Skinny tailed. Typically forages at middle levels. Often difficult to spot hunting in lacy shadows of low bushes.

VOICE: Song a monotonous House Sparrow–like *chi-veK, chi-veK, seeP! chi-veK...* Call, a dry, upward *fiT!* or *wiT!* Not readily separable from Willow or Dusky Flycatcher.

RANGE: Arrives late April, begins breeding early May, departs early September. **West Slope:** Fairly common, woodlands of southeastern Tulare County and near Walker Pass, Kern County. **East Slope:** Fairly common breeder, open forests and sage, below Subalpine.

SIMILAR SPECIES: All other *Empidonax* pump tails upward. **Dusky Flycatcher** greener; small, dark bill. **Hammond's Flycatcher** small, greener, small bill, long primaries, short tail. **Pacific-slope Flycatcher** greenish yellow, entirely flesh lower mandible. **Willow Flycatcher** brownish, faint eye-ring, pale lower mandible.

Fairly small, pale base

mostly dark

pale belly

short primaries

fairly long

ADULT

yellowish wingbars

sulphur

pale edge

JUVENILE

Dusky Flycatcher
Empidonax oberholseri

Midway in size between Gray and Hammond's Flycatchers. Notoriously troublesome to identify, especially worn adults. Tends to feed in sunny areas at lower levels than Hammond's.

THE BIRD: Shaped like a Gray Flycatcher, but pumps tails upward. Bill longer than Hammond's, shorter than Gray. Worn **adult** rather drab, with upper parts dull, gray-green; belly whitish; wingbars often ragged. **Juvenile** and fresh adult are brighter. Gray head and olive-green back contrast slightly. Wingbars and underparts, white or yellowish. Outer web of outer tail feather pale.

FLIGHT: Adroitly twists and turns while hunting insects. Typically forages through interlacing foliage from middle to lower levels.

VOICE: Sings from tall pines and snags. Somewhat monotonous conversational notes: *Tsik, chubReer, tsik, tsik, fitzwee? tsik, chubReer, fitzwee? tsik...* The *tsik* note is strident; *chubReer* burry, vireo-like. Some chirpy notes, House Sparrow–like. Call, quick, upward, airy *siP!* Similar to Willow and Gray Flycatchers.

RANGE: Arrives May, breeds, departs August. **West Slope:** Common in chaparral or forest with widely spaced pines. Breeds Lower Conifer to Subalpine. More common and widespread than West Slope–breeding Hammond's. **East Slope:** Breeds in pine forests and aspen groves, from foothills to tree line.

SIMILAR SPECIES: **Gray Flycatcher** grayer, longer bill, pumps tail downward. **Hammond's Flycatcher** smaller bird, bill, and tail. **Pacific-slope Flycatcher** greenish yellow; large eye-ring; wide, pale lower mandible. **Willow Flycatcher** browner; faint eye-ring; wide, pale lower mandible.

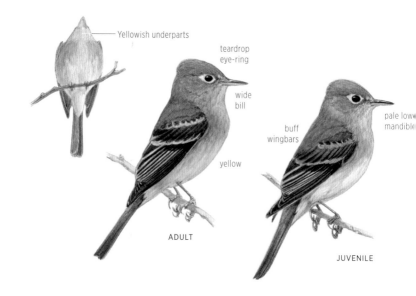

Yellowish underparts

teardrop eye-ring

wide bill

buff wingbars

yellow

pale lower mandible

ADULT

JUVENILE

Pacific-slope Flycatcher
Empidonax difficilis

A bird of cool shade, usually near water. In late 1980s, Western Flycatcher was split into the Pacific-slope and Cordilleran Flycatchers. Simple to differentiate from other *Empidonax*, they're impossible to separate from each other, except by voice and range.

THE BIRD: Smaller than Willow Flycatcher, about Dusky size. Olive green and yellow, with bold almond-shaped eye-ring. The wide bill is orangey below. **Adult's** appearance changes with feather condition. Fresh, it's quite yellow on throat and belly, with blackish-gray wings and whitish wingbars. Worn, appears dull olive-gray above, whitish below, with dull grayish wings and drab wingbars. **Juvenile** shows brighter yellow throat and underparts. Its wingbars are buffy, tertials edged white.

FLIGHT: Bird reveals itself when foraging. Will feed fairly low, but tend higher in leafy canopy or conifer boughs. Listen for its bill snap as it captures insects. Flitting bird shuffles wings and flips its tail, even when "sitting still."

VOICE: A high, thin, three-note call: *see-a-wiT!* Song, repeated three-part phrase *Pa-tik, siT, pa-seeP?*

RANGE: Arrives early April, breeds, departs early September. **West Slope:** Breeds Foothill to Upper Conifer. Favors moist ravines, streamside forests, and mixed conifer. **East Slope:** Does not breed regularly. Migration uncommon at low elevations.

SIMILAR SPECIES: Cordilleran Flycatcher rare, different range and song. **Gray**, **Dusky**, **Hammond's Flycatchers** less yellow, narrower bills, thin eye-rings. **Willow Flycatcher** browner, weak eye-ring. **Hutton's Vireo**, horizontal posture.

round crest

white

brown edges

ADULT

JUVENILE

Black Phoebe
Sayornis nigricans

The "water phoebe." Nice to have around, a friendly bird of farms, fields, and lazy waterways. As humans adorn the landscape with barn, bridge, and pond, the Black Phoebe benefits. From sunny clothesline or rickety fence, it hovers and swoops, hawking winged morsels from the sky or surfaces of mirrored pools. This humble companion invites beginners to look deeper into the world of birds. Confiding and strikingly patterned, it affords easy views, making identification straightforward for a fledgling naturalist. A seed is then planted.

THE BIRD: Just smaller than Say's Phoebe. **Adult** wears tuxedo-like plumage. Black with contrasting belly. Wings and tertials edged white, but paleness diminishes with wear. Singing or feeding, bird reveals bright orangey mouth lining. **Juvenile** adult-like, but wing coverts edged cinnamon. This color soon fades.

FLIGHT: Recalling a large butterfly, bird dilly-dallies low, frequently changing direction. Lands with smooth pump from spread black tail. With no apparent site fidelity, forages on the run.

VOICE: A burry, two-note *seets-seeeer*, second note down-slurred. Also, repeated *piTS! Zoo*. Flight song variable, rapid, twittering. Call, a strident, down-slurred *PSEW!*

RANGE: Widespread and increasing. **West Slope:** Common resident, Foothill to Lower Conifer. After breeding, uncommon to Upper Conifer, rare higher July to October. **East Slope:** Fairly common Reno and Owens Valley. Elsewhere uncommon migrant and post-breeding wanderer, occasionally wintering at low elevations.

SIMILAR SPECIES: None.

translucent
primaries

hovers

wide,
black tail

cinnamon

orange
wing edges

ADULT

JUVENILE

Say's Phoebe

Sayornis saya

Opposite the water-loving Black Phoebe, this "dry phoebe" is at home in wide-open spaces. With a living room big as all outdoors, it inhabits panoramas bathed in pigments reflecting its own. Soft notes wafting across a yawning landscape? Look for a lone bird perched atop a prominent station not far off the ground, gently pumping its spread tail.

THE BIRD: Smaller than Ash-throated Flycatcher. Head and back earth brown, **adult** shows frosty bloom to wing coverts. Depending on wind, temperature, or bird's mood, crown varies from crested, rounded, or flat. Compared to adult, **juvenile** has shorter tail and wings.

FLIGHT: Moseying on silvery wing, pursues insects. Sallies gracefully with aerial pirouettes and powerful ascents. Sometimes appears as if struggling against a stiff breeze, even in dead calm! Capable of hovering, especially in a light breeze.

VOICE: Song a repeated *pip, pipit, uh yeeeer.* Last down-slurred note trails off. Song includes *Myiarchus* flycatcher–like *breeer* notes. Keen observers are alerted by soft airy call. Down-slurred, mournful *pieeeeeer* can be heard over great distances.

RANGE: Primarily a winter bird of foothill grasslands. **West Slope:** Breeds uncommonly, South Fork Kern River and mountains south to Piute Mountains. **East Slope:** Fairly common breeder in lowlands from Reno south to Owens Valley, uncommon in winter. Very rare elsewhere in winter.

SIMILAR SPECIES: Western Kingbird larger, yellow underparts, white outer tail; chatters.

white brow

unmistakable

faint streaks

JUVENILE

streaks

rose

splotchy

FIRST-YEAR MALE

MALE

FEMALE

Vermilion Flycatcher
Pyrocephalus rubinus

Although female and young are subtle, adult male demands attention with clashing red-and-black motif. Although kingbird sexes differ in shape of primary feathers, this is our only flycatcher where ensembles clearly differ. Built like a small phoebe. Favors oases and watercourses through arid lands.

THE BIRD: Wood-Pewee size, **adult male** is unambiguous. Wing coverts edged white. **Adult female**, muted gray above with delicately streaked pale breast. Blackish tail often has pale web to outer feather. **Young female** shows pinkish-rose or yellow underparts. Disheveled, **young male** has irregular red mottling. **Juvenile** dull gray with coverts edged white.

FLIGHT: The flight display is unique and sensational if not somewhat amusing. Male takes flight with body feathers inflated. Blimp-like, wings ablur, he slowly rises, floating with the grace and directional control of a swollen puffer fish.

VOICE: Call, sharp *pseep!* Song, series of distinct notes accelerating and running together: *pip, Pip, PIP, PIP, IT-CHEE-YA!* with strident emphasis on *CHEE-YA!*

RANGE: Breeds South America to desert regions of southern California, barely reaching southern tip of Sierra. **West Slope:** Previously regular breeder in South Fork Kern River Valley, now uncommon and declining. **East Slope:** Very rare. Handful of migrants every few years, Mono Basin to Owens Valley.

SIMILAR SPECIES: Kingbirds and **phoebes** larger.

olive-gray

large bill

sulphur

rust

dark tips

Ash-throated Flycatcher

Myiarchus cinerascens

Resembles a small, lanky kingbird with large, bushy crest. Looking this way and that, *Myiarchus* flycatchers crane their necks, frequently at strong angles. In arid conditions, birds appear skinny, long legged, and rangy. In colder weather, they fluff up to become rounder.

THE BIRD: Larger than Say's Phoebe, smaller than kingbirds. When it is bathed in full sun, behold the subtle beauty of its sulfur belly, rusty wings, and orangey spread tail. Grayish-brown crown and back are blushed olive, while throat and breast ash gray. Distinctly whitish wingbars and tertial edges become worn, late summer and fall. **Adult** shows "fishhook" dusky tip to orangey tail feathers. **Juvenile** adult-like with fresh feathers.

FLIGHT: Long tailed; often flies with head elevated, crest swollen. Rounded wings flash orange. Captures large flying insects, especially butterflies and wasps. Returning with leggy, winged, or spidery groceries, adults feed hungry chicks nestled within tree cavities.

VOICE: Distinctive. Gives softly blown referee's whistle. Also, bright, burry *Chi-breeeer*, with last note descending. Gives repeated, uplifting, rising *priP!*

RANGE: Arrives early April, breeds, departs August. **West Slope:** Frequents semi-open, oak-dominated Foothill and Lower Conifer. After breeding, uncommon to Upper Conifer. **East Slope:** Uncommon migrant. Breeds Inyo County, rare north. After breeding, may appear at higher elevations.

SIMILAR SPECIES: **Brown-crested Flycatcher** breeds Kern River Valley; bigger; larger bill; orange runs clear to tail-tip. **Kingbirds** large, brighter underparts, black tails.

rust

rich
brown

huge
bill

slight
contrast

sulphur

rust extends
to tips

Brown-crested Flycatcher
Myiarchus tyrannulus

If you are in this bird's neighborhood, you will likely hear it well before spotting it. Look for a large Ash-throated Flycatcher with a deep, swollen bill and rousing *FWHIP!* call. Aroused, it frequently elevates its head, raises its crest, and pivots dramatically.

THE BIRD: Large, kingbird size. More saturated in color than Ash-throated. Differs with larger bill and browner upper parts. Darker breast contrasts with yellow belly. **Adult's** wings show fairly bold wingbars. Dark-tipped primaries are orangey. Orangey tail has color extending to tip. **Juvenile** adult-like in late summer and fall, but feathers are fresher.

FLIGHT: Large headed with orangey wings and long, rounded tail. Strong, climbs sharply with jerky movement. Hunting for insects, sometimes forages low to the ground, dramatically swooping and dashing.

VOICE: A loud, bright *FWIP!* Complex calls are strong, husky phrases of robust, burry, rolling notes: *BREER, wiP, wiTIP! BREEER! prip, PRIP!* Some have thrasher-like quality.

RANGE: Northern limit of bird's range barely reaches southern Sierra. A bird of riparian and lonely desert oasis. **West Slope:** This cavity nester formerly bred at Kern River Preserve. Recently breeders have been seen south at the Kelso Creek Sanctuary. **East Slope:** No breeding records. Migrants very rare at far-flung sites and desert seeps.

SIMILAR SPECIES: **Ash-throated Flycatcher** smaller, smaller bill, orangey tail tipped dusky. **Kingbirds** blackish tails, yellow bellies, short legs.

ash-gray

faint
olive

pale
yellow

black with
white edges

Western Kingbird
Tyrannus verticalis

From barbed-wire fences along sunny country roads, the chattering from this boisterous bird enlivens Sierra foothills. Breeding pairs communicate vociferously, often while on the wing. Harassing a passing hawk or pirouetting over golden fields of grass, this bird enjoys a big presence in California's warm heartland. On hot days, bird juts its shoulders forward linebacker-like.

THE BIRD: Larger than Say's Phoebe. Bill, medium size. Rather pale, **adult** has ash-gray head. White throated; the breast is grayish, belly pale sulfur. Blushed green, the gray back darkens into strikingly black tail with diagnostic white outer feathers. **Juvenile** adult-like with pale scaled wing coverts. Wings and tail slightly shorter than adult.

FLIGHT: Flying overhead, appears similar to American Robin. Display flights and social interactions undertaken on quivering wings as bird slows almost to a hover. Male shows slender emarginated primary tips.

VOICE: Calling before dawn, this bird summons a new day. In aerial disputes, birds anxiously bicker with high-pitched, rapid, chattering notes. Gives explosive emphasis on last note: *tik-tik, ti-kree KA-DIK!*

RANGE: Arrives to breed mid-March, departs mid-September. **West Slope:** Common spring and summer to Foothill oak savanna. Rarely higher after breeding. **East Slope:** Fairly common breeder, open lowlands. Spring migrants arrive May, later than on West Slope.

SIMILAR SPECIES: **Cassin's Kingbird** rare, local, dark-gray chest, brown tail tipped buff. **Say's Phoebe** smaller, brown and cinnamon.

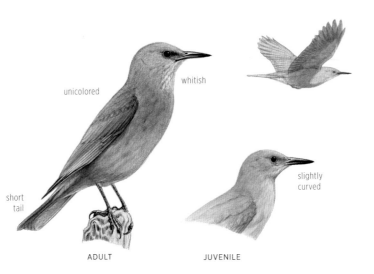

unicolored

whitish

short tail

slightly curved

ADULT

JUVENILE

Pinyon Jay

Gymnorhinus cyanocephalus

Essentially worldwide, corvids have about 120 species, with 10 in the Sierra. Sexes similar. All are somewhat to extremely gregarious. Intelligent, corvids retrieve seeds cached far in the past. While whisper songs are complex, most vocalizations are hoarse. All construct bulky stick nests. Pinyon Jays are heavier than scrub-jays. Sometimes pairing for years, these nomads breed, feed, and rove in highly vocal flocks. Sturdy, chisel-like bills with unfeathered nostrils are used for extracting pine nuts. Foraging groups post sentries to stand watch. Harvesting thousands of pinyon pine seeds in fall, Pinyons cache them for winter consumption, benefiting tree and bird. Astonishingly, these far-flung caches are relocated, even beneath deep snow. Nonbreeding birds disperse when pine crops fail.

THE BIRD: Overall pale blue. **Adult** most intensely sky-like on cheeks, forehead, and primary edges. Throat whitish. **Juvenile**, overall dusty gray touched blue on wings and tail.

FLIGHT: Forms flocks of up to several hundred birds. With short tails, shaped like small crows.

VOICE: Loud, crow-like *HEAR... HEAR, HEAR* and jay-like *zrEEK, zrEEK!*, each note rising. Feeding, utters querulous Bald Eagle–like "chirping."

RANGE: Irruptive. **West Slope:** Fairly common year-round visitor to high country in Kern and Tulare Counties. **East Slope:** Widespread, locally fairly common resident. Breeds early February through August. Most reliable in Mono and Alpine Counties.

SIMILAR SPECIES: **Mountain Bluebird** gregarious, smaller. **European Starling** in flight faster, blacker.

crested
blue
blunt
"lips"

ADULT   JUVENILE

Steller's Jay
Cyanocitta stelleri

Spirit of the Sierra, a bird of many moods. Without a whisper, blends with the shadows and bides its time, watching and waiting. At other times... not so much. A tattletale, it points out things that otherwise go unnoticed. Pay heed to its shrieking cry, as the object of scorn may be an owl, snake, or weasel. Its crest expresses emotion—erect when curious, flat when nervous. Opportunistically profits from discarded sandwich, pine-nut cache, even unattended nestlings.

THE BIRD: Slightly heavier than California Scrub-Jay. Forehead lined blue, **adult's** inky plumage ensures that the bird recedes into darkness. Under, lustrous blue sheen; sunlight reveals delicate barring on wings and tail. Grayer below, **juvenile** adult-like with unbarred blackish coverts.

FLIGHT: Dark, with rounded wings and broad tail. With drawn-out glides, spills altitude with swooping "stair-stepping" drops. Travels singularly or in small groups, infrequently forming flocks. Distended throat indicates full crop.

VOICE: Vocabulary complex. Gives rapid *shreK! shreK! shreK!* and agitated *RAAAAAAH!* Imitates Red-shouldered Hawk with *eAR! eAR! eAR!* Whisper song extraordinary, complex, and thrasher-like with rapid mimicking.

RANGE: Ranges from Alaska to Nicaragua. Sierra resident *Blue-fronted* (*C. s. frontalis*) is one of fifteen subspecies. **West Slope:** Locally abundant, Lower Conifer to Subalpine. Most retreat below snow line in winter, some to foothills. **East Slope:** Fairly common in pinyon-juniper and aspen groves, often near water.

SIMILAR SPECIES: None.

white
brow

bold
collar

ADULT

JUVENILE

California Scrub-Jay
Aphelocoma californica

Common, widespread, and seemingly always about, this sentinel sits patiently observing its surroundings. Cold and fluffed, generous gray flanks often conceal blue wings. A sneak, a songster, a forester, a watchdog, and at times a predator. Often feeds in pairs or family clans on seed, fruit, insects, carrion, eggs, or nestlings. Benefits from handheld peanut offerings. Spending months caching thousands of acorns, perhaps the most effective reforester of oaks in the Sierra.

THE BIRD: Jays typically hop. Nearly Steller's Jay size. White browed, the bicolored **adult's** crown, nape, wings, and tail are glossy blue. Semi-collar frames white throat. **Juvenile** has a grayish head and upper parts, with loose feathers often appearing scruffy.

FLIGHT: Appears labored. Flaps hard with long, drawn-out glides between points. Upper parts blue, back tan, underparts dull. Often transports acorns from oak to cache.

VOICE: A loud, repeated, scratchy, questioning *jreeK?! jreeK?!...* usually accompanied by full-body dip. In flight, often gives "bossy" *SHRUK! SHRUK! SHRUK!* Whisper song captivating, an unlikely series of quiet, jumbled, tumbling notes and trills.

RANGE: Formerly Western Scrub-Jay, *Interior* subspecies (*A. c. super-ciliosa*) occurs in the Sierra. **West Slope:** Common to locally abundant resident, Foothill to Lower Conifer where oaks abound. Especially common near human habitation. **East Slope:** Fairly common resident of pinyon-juniper woodlands, Alpine County north.

SIMILAR SPECIES: **Northern Mockingbird** and **Loggerhead Shrike** similar silhouette; little else to confuse.

pale
blue

subtle
contrast

faint
collar

bluish

Woodhouse's Scrub-Jay

Aphelocoma woodhouseii

Equal in size to the California Scrub-Jay, and in general appears as a "washed-out" version of it. With similar breeding behavior, this non-migratory bird was previously lumped together with the California as a single species. Other widespread birds like the Bewick's Wren, Spotted Towhee, or Song Sparrow, whose ranges extend east of the Sierra into the arid Southwest, also appear slightly bleached. Like other jays, Woodhouse's caches an array of seeds, pine nuts, and acorns. Also consumes insects and small vertebrates.

THE BIRD: Compared to California Scrub-Jay, **adult** Woodhouse shows less cheek-to-crown contrast. The upper parts are paler blue; the brow line is weak, breast collar indistinct. The underparts are dingy, and the vent blushed blue. **Juvenile** shows a fleshy gape and is likely to be following parents, begging. Briefly held juvenile plumage shows entire head, back, and underparts brownish gray; wing edges and tail are blue.

FLIGHT: California Scrub-Jay–like.

VOICE: Much like California Scrub-Jay's, but somewhat abbreviated, more nasal.

RANGE: Formerly considered a subspecies of Western Scrub-Jay, ranges from western Great Plains and southwestern deserts to southeastern edge of Sierra. **West Slope:** Regular on Kern Plateau above 5,000 feet. **East Slope:** Fairly common resident, Alpine County south. Breeds in pinyon-juniper woodlands, often around human habitation.

SIMILAR SPECIES: **California Scrub-Jay** predominately West Slope. Plumage contrasting, colors saturated, brow and collar distinct.

labels in image: white, gray face

ADULT JUVENILE

Clark's Nutcracker
Nucifraga columbiana

A bird with a big presence. Highly vocal, its rasping call is often heard well before this tricolored bird is seen. With chisel-like bills, Clark's gather thousands of pine seeds, which are distributed and buried in caches for later consumption. Scan far-off ridgelines for nutcrackers perched on exposed rocks or snags.

THE BIRD: Hops more than walks. Smaller than American Crow, flicker size. **Adult** gray, shows a white face. Attended by adult and lacking white face, **juvenile** is identified by annoying begging.

FLIGHT: Rowing steadily, flight is crow-like. Wingbeats nearly meet below belly on downstroke. Doesn't soar, but this showy aerialist benefits from updrafts created by wind currents over mountainous terrain. Shows unambiguous black wings with flashing white secondaries. Black central tail feathers are bookended by white. With a pouch under its tongue for carrying food, bird with swollen throat is in essence carrying groceries.

VOICE: Loud, coarse, rolling "back-of-throat" *Raaaaaah!* With upward inflection, *CraaH, CraaH...* Also, downward, nasal *Naaaay...* Whisper song, quiet, sweet intricate trills, often imitating local species.

RANGE: Both slopes: Inhabits dry, open pine forests. **West Slope:** Post-breeding birds cross crest from East Slope to forage. Fairly common, Upper Conifer to Subalpine through November. **East Slope:** Fairly common. Breeds in Jeffrey and ponderosa pine forests up to Subalpine. After young fledge in May, family groups may cross crest.

SIMILAR SPECIES: None.

JUVENILE

blac
bill

ADULT

Black-billed Magpie
Pica hudsonia

Fairly gregarious, primarily at food sources, especially roadkill. Magpies dazzle as their striking pattern flashes. Appears dressed in a well-tailored suit of black and white. Burnished by rainbow sheen; greatly elongated train-like tail adds a classy flourish. Proportions and plumages similar to the Yellow-billed Magpie; this bird is heavier and weighs more than a Clark's Nutcracker, but less than an American Crow.

THE BIRD: Black billed, **adult** shows contrasting black-and-white plumage. **Juvenile** appears nearly adult-like, but its bill is smaller, eyes gray, gape pale, and tail shorter.

FLIGHT: Dramatic, eye-catching pattern and silhouette. Progresses on deep, flowing wingbeats. Largely black above, with bold white scapulars creating "racing stripes." Black primaries, strikingly centered white, produce a flash with each wingbeat. Lengthy central tail feathers create a distinctive shape.

VOICE: A repeated up-slurred questioning and scratchy *wrEY? wrEY?* and forceful *NAY? NAY?* Gives "simmered-down" versions of these louder notes. Whisper song comes with soft trills, rapid phrases, and strained notes.

RANGE: Widespread in western North America. Range extends to base of Sierra. **West Slope:** Crosses crest in eastern Nevada, Sierra, Lassen, and Plumas Counties where resident. **East Slope:** Fairly common resident in sagebrush steppe, agricultural lands, ranches, and riparian groves near creeks and springs, Honey Lake south to Owens Valley.

SIMILAR SPECIES: **Yellow-billed Magpie** West Slope only. Nearly identical, slightly smaller, bill yellow.

bold pattern

yellow

JUVENILE

ADULT

Yellow-billed Magpie
Pica nuttalli

Enhances the Golden State simply by bestowing beauty. If a new State Bird of California is ever needed, this species should be strongly considered, as its entire range lies within the state's borders.

THE BIRD: Eye-catching in plumage, rich in personality, **adult** is slightly heavier than California Scrub-Jay. Boldly struck in logo-like patterning, it is the perfect symbol to represent the California heartland. Sauntering below massive valley oaks, this "rainbow crow" parades cobalt-blue wings and green tail tipped in purple. The small bill is banana yellow, as is the area of skin cradling the eye. Following parent, mouth agape, wings quivering, **juvenile** appears adult-like with smaller bill, and eye encircled by yellow skin.

FLIGHT: Gregarious; groups arrive to evening roosts. With crow-like flapping, translucent primaries flashing with each wingbeat, Yellow-billed moves level and steadily with long tail trailing.

VOICE: Up-slurred, peevish, questioning *JZEEEK? JZEEEK?* Also, strident, rasping *jziik? jziik?* or *wrenk? wrenk?*

RANGE: Range restricted to Sacramento and northern San Joaquin Valleys, south Coastal Range and western Sierra foothills. **West Slope:** Formerly common local residents of Foothill to about 2,000 feet in central Sierra. Favors oak savanna, community parks, and leafy suburbs with fruiting trees. Entire population declined alarmingly after 2005 West Nile virus outbreak. **East Slope:** No records.

SIMILAR SPECIES: **Black-billed Magpie** essentially East Slope. Nearly identical, slightly larger, black bill.

square
tail

American Crow
Corvus brachyrhynchos

With their lives intricately interwoven with those of humans, it's difficult imagining a world without crows. Gregarious in winter, they stroll front yards, harvest plenty from farms, mass in "Halloween trees," and roust drowsy owls. Flocks dissipate in spring as birds pair up to breed, then regroup in fall. Opportunistic and shrewd, crows watch, calculate, and figure things out.

THE BIRD: Walks with streetwise swagger. **Adult**, black with wings and tail glossed bluish. Disheveled, fleshy gaped, and peevish, **juvenile** has blue eyes. Some with albino feathering have interesting calico markings.

FLIGHT: Winter flocks congregate with no apparent formation. Crows flap with wingtips at sides; ravens "paddle" with wingtips below and behind, rowboat style. Ravens can soar; crows can't. (Soaring is gaining altitude on thermals without flapping.) Crows glide or sail on air moving upward over landforms.

VOICE: Vocabulary wide, gives iconic *KAW!* or *rah!* Utters agitated, quavering *ARrrrrr!* Produces rattles like woodpecker drumming. Whisper song, quiet, hollow, "back-of-throat," frog-like *churr*.

RANGE: Widespread across North America. **West Slope:** Common to locally abundant residents of foothills in developed areas to 3,000 feet. Rare higher. **East Slope:** Fairly common resident. Increasing, Honey Lake, Reno, and Carson and Owens Valleys.

SIMILAR SPECIES: **Common Raven** over twice a crow's weight, longer wings, narrower tips, wedge-shaped tail, larger head and bill. **Great-tailed Grackle** one-half crow's weight, yellow eye, long tail.

sizable

"beard"

long wings

soars

wedge

Common Raven

Corvus corax

A large, black nomadic bird. Alone or in pairs, a creature of wide-open spaces, on the move, covering ground. These ingenious, resilient birds of legend and lore are denizens of deep canyons, sweeping deserts, and Alpine crests. Omnivorous—consumes grain, fruit, insect, fish, reptiles, small mammals, carrion, and nestlings. Ravens hop, walk, or gallop.

THE BIRD: America's largest songbird, Red-tailed Hawk size. Appears "bearded." If you encounter a family group after breeding season, note "perfect" full-size **juveniles** and "trashed" **adults**. Infrequently, ravens gather in flocks, usually at trash or road kills.

FLIGHT: Capable of soaring. Spirited, this aerialist uses gravity, inertia, and momentum as playthings. Commuting or courting, this stunt pilot executes heart-stopping barrel rolls while hurling across frowning precipices. Long-fingered wingtips flap down and back, "paddling" rowboat-style. Head sizable with large, hooked, blade-shaped bill. Tail long and wedge shaped.

VOICE: Calls include throaty *GRONK!*, a questioning *wrok?*, a high-pitched crow-like *raH!*, clacking "wooden castanets," and rolling croaks and clucks. Whisper song, "tiny quiet," wondrously intricate trills, electronic buzzes, assembled phrases, and bill snapping.

RANGE: Most of Northern Hemisphere's land masses. **West Slope:** Common resident, increasing in deciduous and conifer forests, towns, and meadows from Foothill to Subalpine. **East Slope:** Common resident, lower elevations. Uncommon visitors to Alpine, mostly fall.

SIMILAR SPECIES: **American Crow** gregarious, smaller, lacks "beard," square tail, different voice, can't soar.

white

white
corners

black
bill

black
mask

buff
wingbar

gr

faint
barring

ADULT

JUVENILE

Loggerhead Shrike
Lanius ludovicianus

About thirty shrike species occur on Earth, two in the Sierra, one of which is rare.

THE BIRD: Sexes similar, shrikes have stout, hooked bills; blocky heads; and bulky bodies. **Adult** gray, black, and white. **Juvenile** shows buff and delicate barring until September. Any shrike with barring after September is Northern Shrike.

FLIGHT: Hunter of wide-open spaces. Flies low with bounding undulations. Landing, swoops upward, wings fully spread, showing bold spots and tail markings. Capable of hovering. Intimidating. Behind fearsome black mask, aggressively pursues prey. Dead-set on capture, shrikes overwhelm by outright aggression. Victims are carried away and wedged into tree fork or impaled onto thorn for later consumption. These meat-eating songbirds entice mates by displaying a butcher's larder of skewered insects, small reptiles, birds, mammals.

VOICE: Not vocally gifted. Monotonous *chur-chur*, meadowlark or thrasher-like rolling *chtttttttr*. High, thin *chee-verr*, first note level, second down. Alarm, rasping down-slurred *aannnnngh!*

RANGE: Foothill grasslands, farms. **West Slope:** Fairly common Kern River, rare elsewhere. After breeding, very rare, Upper Conifer meadows. Winters low elevations. **East Slope:** Presumably breeds. Uncommon spring and summer, sagebrush and pinyon-juniper woodland. Rare winter except Mono Basin and Owens Valley, where fairly common. Numbers have declined.

SIMILAR SPECIES: **Northern Shrike** rare, winter only, large, pale, pale bill base. **First winter** brownish. **Northern Mockingbird**, no mask, pale eye, long tail.

white patches

pale eye

white edges

JUVENILE

ADULT

Northern Mockingbird

Mimus polyglottos

Mimids, a New World family of about thirty species, range from southern Canada to South America and the Caribbean. Includes thrashers, mockingbirds, and catbirds.

THE BIRD: Referred to by the Aztecs as *Cenzontle*, "the bird of four hundred voices," which seems appropriate. Enlivens neighborhoods singing from power line or garden thicket. Presence strong. Serenades morning, noon, or night with volume, creativity, and a touch of humor. Master of imitation; its repertoire reflects local birds, car alarms, or ringtones. Running across lawns or dive-bombing the neighbor's cat, mockingbirds associate with humans. Sexes similar. Slightly smaller than scrub-jay, **adult** is gray, black, and whitish with short, gently curved bill. Brownish, **juvenile** is spotted below.

FLIGHT: Spirited display often performed from telephone pole. Singing, male flashes white patches, repeatedly rising on exaggerated wingbeats. Show complete, wings high, legs dangling, it drops. Flying farther, appears long tailed and round winged. Moves low with shallow rollicking.

VOICE: Song, cheerful phrases pieced into lengthy performances. Repeats phrases, adds new lyrics, and circles back: *Dee-dull, Dee-dull... fweet? fweet? jeer, jeer, Pew, Pew, pew, pew, pew.* Call, forced *TCHEK!*

RANGE: Frequents farmland, suburban gardens. **West Slope:** Fairly common Foothill resident. Uncommon Lower Conifer, very rare higher. **East Slope:** Fairly common Reno through Carson Valley. Breeds Owens Valley. Rare but regular in fall, Honey Lake, Sierra Valley, Mono Basin.

SIMILAR SPECIES: **California Thrasher** song not as complex.

white corners

pale eye

diminished spotting

heavily spotted

WORN ADULT

cinnamon

white wingbars

long tail

ADULT

JUVENILE

Sage Thrasher

Oreoscoptes montanus

California Towhee size, our smallest thrasher is a bird of sagebrush. Often heard first, then spotted atop the tallest bush. Bird's form changes from round and "inflated" in cold weather to elongated and "leggy" in warm. Foraging on foot, holds head high. Pelted by blowing sand, baked by unrelenting sun, and abraded by combative habitat, adults look beaten up by late summer! Migrate, court, build nest, brood eggs, raise chicks, molt, migrate...life goes on.

THE BIRD: Dusted in earth tones, **fresh adult** is distinctly spotted. Flanks and underparts cinnamon-clay. **Worn adult** is drab, with trashed feathering, reduced spotting, and tattered wingbars. **Juvenile** like fresh adult, with streaked back.

FLIGHT: Perched birds often lift one wing high above their backs. Whether a signal, display, or stretch, this "raised hand" is visible from distances. Flies low, progressing with shallow undulations. Appears brownish, round winged, and long tailed.

VOICE: Song carries on a breeze. Stream of rich notes punctuated by lengthy stop. Classic thrasher with mimicry of local birds. Call, a dry, hard *CHEK!*

RANGE: Great Basin to eastern edge of Sierra. Arrives late February, breeds, departs early October. **West Slope:** Rare visitor, mostly foothills in fall; some winter at berry bushes, departing early spring. **East Slope:** Fairly common, sagebrush flats throughout breeding season. Rare elsewhere.

SIMILAR SPECIES: Northern Mockingbird song more variable. **Juvenile**, wing patch.

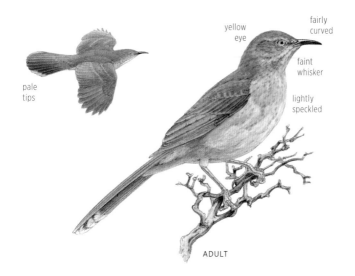

yellow eye

fairly curved

faint whisker

lightly speckled

pale tips

ADULT

Bendire's Thrasher
Toxostoma bendirei

Larger than Sage, this medium-size thrasher is LeConte's size. A bird of desert with open soil and grassy habitat. Like all thrashers, comfortable on the ground. Foraging on foot procures insects by prodding and digging under dirt, at its surface, or higher among the brambles.

THE BIRD: **Fresh adult** upper parts gray-brown to warm ginger. Bill slightly curved. Yellowish staring eye. Face marked by faint brow line, whisker. Breast, flanks veiled with vague dots. **Worn adult's** spotting fainter than fresh adult's. Fairly long tail shows whitish corners. Darker-eyed **juvenile** has gray wing coverts edged buff.

FLIGHT: When not running, flies low, typically from bush to bush. Round winged and rather long tailed, covers ground with shallow bounding and fairly long glides.

VOICE: A steady stream of sweet singsong phrases. Seemingly without taking a breath, adds, replaces, or repeats elements from one performance to the next. Call a rapid *chid-d-dip*.

RANGE: Mojave Desert; breeding range barely touches southern edge of Sierra. **West Slope:** Breeds occasionally South Fork Kern River Valley, south of Weldon. Infrequent, Butterbredt Canyon and Kelso Valley. **East Slope:** Desert canyons, Inyo and Kern Counties. Very rare away from desert.

SIMILAR SPECIES: **Sage Thrasher** smaller, dark breast spots, grayer, wing-bars. **Northern Mockingbird juvenile**, white wing and tail feathers.

long, rounded

long, curved

long legs

ADULT

California Thrasher

Toxostoma redivivum

California Scrub-Jay size, our largest thrasher scrambles through shadowy thickets pursuing insects and spiders. As if atoning for somber plumage, voice jubilant. Although difficult to view well, this covert mimic can be inquisitive. Stay alert: They sometimes give you the once-over through a screen of tortured branches.

THE BIRD: Dark eyed. **Adult** gray-brown with cinnamon vent. Bill long and strongly curved. Brow and cheeks flecked pale. White throat, dark whiskers. **Worn adult** in late summer appears beaten up, with broken feathers. **Juvenile** is adult-like with shorter tail, bill, and fleshy gape. Body feathers loose, wing coverts tipped buff.

FLIGHT: Moves low with labored flaps and long glides, usually undercover. Wings rounded.

VOICE: With magnificent melodies, California's lead singer echoes down steep canyons. Performances are broken into separate phrases by inserting snippets from local species. Song may begin as thrasher, but transforms into flicker, quail, jay, then back to thrasher. Calls include strident *jirr-RET!*, nasal catlike *nee-yah*, and strong *CHEK!*

RANGE: Sedentary to Foothill chaparral and riparian. **West Slope:** Fairly common below 3,500 feet, Foothill to Lower Conifer. Some occur Kern County's Walker Pass around 5,000 feet, and Butterbredt Springs. **East Slope:** Rare, but locally uncommon resident in desert canyons such as Sand Canyon, northeastern Kern County.

SIMILAR SPECIES: **LeConte's Thrasher**, desert, ranges barely overlap; smaller, pale. **California Towhee** bill conical, face cinnamon; nonmusical voice.

slender, curved

sandy tan

thin, black whisker

long, dark

cinnamon

ADULT

LeConte's Thrasher
Toxostoma lecontei

Melds effortlessly into its arid habitat of dry sand and thorn scrub. Afoot, moves about like a miniature Greater Roadrunner sprinting quickly through the sand, head and tail lowered. Pausing, it slowly raises then lowers the tail. Continuing, it scampers through a living room of Joshua trees, down a hall of creosote, across a den of sagebrush, and out the foyer into a yawning solarium of exquisite desolation.

THE BIRD: Slightly larger than Northern Mockingbird; its slender, strongly curved bill casts a distinct silhouette. **Adult** is pale tan with a black whisker and cinnamon vent. Long tail darkens toward tip. **Juvenile** adult-like, with shorter bill, wings, and tail.

FLIGHT: Somewhat ungainly, moves low with labored flapping. Touching down in a bush or hitting the ground running, bird vanishes into thrasher-colored habitat.

VOICE: Pure in quality, gives repeated singsong phrases, unburdened by imitations of other birds. Often sings without long pauses. Call, a questioning *foyp?* or double *foy-ip?*

RANGE: Desert range barely extends into southern Sierra. **West Slope:** Uncommon resident, Canebrake and Kelso Creeks in Kern River watershed. **East Slope:** Fairly common but very local, desert canyons of northern Kern and Inyo Counties.

SIMILAR SPECIES: California Thrasher, range, larger, brown. **Bendire's Thrasher** limited range, shorter bill, pale eyes.

deep blue

white

gray

whitish

spots

pale stripe

♀

MALE FEMALE JUVENILE

Western Bluebird

Sialia mexicana

Thrushes are a family of about 150 species; seven occur in the Sierra. Some resident, others irruptive, a few highly migratory. All consume insects and fruit. Most are celebrities in the singing arena; a few, prodigies.

THE BIRD: Lovely, these pleasing companions go about their lives in peace and in proximity to people, livening the day. Often encountered in close-knit family groups. Friendly, they get along famously with Yellow-rumped Warblers working winter fence lines. Nests in tree cavities or artificial boxes. About Hermit Thrush size. **Male** ultramarine blue, orangey, and whitish. **Female**, pastel blue-gray, peach, and whitish, with blue wings and tail. **Juvenile** female-like with distinct breast and back spots.

FLIGHT: Bluebirds space widely in flight, progress slowly, and show translucent stripe up the center of the wing. Hunting, bird hovers. Landing, flicks wings until settled.

VOICE: Not a gifted songster. Sounds forced and awkward, with strident, choppy notes. *CHEW! Chew, PEW! Chew..., PEW!* Excited chatter: *chik, chi-DIK! Chik, chik.* Flying, gives soft, pleasing, far-carrying *Pew!*

RANGE: **West Slope:** Common to locally abundant Foothill resident. Uncommon Upper Conifer. Often abundant winter. Late summer, fall, some to Subalpine. **East Slope:** Uncommon but regular, pinyon-juniper, April to October, Tahoe Basin, Sierra and Carson Valleys. Rare, local, spring and summer, Owens Valley, uncommon south. Winter rare north of Inyo County.

SIMILAR SPECIES: **Mountain Bluebird female** grayer, breast pinkish clay, longer primaries.

white

hovering

unspotted

"GRAYISH" FEMALE

long wings

pinkish

spots

MALE

FEMALE

JUVENILE

Mountain Bluebird
Sialia currucoides

Soft spoken, with a gentle demeanor. Breeding birds tend to family obligations as "households," stay fairly close together. Winter birds can form large foraging flocks. Spreading across wide-open areas, birds hop, hover, or flycatch, foraging for winged morsels, caterpillars, or berries. Comfortable on the ground, atop sage, fence post, or lichen-encrusted rock, Mountains stand vertically for loftier views.

THE BIRD: Western Bluebird size. Appears thinner, less potbellied. With azure wings and tail, radiant **male** appears cut from a clear blue sky. Cloud-white tummy completes atmospheric analogy. Most **females** overall gray. Some slightly pinkish on face and breast. **Juvenile's** head and upper parts brownish gray, little to no spotting on back.

FLIGHT: With long primaries and pale wing stripe, spends time on the wing capturing insects or hovering. Along with phoebes and shrikes, capable of extended hovering.

VOICE: Soft repeated *cheer, chur, cheer, jear, chur...* Also *tew, tew, pit-tew, tew, pit-tew...* With meadowlark quality, *tearP...pit-tearP, pit-tearP!* Flight call, soft, pleasing, down-slurred *pew.*

RANGE: Arrives March, departs October for lower elevations, southern California or Baja. **West Slope:** Fairly common breeder, open forests in Subalpine and Alpine. Rare in migration. **East Slope:** Uncommon breeder from Subalpine and Alpine to Great Basin. Fairly common in winter, Honey Lake, Carson and Owens Valleys, and southeastern Sierra deserts.

SIMILAR SPECIES: Western Bluebird female breast orangey, blue deeper. **Juvenile** back spotted.

eye-ring

white edges

bold stripe

heavily spotted

complex pattern

long tail

ADULT

JUVENILE

Townsend's Solitaire

Myadestes townsendi

Appropriately named, the solitaire is usually unaccompanied. Perched high atop tall snags or fluttering down to a bed of pine needles, it's slender and elongated. Fond of juniper berries, it's often found foraging with other fruit eaters at food sources.

THE BIRD: Slightly smaller than Northern Mockingbird. Sexes similar. **Adult** appears dressed in a gray "vintage tweed." Bill and legs short, thin, and black. Slender white "monocle" imparts an earnest appearance. Black wings intricately patterned white and buff. Tail long and gray with black-and-white outer feathers. Variable, **juvenile** briefly holds spotted plumage. Disheveled or beautiful, motionless young all but vanish against tortured bark.

FLIGHT: Boldly patterned wings and tail unique. On warm days, solitaire flycatches from prominent perches procuring insects. Often dilly-dallies at lofty heights, leisurely fluttering, frequently singing, and usually going...nowhere.

VOICE: Not particularly thrush-like. A forceful, robust, grosbeak-like series of jubilant notes, some burry and vireo-like in a continuous thread. Tooting high-pitched call *very* Northern Pygmy-Owl–like. Unlike other thrushes, solitaires sing through the fall and winter.

RANGE: Prefers open forested ridges. **West Slope:** Fairly common Upper Conifer to Subalpine. Uncommon to Alpine until November. Breeders cross Sierra, becoming locally fairly common in junipers, September to March. Rare to foothills in winter. **East Slope:** Breeds fairly commonly April to August.

SIMILAR SPECIES: See **Northern Pygmy-Owl** call.

warm russet

faint spots

cold olive

dark spots

olive flanks

RUSSET-BACKED

OLIVE-BACKED

Swainson's Thrush
Catharus ustulatus

Usually heard well before being seen, the forest's lead singer is the lord of the underworld. Covert, skulking, and down-to-earth, it exhibits the classic thrush "hop, hop, stop" movement, often with smart wing-flick.

THE BIRD: Sexes similar. Slightly larger than Hermit Thrush. **Adult**, bold spectacles, lores, and breast rich buff. *Russet-backed*, warm upper parts, wings, rump, tail. Breast spotting, anemic. *Olive-backed*, cold grayish-olive head, upper parts, and flanks. Dark breast spots. **First-year bird** shows a tiny pale spot on each greater wing covert.

FLIGHT: From above, unicolored warm russet or olive, depending on subspecies. Flashing through underbrush, shows pale stripe up middle of underwing.

VOICE: Sublime. Ethereal, airy, flute-like song begins with introductory notes. Rotating sound climbs up and away beyond range of human hearing. Call, a questioning *fwip?* or *foip?* with water-drop quality. Gives *fwwEar* calls and goat-like *fwiT, w-a-a-a-a-a-aaa.*

RANGE: Nonexistent in winter. Historically widespread, now diminishing. Small numbers breed near water in shady forests at scattered locations, central and northern Sierra. Two subspecies occur: *Russet-backed* (*C. u. ustulata*) and *Olive-backed* (*C. u. almae*). **West Slope:** *Russet-backed*, rare breeder. Winters to Central America. Spring migrants common, Kern River Valley. **East Slope:** *Olive-backed* breeds rarely, western Tahoe Basin and eastern Plumas, Placer, and El Dorado Counties. Possibly Mono Basin. Winters South America.

SIMILAR SPECIES: **Hermit Thrush** winters; rusty tail, heavily spotted breast.

buff
stripe

grayish

brown

heavy,
dark
spots

rusty
tail

ALASKA

SIERRA

Hermit Thrush
Catharus guttatus

Bound to the shadows, a wing-flicking "ball on stilts." Slightly smaller than Swainson's Thrush. Frequently inquisitive and well worth overtures of friendship. Several subspecies occur in North America, two or three in the Sierra. Breeding birds show pale grayish head and back. Winter birds are dark warm brown, and occur below snow level through Foothill oak or neighborhood. Any spot-breasted thrush in winter is Hermit.

THE BIRD: Often cocks tail. Sexes similar. **Adult** has rusty rump, tail, and primaries. Throat and underparts whitish, flanks grayish. Breast shows strong black spots. Late-summer **juvenile**, dark-gray upper parts spotted white. Adult-like, **first-winter** bird shows tiny whitish tips to wing coverts.

FLIGHT: Largely brownish with rusty tail. Below, pale stripe up wing's center obvious.

VOICE: With flute-like quality, sublime. Song begins with a pure, long, level, ringing note. It then tumbles closer to Earth than the "upward spiraling" of Swainson's. Call, a double *chuP, CHUP!* Also, shrill, rising Spotted Towhee–like *shreeeEEE!*

RANGE: Wintering in Mexico, the subspecies *Sierra* (*C. g. sequoiensis*) breeds both slopes, May to September. **West Slope:** Fairly common from Lower Conifer to Subalpine. **East Slope:** Breeds in riparian, aspen, and pine forests, departing mid-August. From Alaska, wintering *Alaska* (*C. g. guttata*) arrives both slopes in September, departs April. Very rare East Slope.

SIMILAR SPECIES: **Swainson's Thrush** never winters; buff spectacles and breast. Call, *foip?*

white · yellow · black · gray · "spectacles" · light rust

MALE　　　　JUVENILE　　　　FEMALE

American Robin

Turdus migratorius

Sings predawn, welcoming the new day. Pay attention, for when something is amiss, they alert and inform. Familiar with its full reddish breast and expressive face pattern, most folks can identify a robin. Content around home gardens with widely scattered trees. Frequenting lawns, it procures insects or competes in an earthworm tug-of-war.

THE BIRD: Rotund, Varied Thrush size. **Male** shows black head and rich color saturation. Darker billed, **female** exhibits dull head like a subdued male. Fleshy lipped, recently fledged **chick** shows black spotting below, white streaks above, and fluff atop its head.

FLIGHT: Lateral "flicking" wingbeat, reminiscent of kingbirds. Pushed by winter's "squeegee," waves of robins sweep down from points north. From great heights, they descend to Earth. Pattern simple, lacks "classic" thrush wing stripe. Snowy vent contrasts with tail.

VOICE: Rich, lilting, and flute-like. Can carry on. Less musical than Black-headed Grosbeak, less burry than Western Tanager. *Jeer-it! fee-let, jurr-rit, CHUK! ferr-riT!* Calls include forceful *shruK-shruK!*, descending *CHUK-CHuk-chuk*, alarming *jrEEK, jrEEK!*

RANGE: **Both slopes:** Common widespread resident. **West Slope:** Foothill to Alpine. Winter arrivals from the north descend below Upper Conifer, becoming locally abundant in berry-rich areas. **East Slope:** Common spring and summer below Alpine. Irregular in fall. Fairly common winter at low elevations with little snow and abundant junipers.

SIMILAR SPECIES: **Varied Thrush** in flight, head longer and tail shorter. Shows bold orangey wing stripe.

short tail

boldly marked

♀

prominent head

eyebrow

ornate

black

brown

diffuse band

scalloped

MALE   FEMALE

Varied Thrush

Ixoreus naevius

The "Hollywood Robin." Although attractively patterned, it cloaks its beauty by going undercover. A movement in the shadows may just be this bird. Let your eyes adjust, and behold a thrush foraging in the shelter. Cheeky and "out there," robins parade overtly while Varied Thrushes are demure and retiring. Infrequently gives queer "electric" call. If one materializes, get on it quickly! Apprehensively, they draw near to peer at you, then vanish with a disgruntled *CHUK!*

THE BIRD: American Robin size, the steel-blue, black, and orange **male** displays a broad brow, thick breast band, complex wing pattern, and delicately scaled flanks. Her breast band less distinct, **female** appears male-like with bluish plumage replaced by pale grayish olive.

FLIGHT: Compared to American Robin, conical headed, large chested, and short tailed, with jerking meadowlark-like flight.

VOICE: Haunting. Repeated every few seconds and on different pitches, a long, level, harmonic ringing *Vreeeeeeeeeeng*. Call, a hefty *CHUK!*

RANGE: Irruptive. Some winters, uncommon. Others, nonexistent. Breeds in coniferous forests, Alaska to northern California. Does not breed in the Sierra, but winters. **West Slope:** Common October to April, typically below snow line with berries and acorns present. Widespread in migration, usually conifer and riparian below 5,000 feet. **East Slope:** Rare visitor to aspen, pine, juniper, and riparian, October through December.

SIMILAR SPECIES: **American Robin**, no breast band, plain wings. **Hermit Thrush** call, *chuP*, less forceful.

short
tail

thin

long,
pinkish

pale
billl

scaled

ADULT   JUVENILE

American Dipper
Cinclus mexicanus

Unique, dippers are a family with five species dispersed in the Americas and Eurasia. Grayish, brown, or chestnut, some are boldly punctuated by white. Unlikely in appearance, wondrously adapted. This aquatic songbird survives in a realm where granite rock and surging ice water relentlessly criticize one another. In tempestuous currents, bird swims effortlessly across the surface like a tiny duck. Diving, it submerges. Using its wings, it "flies" underwater searching for insect larvae. Blending into an environment in motion, it rhythmically bobs its bulbous body.

THE BIRD: Communicative or not, blinking white eyelids are highly visible. Black billed, **adult** has faint brownish hue to head. Fleshy billed, **juvenile** is paler and variably scaled below. Coverts edged white.

FLIGHT: When the dipper is rocketing a foot or so above surging waters, its rapid wingbeats appear as a blur. As it "flies" underwater, its flaps are deep and cleaving. Encountering a dipper away from its turbulent world is almost unheard of.

VOICE: Over tremendous rush of water, calls appropriately clear, loud, and ringing. Vocabulary expansive, thrasher-like in quality. This gifted vocalist sings sweet phrases composed of buzzy trills and question-and-answer jabber. Flight call, strident run-together notes: *jit jit jit jit jit jit*. Call note, *tzeeK!*

RANGE: Residents of turbulent streams the length of the Sierra. **Both slopes:** Uncommon Foothill. Fairly common Lower Conifer to Subalpine. Some at middle elevations year-round. Most winter below snow.

SIMILAR SPECIES: None.

crest

streaked

gray rump

whitish

red, waxy

yellow

ADULT

JUVENILE

Cedar Waxwing

Bombycilla cedrorum

Three species worldwide, waxwings occur across Eurasia and North America, breeding at higher latitudes and wintering south. Two occur in the Sierra, one common, one rare. Gregarious, sometimes into the hundreds, waxwings swirl across the landscape in a seemingly endless quest for fruit. Ripe berry-producing plants are inundated, then denuded of produce. Notorious for "adorning" cars with droppings!

THE BIRD: Appears exotic. Expressively fans crest depending on temperature or emotion. Aesthetically tailored, this bluebird-size creature appears airbrushed. Embellished with black "mascara," **adult** is enhanced by waxy droplets to the tips of each secondary; the tail is tipped yellow. **Juvenile**, an anemic version of the adult, is dull gray-brown and pale bellied, with mottled streaks to breast and flanks; crest, paltry.

FLIGHT: Short tailed and triangular winged, moves in vocal, well-choreographed flocks. Flycatches, especially days "raining" with flying termites.

VOICE: A thin, wispy, drawn-out, high-frequency *tseeeeeeeeee*, with quavering quality.

RANGE: Breeds north of the Sierra. Possible to encounter any month, except perhaps July. Some depart north, as late as June. Others return to winter by August! Possibly breeds Lassen and Mono Counties. **West Slope:** Fairly common from Foothill to Lower Conifers. Rare higher. **East Slope:** Uncommon, local, and regular fall to spring, Reno and Owens Valley, occasionally lower.

SIMILAR SPECIES: **Bohemian Waxwing** rare, larger, cinnamon vent, ornate wings. **European Starling** in flight, larger, black plumage.

white

spiky

red eye

glossy

faint patch

pale edges

JUVENILE MALE

MALE

FEMALE

Phainopepla
Phainopepla nitens

The silky-flycatchers, a New World family, are four species ranging from California to Central America. Phainopepla occurs in the Sierra.

THE BIRD: With a funny name, Phainopepla ("fay-no-PEP-luh") infrequently offers up its beauty. Slightly smaller than Western Bluebird, this ruby-eyed creature is demure. With bluebirds, these friends of mistletoe consume fruit and then "pass" the seeds to trees, where they attach and grow. Flocks occur in areas high in fruit or flying insects. Expressively crested, long tailed, and ruby eyed. Silk and satin in its purest form, black **male** is glossed blue. **Female**, a dark-gray version of the male, shows wing coverts edged white. **Immature male** in late summer and fall appears female-like, but splotched by dark feathers.

FLIGHT: Gracefully flutters and hovers among fruiting trees. Covering ground, dilly-dallies, jerking side to side. Male wings show unambiguous white "pom-pom"; female, less so. Landing, flicks and fans tail simultaneously. Captures insects flycatcher-style.

VOICE: Short phrases with downward starling-like *churs* and flute-like thrush contributions. Call, a soft, questioning, water-drop *FoiP?*

RANGE: Chaparral with mistletoe-laden oaks. **West Slope:** Fairly common. Widespread to foothills, fall through winter. Uncommon north of Yuba County. Breeds May and June, Amador to Mariposa County. Some reside Kern River area; others move to desert to breed, early spring. **East Slope:** Breeds uncommonly May to July in Joshua tree, desert riparian, Owens Valley south.

SIMILAR SPECIES: None.

gray

white
brow

Mountain Chickadee
Poecile gambeli

Parids (chickadees and titmice) are a family of around sixty species worldwide; four occur in the Sierra. Sexes appear similar, in black, gray, or brown; these familiar, rounded-bodied birds have short bills. Wings are short, legs sturdy and gray. Not prone to long migrations, some stage irruptions when food stocks falter or weather demands. Cavity nesters.

THE BIRD: Eyes and ears of the forest, chickadees eagerly confront danger. They monitor comings and goings whether goshawk lurking or fox trotting. Foraging and vocalizing with kinglets, creepers, and nuthatches, they knit a blanket of communication throughout the forest. **Adult** slightly larger than Chestnut-backed Chickadee. White brow unique among chickadees. **Worn adult** shows tattered brow. On **juvenile**, diagnostic brow reduced or missing.

FLIGHT: Flaps for all its worth, progressing in slightly jerky fits and starts. Appears chunky, bull headed, and thin tailed.

VOICE: Song sweet, pure *cheeseburger*. First note strong, level; next two down-slurred *SEE! pur-pur*. Call a harsh, agitated, scratchy *zchee, zchee, zchee* or *chit, chit, churr* or *ts, ts, ts, CHURR! CHURR!* Sometimes intermingled with sweet warbling. Difficult-to-hear, high-frequency *see eee eee*.

RANGE: Common to locally abundant, both slopes. **West Slope:** Resident, Lower Conifer to Subalpine. Frequents pine, fir, sequoia, and black oak. **East Slope:** Common, pine, aspen, cottonwood. Uncommon pinyon-juniper woodlands.

SIMILAR SPECIES: **Chestnut-backed Chickadee**, chestnut back, flanks. **Golden-crowned Kinglet** call very similar.

white cheeks

chestnut

Chestnut-backed Chickadee
Poecile rufescens

Encountered less than Mountain Chickadee. Handsome. Adds a splash of color to dappled canopy or lacy conifer. Primarily associated with California's coastal community, this species likes its forests mature and moist. Forest birds pay close attention to and associate with chickadees. Whether to increase foraging success or determine threats of danger, different species join these hunting parties of locals. Want to maximize the diversity of species you encounter? Get with the chickadees and roll!

THE BIRD: Boldly patterned. Slightly smaller than Mountain Chickadee. Appears as if wearing a sleeveless vest that does not quite meet across its portly tummy. Feeding, often hangs upside down. On **fresh adult**, wings show frosty-white area, a feature not shared by Mountain. **Juvenile** has a dark sooty crown and chestnut feathers, less intensely reddish than adult.

FLIGHT: Same as Mountain Chickadee.

VOICE: Pure chickadee. Compared to Mountain, call higher, thinner, not gruff. Clearly proclaims *chik-a-dee-dee*. Gives high, thin *tsee-tsee-tsee*, last note descending. Also *chicka-chicka-dee*. Song less intricate than Mountain.

RANGE: First recorded in the Sierra in the mid-1900s. Has expanded range south at least to Madera County. **West Slope:** Fairly common and highly local from Lower to Upper Conifer, uncommon higher. Distribution patchy and discontinuous. Frequents moist stands of mature conifer, madrone, oak, alder, dogwood, and maple. **East Slope:** Very rare. Few records.

SIMILAR SPECIES: **Mountain Chickadee**, white brow, lacks chestnut.

WEST SLOPE

Oak Titmouse

Baeolophus inornatus

In the mid-1990s, Plain Titmouse was split by the AOS into two species, the Oak and Juniper Titmouse. The species are physically separated by extensive forests and rock scree of the Sierra crest. Aptly named, Oak Titmouse is largely wedded to oaks. Forages by clinging under and over gnarled trunks or hanging from twigs. Alone or in mixed assemblages of insectivores, titmice seem cheerful and bright. Highly vocal, they communicate their emotions and locations.

THE BIRD: Slightly larger than Mountain Chickadee. Shaped like Hutton's Vireo, but heavier. One of the most somber Sierra birds, its expression changes when it raises or lowers its crests. Slightly darker above, bird is overall gray with wings and tail blushed brownish. Alone in a gray face, the eyes are black and beady. **Juvenile** similar to adult.

FLIGHT: Hurried, bounding, twisting. Chickadee-like, chunky, bull headed, and fairly long tailed.

VOICE: A familiar Foothill sound, chickadee-like, but less practiced. Various calls include a forceful *Fid-it! Fid-it! Fid-it!*, level *fweet! fweet!*, repeated *tsee, tsee, fwEEo, fwEEo*, and rapid, descending *tsee, tsee, tsee*.

RANGE: Primarily sedentary. **West Slope:** Common Foothill resident, blue and live oak woodland. Uncommon, Lower Conifer in black oaks. Southern Sierra to 7,000 feet. **East Slope:** Uncommon small populations, Inyo County and Kern River Valley's Walker Creek. Otherwise no records.

SIMILAR SPECIES: **Juniper Titmouse** virtually identical, East Slope only.

EAST SLOPE

Juniper Titmouse
Baeolophus ridgwayi

Based on different range, habitat, and voice, split from Oak Titmouse. Perhaps paler, Juniper looks virtually identical. Living in a harsh environment, birds must be resilient and tenacious to survive where water is scant and night's biting cold swaps places with the day's mad heat. As unrelenting winds sting and gnarled junipers clutch the earth, this hardy bird thrives, bringing its rollicking call and strident note to a tremendous space. Moving about alone or in family tribes, these birds pick, prod, and procure seed and insect from cranny and crevice.

THE BIRD: Larger than Mountain Chickadee. Overall gray with bead-like eyes, bird frequently lowers or raises crest depending on emotions. Flat when hot or anxious, erect when inquisitive or cold.

FLIGHT: Like Oak Titmouse.

VOICE: Songs include level *pee-o, pee-o, pee-o*; clear, rolling, robust *chiddler, chiddler, chiddler*; and additional variations. Calls include sweet wren-like chatter and Pygmy Nuthatch–like *pa-dip, pa-dip, pa-dip*. Chickadee-like, it gives *chi, chi, chi-dik, chi-dik* and forceful *CHI! CHI! CHI!* notes.

RANGE: Reaches western edge of its range in the eastern Sierra, north to Modoc County. Here, its range overlaps with Oak Titmouse. **West Slope:** No records. **East Slope:** Seen in breeding season in Mono Basin. More frequent fall and winter. Rare to Bishop. Fairly common east of region, Mono County, Owens Valley. Uncommon Lassen County.

SIMILAR SPECIES: See **Oak Titmouse**.

light corners

bold stripe

gray cap

extensive reddish

MALE

FEMALE

Red-breasted Nuthatch
Sitta canadensis

Forest birds, about thirty species of nuthatches occur worldwide. Three occur in the Sierra, all colored white, blue-gray, black, brown, and rust. Wings are rounded, and tails short and boldly marked. Birds procure insects and pine nuts using slightly recurved bills.

THE BIRD: Whether creeping, hitching between plates of pine bark, or hanging from the frowning limb of a massive oak, this bird's at home in a vertical world. Carousing with a rowdy gang of chickadees on "owl patrol," these nuthatches appear desperate, quickly pivoting and flicking their wings. Perturbed, excited, and face marked with a focused glare, it vocalizes incessantly. Noticeably smaller than White-breasted Nuthatch, but just larger than Pygmy. Sexes subtly but noticeably different. **Female** show gray crown blending with back. **Male's** black crown contrasts with back.

FLIGHT: Feeding, creeps and flutters short distances. Flying farther, moves in hesitant, jerky manner. Like all nuthatches, Red-breasted's large head opposite short tail imparts front-heavy look.

VOICE: Often discovered by loud, continuous, rapid or leisurely *YANK! YANK! YANK!* Foraging, gives soft, contented, squeaky *yenk, yenk, yenk* while chiseling.

RANGE: **West Slope:** Common resident from Lower Conifer to Subalpine. Irruptive, post-breeding birds move higher or lower depending on food or weather conditions. **East Slope:** Fairly common to Subalpine. Intermittent in pinyon-juniper depending on cone crops. Some winters common, others absent.

SIMILAR SPECIES: **Pygmy Nuthatch** gregarious, brownish crown.

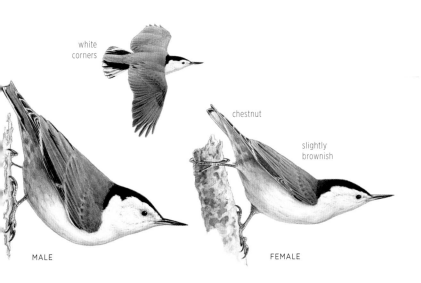

white corners

chestnut

slightly brownish

MALE

FEMALE

White-breasted Nuthatch
Sitta carolinensis

In style with its classic blue-gray "suit" and black "top hat," a restless partygoer decked out in formal attire. With jerky quartering movements, forages in unlikely positions, often sideways or upside down. Food located, it stops, rears head, and repeatedly drives chisel-like bill downward until bark relents and wriggling morsel is procured. Identified by voice and range, two subspecies, *Slender-billed* (*S. c. aculeata*) and *Inyo* (*S. c. tenuissima*) occur and may someday be split into separate species. Subtle differences may lie in flank darkness, back color, or bill size; otherwise essentially identical.

THE BIRD: Smaller than Downy Woodpecker, twice weight of Red-breasted Nuthatch. Sexes largely similar. **Male** crown contrasts with back; **female's** blends. **Juvenile** female-like, but tail and wings shorter.

FLIGHT: Flies more swiftly and directly than smaller nuthatches. Birds are white bodied and dark winged. From below, wrists display a black-and-white spot.

VOICE: *Slender-billed*, one to four nasal, burry, down-slurred notes: *weear, weear...* Also gives a rolling *middddew*. Song, rapid nasal *chew-wee, chew-wee...*, second note rising. *Inyo*, long, rapid, high-pitched *chur-chur-chur-chur* and soft burry chatter: *midddt*.

RANGE: Sedentary. Resident both slopes. **West Slope:** *Slender-billed*, common Foothill oak, riparian woodlands. Uncommon Lower Conifer. Absent from fir forests of Upper Conifer. **East Slope:** *Inyo*, fairly common to Subalpine. Subspecies barely come into contact near crest in southeastern Tulare and Plumas Counties.

SIMILAR SPECIES: **Smaller nuthatches**, faces marked.

whitish
spot

brown

mask

Pygmy Nuthatch
Sitta pygmaea

Other nuthatch species are loners encountered in pairs or small parties. By contrast, Pygmy Nuthatches are usually gregarious, found in gatherings numbering a dozen or more. Forest birds accompany these roving pygmies. Keeping assemblages of wandering songbirds cohesive is likely challenging, but this nuthatch does so with "peeping" calls. Birds convene on trunk or cone, profiting from insects or seeds that lie before them. With large, strong feet for clinging and sharp chisel bills, they're supremely equipped for removing seeds from sharp, sticky cones.

THE BIRD: Just smaller than Red-breasted Nuthatch, chickadee size. Sexes similar. Grayish-brown crown has white spot on nape. Face shows black "robber's mask." Upper parts "nuthatch blue," underparts fawn and gray.

FLIGHT: Bushtit-like, these birds stream forth from trees singly or in pairs along with mixed assemblage of songbirds. Combination of whitish nape and bold, white tail spots, unique.

VOICE: Lengthy, uninterrupted, toy-like peeping notes: *peep, peep, pip, peep, pip, peep, peep*... Some increase in tempo, running into trill of *pips*.

RANGE: Residents of mature, long-needled pine forests with abundant snags. **West Slope:** Local in ponderosa and Jeffrey pines, Plumas and Sierra Counties. In the south, Madera to Kern County above 6,000 feet. Records at 3,000 feet suggest post-breeding wandering. **East Slope:** Common residents to Subalpine in habitats similar to West Slope, including aspen groves.

SIMILAR SPECIES: **Red-breasted Nuthatch** slightly larger, white brow, reddish breast.

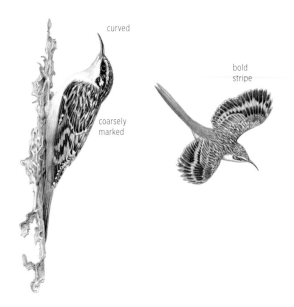

curved

bold stripe

coarsely marked

Brown Creeper
Certhia americana

Brown Creeper is our only member of the Old World family Certhiidae. Nuthatches hitch up or down, creepers upward.

THE BIRD: Sexes similar. Lighter but longer than Pygmy Nuthatch, creepers are small. Like a wood chip brought to life, they vanish against bark. Diverse flocks of insectivores often have them in attendance. Lifting moss or bark, creepers peer underneath for leggy tidbits. Insects avoiding chickadees picking or creepers creeping may live to see another day. These species with white underparts—woodpeckers, nuthatches, and creepers—feed close to bark, illuminating the possibility that alabaster breasts reflect light into dark crevices, helping to light the way. All birds, note curved bill, white brow and ear-spot. Toenails long and spidery, tail long and stiff.

FLIGHT: Plummets stone-like from treetop to base. Look quickly for the buffy zigzag wing stripe and cinnamon rump. Easily flycatches and loves a "good-old termite hatch."

VOICE: One or two exceedingly high, thin, rising *tseeeee!* notes. High in frequency; many cannot hear it. Song easier to hear: *see, see, pitta-pa see?*, put to words, *trees, trees, beautiful trees.*

RANGE: Mature conifer, broadleaf forests. **West Slope:** Common resident Lower and Upper Conifer. Uncommon or rare, Subalpine. Some winters, uncommon to Foothill. **East Slope:** Fairly common, ponderosa, Jeffrey pine, aspen, and cottonwood groves. Rare away from pinyon-juniper.

SIMILAR SPECIES: **Golden-crowned Kinglet** call. **Mountain Chickadee** call.

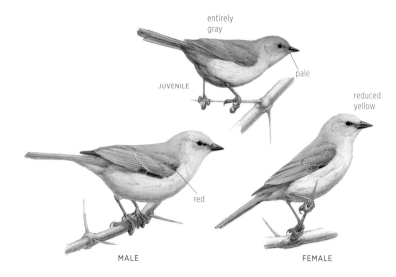

entirely gray

JUVENILE

pale

reduced yellow

red

MALE

FEMALE

Verdin

Auriparus flaviceps

Verdin is the only New World member of this Old World family, Remizidae.

THE BIRD: A diminutive bird of the Mojave Desert. Tough as nails, it's resilient in the face of daily temperature swings from freezing to well over 100° F. Tenacious and nimble, forages through some of the thorniest stickers and prickliest brambles a desert can throw at it. Solitary, in pairs, or in small groups, these agile birds forage for insects, seeds, and fruit. With entrance hole located at the side, its globular stick-nest is constructed into a grapefruit-size ball secreted in cactus, mesquite, or a nest predator's worst nightmare, cholla cactus. Just larger than a kinglet. **Male** gray with a yellow crown and face. Often conceals chestnut lesser wing coverts. **Female** is male-like with diffused yellow face. Slightly darker above, **juvenile** is overall gray with pale at bill's base.

FLIGHT: A wee gray bird, not unlike a tiny titmouse; flies fairly low with labored flaps.

VOICE: Song, lisping *tsu, tsee, see, seeu* notes. Call, rapid *tsik, tsik, tsik, sik, sik*, with hummingbird-like quality. Also, peevish down-slurred *tsew.*

RANGE: Inhabiting deserts, reaches extreme northwestern edge of its range in southeastern Sierra. **West Slope:** No records. **East Slope:** Uncommon local resident of desert canyons west of Highway 14 and US 395 from Kern into southern Inyo County.

SIMILAR SPECIES: **Bushtit** with yellow pollen on face, smaller, gregarious.

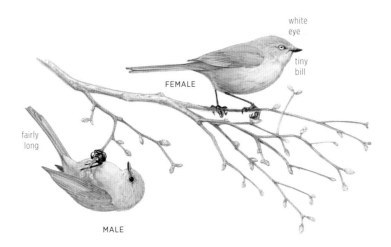

white
eye

tiny
bill

FEMALE

fairly
long

MALE

Bushtit

Psaltriparus minimus

Bushtit is our only member of this Old World family, Aegithalidae.

THE BIRD: Tiny. After hummingbirds, the Sierra's smallest bird. Energetic and bestowed with a community spirit toward their families and greater songbird commonwealth. Pairing off to breed, Bushtits build hanging nests from woven cottony fiber, lichen, and spider silk. Growing up inside a "crowded sock," chicks are obliged to cuddle. In the nonbreeding season, Bushtits form hunting parties that number into the dozens. Sexes are identified by eye color. **Male** eyes are dark, **female** white. The bill is tiny; the tail is slender and proportionally long.

FLIGHT: Flocks appear hesitant to cross open spaces. Once brave enough to make a harrowing journey of, say, 30 feet, they burst forth, wings a blur, progressing with noticeable tail pumping, while another and another make the same commitment until all have crossed the yawning gap.

VOICE: High in frequency, a metallic tinkling *ts, ts, sss, s, ts, tss...* Also, thin, down-slurred *ts, ts, ts...* Gives dry, scratchy *tsip, sip, tsip, tsip*. Alarm, a high, thin shower of twittering.

RANGE: Resident. **West Slope:** Common to locally abundant Foothill to Lower Conifer. Uncommon Upper Conifer. Frequents riparian, oak chaparral. **East Slope:** Fairly common riparian and oak woodlands, fall to spring. Winter records from desert canyons, southern Inyo and Kern Counties.

SIMILAR SPECIES: **Verdin**, desert inhabitant, yellow face.

long
tail

pale
eye

Wrentit
Chamaea fasciata

Neither wren nor tit, Wrentit is North America's sole representative of this Old World family, Sylviidae.

THE BIRD: Reclusive. Wedded to impervious undergrowth, Wrentit lives to discourage satisfying views. Heard far more than seen; sexes are similar, and both sing. Notably inquisitive, it'll size you up, peering through a lattice of twigs. Wrentit couples join foraging parties of insectivores passing through their neighborhood, but only "to the end of the block." **Adult** larger than Bewick's Wren, tail long and cocked. Body dark brownish, head washed gray, throat pinkish buff with faint striations. **Worn adult** often has tail with broken feathers.

FLIGHT: Hesitant to fly more than a few feet. Once a bird "bucks up" with sufficient bravery, it pushes off! On a blur of wings and with vigorous tail pumping, it vaults forth on a terrifying odyssey of perhaps 10 feet, only to dissolve into tangle.

VOICE: Voice of the chaparral. A Ping-Pong ball–like loud, clear, whistled series of level notes that steadily quicken in pace. Male often culminates in rapid trill. Female is evenly paced. When anxious or inquisitive, utters agitated ratchet-like notes. Also, lethargic series of well-spaced, level *tee, tee, tee...* notes.

RANGE: Dense chaparral, lush riparian. **West Slope:** Common residents, Foothill to Lower Conifer; rare higher. **East Slope:** Very rare. Few records southwestern Inyo County.

SIMILAR SPECIES: **House Wren** smaller, barred.

bold
brow

heavy
spotting

fewer
spots

JUVENILE

ADULT

Cactus Wren

Campylorhynchus brunneicapillus

Wrens are essentially a New World family. About eighty species range from Alaska to southern Chile, with seven in the Sierra. Usually alone or in pairs; sexes are similar. Plumages barred and earth tone. Slightly curved, bill is slender. Most wrens hold tails cocked. Songs jubilant and complex.

THE BIRD: Large, loud, and nearly Sage Thrasher size, this extrovert is patterned in "striated cactus" motif. With long, curved bill, our largest wren is strongly marked with white brow and brown eye line crossing red eye. Cheeks and back streaked; wings barred. **Adult** breast heavily spotted. **Juvenile** less spotted; eyes are duller.

FLIGHT: Moves low through brush and swale with labored wingbeats and level glides. Wings flat, tail spread, it swoops up to perch, showing conspicuous tail spots.

VOICE: Perched prominently, this big talker drones on and on like an old car that doesn't quite turn over. Creating a sense of impending doom, filmmakers insert Cactus Wren's creepy, low, monotonous drone prior to any devious act, be it murder or misfortune. A level, dry, breathing *reh, reh, reh, reh, reh, reh...*

RANGE: Reaches desert of southern Sierra. **West Slope:** Locally common Joshua woodlands, South Fork Kern River Valley, Chimney Peak, Kelso Creek, Walker Basin, and Piute Mountains. **East Slope:** Fairly common and local, desert washes, Inyo and eastern Kern Counties.

SIMILAR SPECIES: **Sage Thrasher** unbarred, pale eyes, smaller spots.

faint
eye line

speckled

buffy
flanks

Rock Wren
Salpinctes obsoletus

Prominently perched, Rock Wrens can lead you on a musical adventure. When this bird throws back its head, chest swollen, a rock-strewn amphitheater suddenly brims with song. Bounding from one boulder to the next, it stops, bobs, and pivots. Patterned in "marbled rock" motif, it vanishes when not in motion.

THE BIRD: Medium size, slightly larger than Canyon Wren. Infrequently holds tail cocked. **Adult** shows sandy-tan upper parts with tiny white speckles. Faintly streaked, muted breast blends into warm tan flanks. Fleshy-billed **juvenile** is adult-like with shorter wings and tail.

FLIGHT: Flies low with rapid flapping, punctuated by fairly long glides that display its cinnamon rump and buff tail corners. Landing, gives exaggerated bows that end with head high, bill aloft.

VOICE: This skilled soloist contrives one chorus after another. Unrestrained, it changes the tempo, cadence, and pitch of its sweet, burry trills while sampling songs of local species. Curtain call? Bowing repeatedly, it's only too happy to come back for an encore and offer a medley of greatest hits. Call, a bright, rising, springy trill *FTRRREEEEEEP!* Alarm, a downward *Pitseeeeeew.* Other calls thin, strident, and burry.

RANGE: A bird of talus slopes, rocky ridges, and boulder-strewn earthen dams. **West Slope:** Fairly common resident in foothills. Local and uncommon to Alpine fell-fields. **East Slope:** Locally common breeder, uncommon winter.

SIMILAR SPECIES: **Canyon Wren** warm cinnamon, white throat.

rusty

long. thin bill

white throat

Canyon Wren
Catherpes mexicanus

Lives in a world that, for humans, would not be for the faint of heart. Foraging on boulders and sheer vertical walls, this rust and white rock-jumper bursts forth in song. High above horizontal earth, clinging to the polished face of a precipice, this cliff-hanger is sometimes encountered by rock climbers. Partaking in solo moves that make free climbers jealous, this natural spelunker flattens its body and squeezes between granite slabs in search of insects.

THE BIRD: Patterned in "rusty canyon" motif. Slightly smaller than Rock Wren, **adult** is grayish crowned, with body, wings, and tail warm cinnamon. Throat and breast alabaster. Upper parts peppered by white speckles; flanks and tail display thin black barring. Equipped for capturing spiders, the bill is long and slender. **Juvenile** adult-like with shorter flesh bill base.

FLIGHT: Flies low between jumbled boulders. From a cliff face, pushes off and plummets stone-like for hundreds of vertical feet to land safely below.

VOICE: Most memorable. Like a Hollywood version of an alien craft descending from outer space. Spiraling song "circles" downward, while dropping in pitch. At the end of a song or as a stand-alone note, gives a Common Nighthawk–like *beenK!*

RANGE: Fairly common resident. **West Slope:** Favors river canyons with sheer walls from Foothill to Upper Conifer, uncommon higher. Moves downslope in winter. **East Slope:** Uncommon residents from Foothill to Subalpine.

SIMILAR SPECIES: See **Rock Wren.**

white
eye line

white
corners

Bewick's Wren

Thryomanes bewickii

With a small home range, this jaunty bird of brushy entanglement knows its neighborhood. There are few nooks this investigative denizen of the shadows has not peered into, places dark and safe, where few have tread. Mocking twisted labyrinths and singing through manzanita mazes, with one fleeting hop, it vanishes through a lattice of twigs. Periodic extravert or weary of obscurity, this wren sometimes perches unabashedly and pours forth song.

THE BIRD: Slightly longer than House Wren. Upper parts wood brown, cheeks grizzled. Wings and "active" tail, barred. Slender bill slightly curved. **Juvenile** adult-like with shorter bill.

FLIGHT: Moves through brush with hops and flutters. Reluctant to cover open ground, barrels low, directly, and rapidly.

VOICE: Sings all year. When you're birding in the Sierra, an unusual song is often the Bewick's Wren. Capable of a remarkable array of songs. Often composed of two or three distinct elements—a trill, a buzz, then rapid rolling notes: *zit, zit, zit, swEEET! brrrrrr*. Repeats song, then switches to another. Scold note, a dry, agitated, scratchy *jzzzzzzit*.

RANGE: Sedentary. Brushy habitat, forested rivers, post-fire areas, foothill farms. **West Slope:** Common, Foothill to Lower Conifer. May wander higher after breeding. **East Slope:** Fairly common, low-elevation riparian. Uncommon, pinyon-juniper.

SIMILAR SPECIES: **House Wren**, no eye line. **Marsh Wren**, marsh, voice.

lacks distinct
features

nearly
straight

barred,
cocked

House Wren
Troglodytes aedon

After Barn Swallow, this little brown bird has the widest distribution of any land bird in the Americas! North to south, east to west it has wandered, flitted, and crept among the greatest tangles connecting these two vast land masses. To slow down, smell the roses, and appreciate the subtle, coax one into view and get to know this bird. Behold soft gradations, scrawls of delicate barring, and welcome embers of warmth to the tail. A whisper of an eye-ring, a touch of pale to the bill, and this elegant exemplar of understatement is complete.

THE BIRD: **Adult**, Bewick's Wren size, shorter tail. Upper parts grayish brown, underparts paler. **Juvenile** shows fleshy gape.

FLIGHT: Agile in dense cover. In the open, moves directly and purposefully, twisting on axis.

VOICE: An auditory delicacy delivered by a creature seemingly brimming with joy. Bubbly and jubilant, ecstatic notes trip over each other to burst into public space. Highly variable. Song typically longer and more complex than Bewick's Wren, with jumbled notes, liquid trills, and different phrases. Call less scratchy than Bewick's.

RANGE: Arrives March, breeds, departs by mid-September. **West Slope:** Common woodland, riparian, meadows, Foothill to Upper Conifer. Some to Subalpine after breeding. Rare winter. **East Slope:** Fairly common breeder, aspen and riparian. Uncommon to Subalpine. Fairly common desert oases.

SIMILAR SPECIES: **Pacific Wren** smaller, tiny tail. **Bewick's Wren**, white brow.

short tail

cinnamon

Pacific Wren
Troglodytes pacificus

Wedded to cool shadows. While it's difficult to behold this energetic gnome-like creature, it's well worth the effort. If eye-to-eye with this diminutive custodian of the conifers, pause to consider the hallowed halls in which it dwells. Whether broadcasting crystalline notes throughout a lush metropolis of coniferous skyscrapers, permeating forest cathedrals with tumbling trills, or pouring forth liquid rivulets of song beneath 3,000-year-old sentinels, Pacific Wrens fill space with sound. "On the street," this breath of a bird appears mouse-like, hopping beneath lacy ferns or venturing into webby crawl spaces.

THE BIRD: Tiny bird, minute bill, smaller than House Wren. On proportionately large legs, dramatically bobs entire body. Overall cinnamon with paler throat and buff brow. Flanks, wings, and tail are barred. Each covert is tipped with a miniscule white-and-black speck.

FLIGHT: In shaded forest understory, difficult to see well. Flies short distances through dense habitat appearing as a tiny "wound up" dark, tailless bird.

VOICE: Loud, notably long song consists of sweet, liquid, thin, rollicking trills. Call, like clinking stones together. A distinct double *tic-tic*, recalling Wilson's Warbler.

RANGE: Residents in riparian, mature conifer forests, and Sequoia groves. **West Slope:** Fairly common in Lower and Upper Conifer. Some move upslope late summer, fall. Winter, most move downslope. **East Slope:** Uncommon in similar habitats, Reno to Owens Valley.

SIMILAR SPECIES: **House Wren** larger, grayer.

Marsh Wren
Cistothorus palustris

At home in tule, rush, or cattail vegetation, this occupant of reedy wetlands is rarely encountered elsewhere. Proclaiming that a Marsh Wren blends into its habitat would be like declaring that a male Western Tanager doesn't. Tule tan and bog brown, it is the color and pattern of marsh, and vanishes when motionless. With tail held at steep angle, it's often inquisitive, but after sizing you up, disappears with little effort. Heard from marsh to mire, its "sewing-machine" song seems to stitch together all quagmires.

THE BIRD: **Adult**, Common Yellowthroat size. Strongly marked with white eye line, cinnamon upper parts, and black back, striped white. Wings, tail barred. Face and underparts creamy, flanks tan. Newly fledged **chick** often shows fluffy white feathers emerging from crown.

FLIGHT: Flies quickly and close to the mire. Landing, shows rusty rump while vanishing into a "forest" of cattails.

VOICE: Song, one or two introductory notes followed by sewing-machine cadence of *chek-tuk, t-t-t-t-t-t-t-t-t-t-t*. Often more varied, but with telltale "stitching" staccato. Call, dry, agitated chattering notes: *chi, chi, chi...*

RANGE: Resident, cattail, tule, reed marshes. Abundance varies seasonally. **West Slope:** Uncommon breeder in scattered Foothill wetlands. May be encountered higher, late summer and fall. **East Slope:** Fairly common local breeder, lower elevations. Fall numbers drop; some remain through winter or depart in extremely cold conditions.

SIMILAR SPECIES: **Bewick's Wren**, brushy habitat, lacks rust.

black

MALE

white
undertail

white
eye-rim

blushed
brown

white

FIRST YEAR

FEMALE

Blue-gray Gnatcatcher
Polioptila caerulea

A New World family of around twenty species ranging from the United States to South America.

THE BIRD: Pearl of the chaparral. Tiny, kinglet size, hyperactive, and "natty." Found in pairs or among foraging insectivores. Soft blue-gray with frosty wing panel and contrasting black tertials. Pivots side to side, expressing its fairly long cocked tail, flicking and flashing bold white outer feathers. Bead-like eyes are neatly encircled by a crisp white ring, giving bird a wide-eyed expression. **Male's** upper parts are more intensely blue than the **female's**. Looking straight at you, his black "unibrow" imparts a focused Frida Kahlo–like stare. Paler-billed **immature** is female-like washed brownish, with color and contrast subdued.

FLIGHT: Foraging, hops from bush to bramble. Flying in the open, appears pale, progressing in a shallow, rollicking manner while vigorously pumping black-and-white tail.

VOICE: Song, thin, jumbled notes, rich and thrasher-like, including annoyed notes: *fizz-ee-u, fizz-it, tseeeep, fizz-eee-u.* Call, inflected downward, a high, thin, buzzy, and miffed *Fzeeeeu, Fzeeeeu,* sounding peevish, nasal, and perpetually perturbed.

RANGE: Arrives April, breeds, departs by early September. **Both slopes:** Fairly common breeder in scrub or riparian. **West Slope:** Frequents chaparral, oak, Foothill to Lower Conifer. Rare south of Mariposa County. In northern foothills, rare in winter. **East Slope:** Aspen, cottonwood, or willows. Very rare winter. Most records Mono and Inyo Counties.

SIMILAR SPECIES: **Bushtit** smaller, gregarious, gray.

MALE | FEMALE

orange
bold stripe
black square
lacks orange

Golden-crowned Kinglet
Regulus satrapa

Six species of kinglets exist on Earth, two in the Sierra.

THE BIRD: Among the smallest and most common of Sierra songbirds, just larger than Bushtits. Often with other songbirds, forages in upper levels of conifers, so close views are infrequent. Saying it appears delicate would misrepresent the true strengths of this hardy creature. Enduring winter's stinging cold, gathering sufficient protein, and avoiding hawk and owl, it thrives. With a high metabolism, this gymnast probes lichen or bark. Ornament-like, it'll dangle to glean insects from undersides of needles. Eye anointed black, gape with slight whisker. Wings and tail edged chartreuse. Tail neatly forked. **Male** female-like until it flares concealed orange crown patch, a feature **female** lacks. Legs thin, feet pink.

FLIGHT: Hovers momentarily when feeding. Moving through treetops, flocks stream out in twos and threes. Covering longer distances, erratic and jerky.

VOICE: Difficult to hear, impossible for some. Rising in pitch, a series of thin notes: *tsee, tsee, tsee, chit-uh-dee-dee-dee.* Buzzy end of song, chickadee-like. Call, high-frequency Brown Creeper–like *tssssssss, tssssssss…*

RANGE: Resident, high altitude in mature conifer forests. Some move lower in winter. **West Slope:** Common to locally abundant, Lower Conifer to Subalpine. Breeds uncommonly Subalpine. Locally fairly common in Foothill, winter. **East Slope:** Fairly common, ponderosa and Jeffrey pine. Uncommon in dry southern forests.

SIMILAR SPECIES: End of **Mountain Chickadee's** call *very* similar.

crest raised

MALE

yellowish edges

eye-arcs

pinkish feet

black wingbar

Ruby-crowned Kinglet
Regulus calendula

Although one of our smallest songbirds, kinglets make up for their minute size with a larger-than-life personality. Whether in an endless quest for insects, flinging mini blasphemy bombs at owls, or simply surviving bitterly cold nights, a highly resilient ball of feathers.

THE BIRD: Fractionally larger than Golden-crowned Kinglet. **Male** conceals his crimson crest until agitated. **Female** lacks a red crest. Ruby-crowned appears similar to Hutton's Vireo. Separated by behavior, Ruby-crowned offers cursory glances. Hutton's stops, regards you, and sizes you up. Kinglets have one bold white wingbar; Hutton's has two. Kinglets engage in overly dramatic wing-flicking and exaggerated pivoting; vireos less so.

FLIGHT: Flutters short distances or hover-gleans for insects. Flying farther, moves in jerky, zigzagging progression.

VOICE: Song high, thin, sweet *cheer-cheer-cheer, cheda-cheda, che-che-che.* Call, rapid, dry, scratchy notes in an irregular cadence: *chi, chi, chi, chi, chi...* reminiscent of typing stenographer.

RANGE: Breeds May through July, possibly later, higher. **West Slope:** Common in Foothill fall, winter, and spring. Locally uncommon breeder to Subalpine in lodgepole pine and mountain hemlock south to Tulare County. **East Slope:** Common migrant. Visits aspen groves to Subalpine. Patchy south of Sierra Valley to northern Inyo County. Winter, rare at lower elevations. Common near Reno and Owens Valley.

SIMILAR SPECIES: **Hutton's Vireo** larger, blocky head, white lores, thick bill, blue-gray legs, voice.

eye-arcs

flicks
long tail

faint
wingbar

Bell's Vireo
Vireo bellii

This primarily New World family contains about thirty species; five occur in the Sierra. Hutton's winters, the rest migrate as far as Central America.

THE BIRD: Smaller than Warbling, our "least" vireo is Orange-crowned Warbler size. Recalls a gnatcatcher with loose, flicking tail. Small and energetic, it forages for insects, singing repeatedly. **Adult** overall grayish with faint white brow and olive wash to back. Fresh bird shows indistinct wingbars. Worn bird, only the lower. **Late-summer adult** rather worn; some downright trashed. **Juvenile** similar to adult with fresh wingbars.

FLIGHT: Moves low and quickly through willows.

VOICE: Usually detected by distinctive, forced, and rapid song. Has "chewy" back-and-forth cadence: *witch-it-uh, fidg-it-uh, witch-it-uh, widgg-EAR!* Gives repeated, agitated, down-slurred, nasal *nee-yah...*

RANGE: Encountered in breeding season in semiarid riparian with brushy willows. Once common in California's lowland riparian. Nearly extirpated from habitat loss and Brown-headed Cowbird brood parasitism. Increasing in southern California; there's hope for its repopulation with Central Valley breeding successes. **West Slope:** Recently bred near Lakes Success and Isabella in Tulare and Kern Counties. **East Slope:** Nested over a hundred years ago, Owens River. In 2009, bred Big Pine, Inyo County. Due to small population and range, Least Bell's Vireo (*V. b. pusillus*) is state- and federally listed **Endangered**.

SIMILAR SPECIES: Warbling Vireo, no wingbars, doesn't flick tail. **Virginia's Warbler female**, yellowish vent, rump. **Blue-gray Gnatcatcher**, black-and-white tail.

white spectacle

bold wingbars

gray flanks

Plumbeous Vireo
Vireo plumbeus

Related to shrikes and corvids, vireos are birds of leafy forests. They perch horizontally; appear warbler-like; and have hooked bills, strong blue-gray legs. Not notoriously gifted singers.

THE BIRD: Adult appears as a pure-gray Cassin's Vireo. Separated into three species in the late 1990s, Plumbeous, Cassin's, and eastern Blue-headed Vireo were formerly considered one species, the Solitary Vireo. Classic vireo, Plumbeous is blocky headed, gray, silver, ash, and white. Spectacles are broken only at the front. Note diagnostic gray wing edges. Some, extremely faint yellow flanks. In **late summer**, worn gray-ish Cassin's makes identification vexing. Similar voices between them compound the difficulty. Nearly identical to adult, **juvenile** has blushed brownish back.

FLIGHT: Appears bulky and large headed. Gray above, whitish below with white wingbars and tail sides.

VOICE: Burry. Cassin's Vireo–like. Lazy and conversational, with pauses between phrases: *chee-dull-EE? burree-up! fitzz-zeeer…, cheer-EE-uP?* Also, quiet, introspective chatters and annoyed nasal whines. Alarm, a rising then falling dry prattle: *ch-ch-cH-cH-CH! CH! Ch-ch-ch…*

RANGE: Great Basin pine and juniper woodlands. Western edge of range touches eastern Sierra. **West Slope:** Breeds rarely, southeastern Tulare and northern Kern Counties. **East Slope:** Breeds uncommonly, Inyo and Mono Counties, possibly eastern Kern County. Likely reaches northern limit of Sierra breeding range in eastern Alpine County. Unconfirmed breeding north in eastern Sierra and Plumas Counties.

SIMILAR SPECIES: Cassin's Vireo greenish. Worn birds difficult to differentiate.

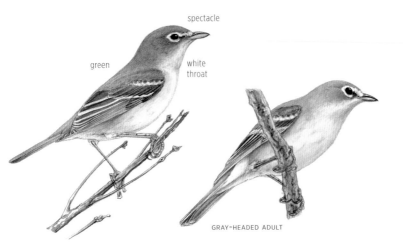

spectacle

green

white throat

GRAY-HEADED ADULT

Cassin's Vireo

Vireo cassinii

A caterpillar's worst nightmare. Methodical hunter with sharply hooked bill, this hop-stop-look predator calmly turns its head this way and that, searching for the vulnerable. Most of us become acquainted with the vireo tribe through our resident Hutton's, so it's always a treat to encounter a Cassin's belting out its gruff song or dining on insects. Vireos capture caterpillars and worry them against branches before consumption. This vigorous shaking often gives the bird's presence away.

THE BIRD: Longer than Hutton's Vireo. Spectacle broken in front of eye. Primaries edged greenish. **Late-summer adult**, worn wingbars and tertial edges. **Juvenile** adult-like, but greener, yellower flanked, wing feathers neatly edged white.

FLIGHT: Moves through canopy in short hops, stops, and flutters. Flying long distances, appears chunky.

VOICE: Husky, vintage vireo. More of a discussion than a proclamation. A one-sided conversation with phrases broken by silent pauses: *chi-burrr!... chi-burr-ree, chi-brEE! urr..., fitz-gee-u..., chu-ree?* Also, utters annoyed scolds and rasping whinnies that increase in "anger," then drop: *jrrr, jrrR, jrrRR! jrrr.*

RANGE: Arrives foothills April, breeds May through July, departs August, some September. **West Slope:** Fairly common to locally common, oak, pine, riparian forests, Lower and Upper Conifer. **East Slope:** Fairly common breeders, Tahoe Basin through Mono County. Elsewhere, uncommon migrants.

SIMILAR SPECIES: **Plumbeous Vireo** gray. **Hutton's Vireo** lacks contrasting throat. *Empidonax* flycatchers perch vertically, sally for prey.

bold

white
wingbars

Hutton's Vireo
Vireo huttoni

With large head, rounded crown, stout bill, barrel chest, short tail, and strong blue-gray legs, Hutton's is built like a chickadee dressed in a Ruby-crowned Kinglet suit. Often located by its repeated song, it's encountered alone, in pairs, or foraging methodically with flocks of insectivores.

THE BIRD: About Warbling Vireo size, almost twice a kinglet's weight. Lacks contrasting underparts. Spectacle broken above eye. Fresh bird shows bold wingbars. Late-summer, fall **adult** is worn, wingbars thin and ragged. **Juvenile** adult-like with weaker face pattern, thicker wingbars, and crisply edged tertials. Tends toward lethargy, *but* if annoyed, appears just as distraught as a pivoting, wing-flicking kinglet.

FLIGHT: Usually shelters, but when flying in the open, bulky bodied, short tailed, and large headed. In other words, chickadee-like.

VOICE: Hear an unfamiliar call or song in the Sierra? *Always* consider Hutton's as a potential candidate. Calls include monotonous up-slurred *zreee? zreee?*; down-slurred, burry, piercing *zeeerp, zeeerp*...; and strident *jeer-reeP!* Call, a nasal, whining, rapidly descending *jzreee, jzreee, jzreee*...

RANGE: Resident, live oak woodlands. **West Slope:** Fairly common Foothill to Lower Conifer. Sometimes moves upslope after breeding to Upper Conifer black oaks. Downslope in winter. **East Slope:** Very rare. Few records, Tahoe and Mono Basins, Jawbone Canyon, Owens Valley, Inyo County.

SIMILAR SPECIES: **Ruby-crowned Kinglet**, disposition, social, smaller, tiny bill, bold wingbar bordered by black. Kinglets glance; Hutton's regards. See **Cassin's Vireo**.

faint
yellow

JUVENILE

subtle
eye line

unmarked
gray

whitish

ADULT

Warbling Vireo
Vireo gilvus

The lord of subtlety, a minimalist's delight. Warbling Vireo offers itself up by pouring forth its jubilant albeit jumbled song. Lethargic, high above in spangled leafy canopy, appears as a small whitish songbird.

THE BIRD: Slighter than Cassin's Vireo, heavier than most warblers. Crown gray, bordered by soft white brow and faint eye line. Black eyes appear bead-like. The small, silvery bill has a tiny hook, used effectively for caterpillar procurement or fruit consumption in migration and winter. **Worn adult** in late summer, gray, lacks the greenish upper parts and yellowish flanks shown by fresh-plumaged **immature**.

FLIGHT: Foraging, hops and flutters short distances pursuing insects. In the open, flies quickly and directly, appearing pale. Different from that of blocky-headed vireos, head tapers to a point.

VOICE: Song, a series of full-bodied singsong phrases, each slightly different. A "mouthful of marbles," notes are garbled and burry. Seems to be rapidly proclaiming *I think I'm really pretty, but I'm not!* Call harsh, angry, rasping, shrike-like *jzzzZZ!...jzzzZZ!*

RANGE: Arrives from the tropics mid-April, breeds, departs early September. **West Slope:** Common breeders in black oak, cottonwood, alder, willow riparian, and aspen. Near wet meadows up to Lower and Upper Conifer. Uncommon to Subalpine after breeding. **East Slope:** Common breeders, riparian and aspen.

SIMILAR SPECIES: Other vireos have spectacles or wingbars. **Bell's Vireo** rare small, faint wingbar, tiny spectacle, active tail.

concealed
orange

gray
head

white eye
crescents

ADULT
ROCKY MOUNTAIN

faint
streaks

buff
wingbars

pale
crescent

ADULT

PACIFIC

JUVENILE

Orange-crowned Warbler

Leiothlypis celata

Exclusively New World, wood-warblers comprise around 110 species; 11 occur regularly in the Sierra. Most are migratory and insectivorous. Although diverse in color, behavior, and habitat preferences, they're similar in size and shape.

THE BIRD: Harbinger of spring. Yellow Warbler size. **Adult**, flared crest of singing **male** orangey, **female's** reduced or lacking. Nearly unicolored, slightly darker above. All show faint breast streaks and whitish crescent at bend of wing. The *Pacific* (*L. c. lutescens*) subspecies is yellow-green, with yellow eye-ring; immature of *Rocky Mountain* (*L. c. orestera*) subspecies exhibits gray head and white eye-ring, inviting confusion with Nashville Warbler. Dark lores impart a stern look. Late-summer, early fall **juvenile**, buff wingbars.

FLIGHT: Appearing greenish, moves fairly directly.

VOICE: Song, bright trill that rises or descends in pitch, like running thumbnail along a stiff comb. Call, sharp *chirt!*

RANGE: More common subspecies, *Pacific* of the west, arrives March, breeds, and moves upslope May-June. *Rocky Mountain* occurs mainly as nonbreeding migrant. **West Slope:** Common breeder, riparian and Foothill chaparral to Lower Conifer. *Rocky Mountain* migrates later. Common fall visitor to Subalpine meadows. Departs October, few winter in lowlands. **East Slope:** *Pacific*, common summer and post-breeding wanderer. *Rocky Mountain* breeds uncommonly, Mono Basin canyons, and migrates commonly to Subalpine. Uncommon winter, Reno and Owens Valley, rare elsewhere.

SIMILAR SPECIES: See **Yellow Warbler female**, **Common Yellowthroat**, **Wilson's Warbler**.

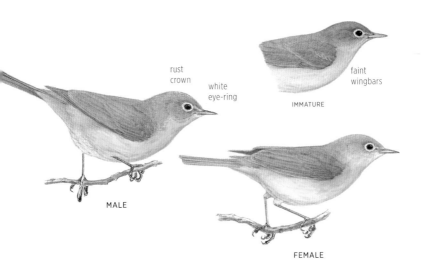

rust crown

white eye-ring

faint wingbars

IMMATURE

MALE

FEMALE

Nashville Warbler

Leiothlypis ruficapilla

The subtly patterned warblers typically occupy low to middle levels, blending where light is subdued and the shadows govern. Our subspecies of Nashville, the *Western* (*L. r. ridgwayi*), behaves and appears much like Virginia's Warbler, with frequent tail-flicking. The nearly identical *Eastern* Nashville (*L. r. ruficapilla*) seldom flicks its tail and is thought by some a different species. *Western* Nashville may therefore be a closer relative to Virginia's Warbler than to *Eastern* Nashville!

THE BIRD: Adult relatively short tailed, slightly larger than Virginia's Warbler. Singing **male** exposes rufous crown patch. Head blue-gray, upper parts olive, underparts contrasting yellow. Area between legs, white. **Female**, subdued version of male. **Immature**, muted version of female. Belly whitish. Drab **juvenile** can pose identification challenges.

FLIGHT: Yellow below, color extends through underwing coverts. Landing, shows greenish-yellow rump.

VOICE: Song, high, thin *fwee-sa, fwee-sa, fweee, se-se-se-se-se-se.* Another version, first notes slower and questioning, last notes rapid, down-slurred, and trilled: *swee? swee?... see, see, see, see.* Call, high, sharp, quiet *tsip.*

RANGE: Arrives April, breeds, departs September. **West Slope:** Breeds commonly, Lower to Upper Conifer and black oak, manzanita. Moves upslope to Subalpine. **East Slope:** Fairly common migrant, especially fall. Breeds commonly in riparian south to Tahoe Basin, uncommonly to Mono County. Drifts upslope post-breeding.

SIMILAR SPECIES: *Rocky Mountain* **Orange-crowned Warbler** greener, broken eye-ring. **MacGillivray's Warbler female**, broken eye-ring, hooded. **Virginia's Warbler** gray, yellow rump.

veiled chestnut

flicks tail

bold eye-ring

yellow

greenish rump

faint yellow

MALE

FEMALE

Virginia's Warbler

Leiothlypis virginiae

Appears bleached. This creature of July sun and juniper scrub adds a "lively touch of gray" to a land where birds can be few and far between. If you lost your pet Nashville Warbler in sun-drenched pinyon-juniper, then miraculously re-found it years later, it just might end up looking like a Virginia's. Although Nashville's does twitch its tail, Virginia's is far more habitual in its posterior dynamics, with a frequently pumping, circular-flicking tail.

THE BIRD: **Adult** slightly smaller than Nashville Warbler. Overall gray, slightly darker above. Thin white eye-ring. Chestnut-capped **male** shows yellow breast. **Female** lacks crown patch, her yellow breast reduced in intensity. **Immature** female-like, but lacks yellow breast.

FLIGHT: Appears largely gray. Landing, shows greenish rump.

VOICE: Song rich, sweet, in two parts. First notes slow, similar, level. Next few drop and quicken: *tsu...tsu...tsu...tsu...tsu—chew, chew, chew.* Sometimes *chiva-chiva-chiva, chee, chee, chee.* Call, sharp, high, strident *TseeT!* or *seeT!*

RANGE: Western limit of Great Basin breeding range, barely extends into eastern Sierra. Arrives mid-April, breeds May to June, departs September. **West Slope:** No breeding records. Very rare migrant at random locations. **East Slope:** Uncommon breeder, pinyon-juniper woodlands Mono and Inyo Counties. Likely in aspen near Monitor Pass, Alpine County. Spring records, Tahoe Basin.

SIMILAR SPECIES: **Nashville Warbler**, olive upper parts, yellow underparts. **Blue-gray Gnatcatcher**, no yellow, black-and-white tail.

FIRST WINTER

thin
eye-arcs

hooded

eye-
arcs

whitish

marbling

FEMALE

MALE

MacGillivray's Warbler
Geothlypis tolmiei

Encountered in winter within a Guatemalan cloud forest, or regarded beneath a protective manzanita, this clandestine creature is fittingly cloaked in a dark hood. No matter how tortured the labyrinth of branches, it often divulges its presence with a sharp *tsiK!* A shade of patience and a "kissing" squeak to your hand usually invite it forward to swap glances of interest with looks of admiration. Singing male occasionally loses his inhibition, allowing for a review. Enjoy it, for when leaves begin to turn and a warbler's bill points southward, obscurity will once again reign.

THE BIRD: Slightly larger than Orange-crowned Warbler. **Adult male** head and breast dark gunmetal, lores black. Bill pink. Upper parts olive green, belly and vent yellow. Legs pinkish. **Female** like male, hood paler. **Immature** like adult female, but duller.

FLIGHT: Infrequently seen flying. Proceeds purposefully. Appears dark green.

VOICE: Loud, clear, usually two parts with second rising: *chur-chur-chur, chee, chee, chee, chee*. Also with last notes falling: *tsee, tsee, tsee, chew, chew, chew...* Call, a forceful *tsiK!* or wet *cheT!*

RANGE: Arrives May, breeds, departs September. **West Slope:** Fairly common Lower and Upper Conifer, rare Subalpine. After breeding, may move to Alpine. **East Slope:** Similar to West Slope, breeds to 10,000 feet east of Yosemite. Fairly common migrant, August and September to Subalpine.

SIMILAR SPECIES: See *Rocky Mountain* Orange-crowned Warbler, **Nashville Warbler**, **Common Yellowthroat**.

Common Yellowthroat
Geothlypis trichas

Encountering this elusive bird in tule marsh or cattail mire is a treat. Female and young are subtle, so identification is often vexing. Male with "robber's mask" unmistakable. Rubber-band call note distinct. Male hitches up reeds to broadcast his distinctive song, offering exalted views. Female is shy, but often approaches to investigate. Scattered over broad regions in appropriate habitat, they're never in large numbers. Birds in migration can be happened on in weedy brush, leafy garden, even desert oases.

THE BIRD: Brownish-olive upper parts and flanks. Legs, pinkish. **Adult male**, face pattern bold. Throat, breast, and vent rich yellow. **Female** lacks bold markings. Eye-ring faint. **Immature male** female-like with black flecking on face, white brow reduced. **Juvenile** like faded female, more unicolored. Some show buff throats and wingbars.

FLIGHT: Typically tethered to cover, flies low. Appears olive green.

VOICE: With a "gitty-up" cadence, song a three-syllable *Chich-away, Chich-away, Chich-away* or *Witch-it-chew, Witch-it-chew*. Call, rubber band–like *tchek* or *tjeK!*

RANGE: Migrant from Central Valley, breeds in Sierra marshes May to September. **West Slope:** Common Kern River Valley foothills, otherwise uncommon. After breeding, some to Subalpine. Uncommon winter. **East Slope:** Common migrant, uncommon breeder, low elevations to Owens Valley. Males recorded 6,000 feet near Truckee and above 10,000 east of Yosemite. Rare winter, Owens Valley, very rare elsewhere.

SIMILAR SPECIES: See **MacGillivray's Warbler female, Orange-crowned Warbler.**

flicks tail

extensive black

orange blush

faint wingbars

JUVENILE

limited black

MALE

FEMALE

Wilson's Warbler

Cardellina pusilla

A yellow bird constantly on the move, our smallest warbler is typically found flycatching and hovering as it forages. Seldom tranquil and seemingly in a never-ending quest for insects, this wee bird appears restless. Usually foraging from low to middle levels, this mite pivots, flicks both wings, and twitches its cocked tail.

THE BIRD: Face uncomplicated, eyes bead-like, cheeks faint green, legs and bill base pinkish. *Pacific*, West Slope–breeding subspecies, shows diagnostic orangey blush to face. **Adult male**, brilliant. **Adult female** less saturated, paler below, smaller crowns. **Immature** less black to forecrown. Breeding east of the Sierra, *Interior West* **adult** birds are yellow faced, lacking orange brow. **Female**, little to no black on crown. **Immature**, no black. **Juvenile**, buff-tipped coverts. Subspecies difficult to differentiate.

FLIGHT: Hover-gleans, flitting tree to tree. Covering distances, appears tiny and yellow-green. Twists, turns, and moves in jerky fashion.

VOICE: Song, rapid series of strident notes that rise in pitch, increase in volume, and quicken in tempo: *chi chi chi Chi Chi CHI CHI CHI!* Call, *TIK* or *TSIK*. *Very* similar to Pacific Wren's double note.

RANGE: Arrives April, breeds until August; few remain until October. **West Slope:** Fairly common breeder along streams and meadows, Upper Conifer to Subalpine. **East Slope:** Widespread fairly common breeder. Common migrant in Subalpine riparian forests.

SIMILAR SPECIES: **Yellow Warbler**, black tertials, yellow tail. **Orange-crowned Warbler** lime.

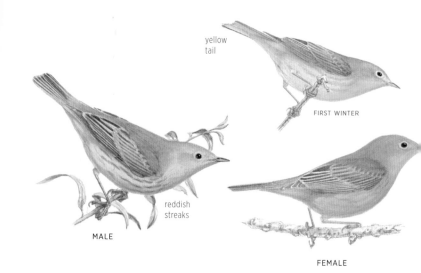

yellow
tail

FIRST WINTER

reddish
streaks

MALE

FEMALE

Yellow Warbler

Setophaga petechia

With the most extensive breeding range of all wood-warblers, Yellow Warbler expresses the extent of a species' variability. Plumages vary depending on age, sex, subspecies, season, feather condition, and individual. Orange-crowned Warbler size. They migrate south in fall, often forming nucleus of hunting parties where numerous species gather to feed.

THE BIRD: Our yellowest warbler displays characteristic yellow tail spots, handy when viewed from below. Note diagnostic dark tertial centers and yellow covert edges. Bead-like eyes on unmarked face impart vacant stare. **Adult male** upper parts green, underparts streaked chestnut. Feet pinkish. Variable, **female** is greenish, slightly paler below, with vague streaks. Paler than female, **immatures** are diverse in appearance; bright green, whitish gray, or milky yellow, some have distinct eye-rings.

FLIGHT: Foraging, hovers momentarily, snatching insects. Flying farther, moves with somewhat zigzagging course, often chipping.

VOICE: Variable. Sweet, high, thin *tsee-tsee-tsee, chew-chew-chew, Tew!* Also *see-ta, see-ta, see-ta, chee-chee-chee, Chew!* or *chu, chu, chu, tsee, tsee, tsee, chu!* Call, strong, downward *tsouP!*

RANGE: Arrives mid-April, breeds wet riparian, shrubby meadows, montane chaparral, departs October. **West Slope:** Breeds fairly commonly, Foothill to Upper Conifer, moving higher after. Rarely to Subalpine. **East Slope:** Spring, common in riparian to Subalpine, then middle-elevation pine, broadleaf forest. Begins departing July. Declining population, habitat loss, and restricted breeding.

SIMILAR SPECIES: **Wilson's Warbler**, cocked tail. **Orange-crowned Warbler** overall lime green.

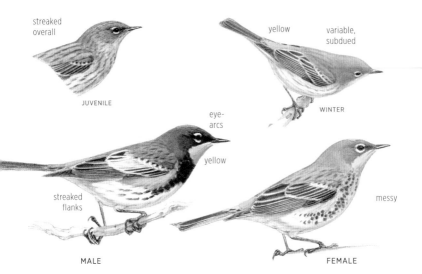

streaked overall

JUVENILE

yellow

variable, subdued

WINTER

eye-arcs

yellow

streaked flanks

MALE

messy

FEMALE

Yellow-rumped Warbler (Audubon's)
Setophaga coronata auduboni

The Yellow-rumped Warbler was once considered two species: Audubon's and Myrtle Warblers. They were lumped together as a single species in 1973 by the AOU (now AOS); however, much of the birding world still considers them separate species. Because of their differences in appearance, voice, and habits, we deal with them separately here.

THE BIRD: **Adult** has round yellow throat spot and large white tail spots. **Breeding male's** wingbars form white panel. **Breeding female** like a diffused gray male. **Nonbreeding**, both sexes have simple face pattern, thin eye-arcs, faint flank streaks. **Juvenile** is heavily streaked gray, appearing disheveled.

FLIGHT: Comfortable on the wing. With tail spread, appears butterfly-like fluttering and flycatching. Covering ground, flies more directly in slightly jerky manner. Landing, note yellow rump and bold white tail spots. Frequently forages with Western Bluebirds along fence rows and over weedy thickets.

VOICE: An anemic, thin, rising *swee-swee-swee-swee-swee, sue, sue, sue*, last notes down-slurred. Or *shu-wee, shu-wee, shu-wee, shu-wee, shu, shu, shu.* Call, a loud rising *tsiP!* Alarm, high, thin *tseet.*

RANGE: Breeds extensively both slopes. Fairly common year-round in most habitats and altitudes. **West Slope:** Breeds in Upper Conifer and Subalpine, May to July. Locally abundant until October. Winter, moves lower where common to Foothill oak riparian. **East Slope:** Rare in winter in low-elevation willow and alder.

SIMILAR SPECIES: **Hermit**, **Townsend's**, and **Black-throated Gray Warbler** songs all similar.

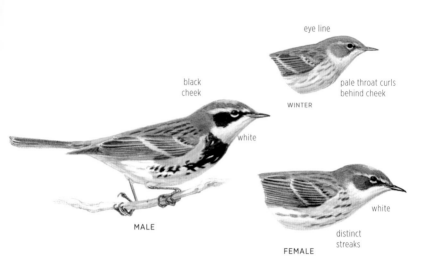

black
cheek

eye line

pale throat curls
behind cheek

WINTER

white

MALE

white

distinct
streaks

FEMALE

Yellow-rumped Warbler (Myrtle)

Setophaga coronata coronata

Beginning birders often lament, "Warblers are hard!" Many cut their teeth on the Yellow-rumped because it is common year-round, frequents most habitats, and pauses for inspection. Becoming *very* familiar with this bird opens doors of understanding to all warbler identification. Slightly larger than Townsend's; note its style of movement and flycatching habits, learn well the chip notes and feather topography. Get a feeling for the anatomy, overall size and weight. Primarily an insectivore; see how it feeds from sapsucker wells or eats fruit in lean times. Appreciate the sexual, racial, and age variations of its plumages. Consider hybrids exhibiting traits of both subspecies. Lastly, behold the radical transformation in plumage from winter to spring.

THE BIRD: Has white throat that wraps around the dark cheek patch, a white brow, and smaller tail spots. **Adult male** shows two wingbars. **Adult female** has gray upper parts and dark flank streaks. **Immature** has more complex face than *Audubon's* and distinct flank streaks.

FLIGHT: Much as *Audubon's*, hovers briefly while feeding. Covering ground, flies more directly, typically chipping at lift off.

VOICE: *Myrtle's* song a high, thin *tsee-tsee-tsee-tsee-tsee, chu-chu-chu-chu*, with second half dropping. Call, a soft, flat *chep*.

RANGE: Does not breed in the Sierra. Found in migration or winter in low-elevation willow and alder thickets.

SIMILAR SPECIES: Black-throated Gray Warbler appears *Myrtle*-like if rump and flanks not seen.

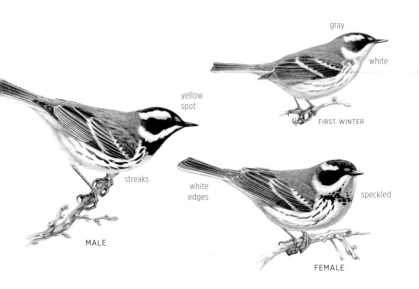

gray

white

yellow
spot

FIRST WINTER

streaks

white
edges

speckled

MALE

FEMALE

Black-throated Gray Warbler

Setophaga nigrescens

With its strong black-and-white face pattern, this bird is positively striking! A true western warbler and undeniable proof that birds with a limited color palette are every bit as fetching as any East Coast "wing-barred wonder."

THE BIRD: Slightly smaller than Yellow-rumped Warbler. Compelling, **male** appears formally tailored. Dapper in form-fitting blue-gray "suit" with shoulders crossed by white bars. From the "lapel," streaks flare back across silk-white flanks. White tail feathers enhance bird's alabaster underparts. The final touch? A stylish yellow punctuation before the eye. No less chic, the attire of the **female** is more modest than male's, an equilibrium of unblemished white and dark. Her throat is crossed by a delicate black necklace. **First winter** duller, flank streaks diffuse.

FLIGHT: From below, strikingly white, flanks streaked black. From above, bluish with bold wingbars.

VOICE: A rapid, rising three-part see-saw series of double or triple notes with buzzy overtones: *jew-vih, jew-vih, jew-vih, gee, gee, zee, zee, zee?* Call, soft *tip* or *stip.* Song similar to *Audubon's*, Hermit, and Townsend's Warblers.

RANGE: Arrives April, breeds May; most depart early August. **West Slope:** Fairly common breeder, live and black oak woodlands from low-elevation river gorges to Upper Conifer. Some to Subalpine in fall. Very rare winter. **East Slope:** Uncommon breeder in pinyon-juniper. Rare, August to October, lodgepole forests to tree line.

SIMILAR SPECIES: *Myrtle* **Yellow-rumped Warbler**, yellow flanks and rump.

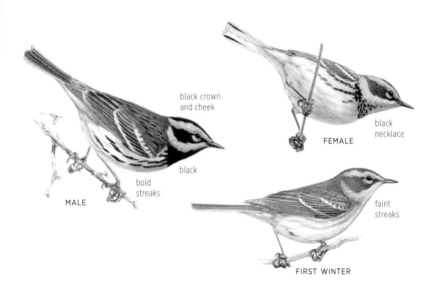

black crown
and cheek

black
necklace

FEMALE

black

bold
streaks

MALE

faint
streaks

FIRST WINTER

Townsend's Warbler

Setophaga townsendi

As opposed to subtly patterned warblers of the understory, "flashy" species like Townsend's tend to inhabit the higher levels where light and shadows create boldly spangled effects.

THE BIRD: Although encountered every month of the year, Townsend's has never been recorded breeding in California! Slightly smaller than Yellow-rumped Warbler. Pattern like Black-throated Gray, but with under-eye crescent. "Technicolor" green color pattern is suited for vanishing in dappled forest light. **Adult male** shows black throat and bold flank streaks. **Adult female** shows yellow throat, blackish-green crown and cheeks. Her breast is crossed by marks or a band. Flank streaks thinner than male's. **Immature** lacks necklace. Crown, cheeks, and back green, flank streaks diffuse.

FLIGHT: In wooded conditions, briefly hovers for insects. Ornate with bold patterning. Outer tail feathers, white. Covers distances in jerky warbler style but fairly directly.

VOICE: Song variable. Buzzy tones, similar to Hermit, *Audubon's*, and Black-throated Gray. Rapid, level series followed by lilting notes, last one higher and explosive: *tzee-tzee-tzee-tzee-tzee-tzee, tsu, tsu, TZEE!* Also, longer notes rising, then abruptly culminating: *fzeeee-zeeeee-zeeeeeeeee, fizzteeK!*

RANGE: Winters to Central America, breeds Pacific Northwest. **Both slopes:** Uncommon migrants to foothill oak woodlands, April to June. Astoundingly, southbound, post-breeding birds arrive by July! Uncommon July to September, to Subalpine. Winter, rare Foothill to Lower Conifer.

SIMILAR SPECIES: **Hermit Warbler**, head yellow, flanks unstreaked. **Black-throated Gray Warbler** lacks green.

Hybrid Townsend's
x
Hermit Warbler

Hybrids between Townsend's and Hermit Warbler occur with some frequency. Birds can show any manner of mixed traits between the parent species. A bird appearing to be a Hermit Warbler with a green back, yellow flanks, or streaks to the sides is a hybrid. Conversely, if a bird that appears to be a Townsend's Warbler shows a gray back, a blank yellow face, or no flank streaks, it is also a hybrid.

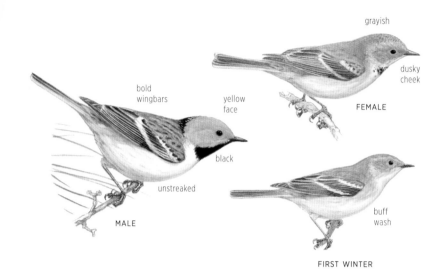

grayish

dusky cheek

FEMALE

bold wingbars

yellow face

black

unstreaked

MALE

buff wash

FIRST WINTER

Hermit Warbler

Setophaga occidentalis

Reaching for the heavens, this bird of lofty conifers seldom surrenders from its realm of fragrant skyscrapers. At dizzying heights high above the forest floor, it hawks insects from the tips of outstretched boughs, making it difficult to observe them from, say, Earth. Mercifully, however infrequently, it ventures down, down, down, toward terra firma, allowing safe views for nature lovers with a fear of heights. Initially appears somber colored and subtle in pattern. However, when its golden dome rises into view, its parenthood instantly becomes apparent.

THE BIRD: Townsend's Warbler size. Yellow faced, **adult male** has black nape and throat, streaked back, white underparts. Largely gray, **adult female** shows yellow face, dusky cheeks, whitish underparts, variably marked breast. **Immature** like subdued female with dull back, buff flanks.

FLIGHT: Foraging for insects, appears butterfly-like hovering or fluttering among pine needles. Unmarked below, white outer tail feathers enhance whiteness.

VOICE: Song with last note distinctly down-slurred: *see-saw, see-saw, see-saw, see-saw, see-SAUL!*

RANGE: Arrives April, breeds May to July, departs September. **West Slope:** Among the most numerous warblers in Lower and Upper Conifer. Afterward may move to Subalpine, joining warbler flocks. **East Slope:** Uncommon local breeder in Tahoe Basin. Rare elsewhere. Rare fall migrant, deciduous woods or desert oases.

SIMILAR SPECIES: **Townsend's Warbler immature**, crown and cheek dark, back greenish, flanks streaked. **Townsend's**, **Black-throated Gray**, and **Yellow-rumped Warbler** songs similar.

label: white stripe

label: white

label: colors subdued

ADULT

IMMATURE

Yellow-breasted Chat
Icteria virens

Yellow-breasted Chat has always found an uncomfortable taxonomic placement within the wood-warbler family. Larger than warblers, it has now been given full family status (Icteriidae) by the AOS. Unclear as to which taxonomic club it's related, some ornithologists suggest New World blackbirds.

THE BIRD: If you hear disgruntled *chek* notes and detect slow movements from behind a maze of branches, remain motionless. With the patience of a saint, you might experience a close encounter of the bird kind. Worth the wait, a chat regards you from behind bold spectacles. Western Tanager size, **adult** sexes similar. Upper parts olive, throat egg yolk, flanks tan. **First winter** similar to adult, colors subdued, bill blue-gray.

FLIGHT: This introvert becomes anything but when it's a displaying male! At showtime, inhibitions vanish, and he bursts forth to perform unlike any other. Rising on exaggerated wingbeats, tail pumping, throat swollen, legs dangling, he pours forth his comical chorus.

VOICE: Thrasher-like, complex, humorous, rapid-fire notes with inquisitive punctuations and strident exclamations: *chur, chur, chur, frEET? frEET?... FRIO! shree? shree?*

RANGE: Arrives April, breeds, departs August. **West Slope:** Central Sierra, fairly common to uncommon in Foothill riparian to 2,500 feet. Recorded in Yosemite Valley after breeding. Largest population, South Fork Kern River riparian. **East Slope:** Uncommon spring, rare fall. Breeds rarely, northern Inyo County. Possibly expanding into recovering riparian streams, Mono and Alpine Counties.

SIMILAR SPECIES: None.

bounding flight

white edges

olive-gray

heavily streaked

two-toned

pinkish

pumps tail

dark

NONBREEDING ADULT
Western

BREEDING ADULT
Rocky Mountain

American Pipit

Anthus rubescens

Pipits and wagtails constitute a mostly Old World family of nearly seventy species. American Pipit is our sole representative.

THE BIRD: Found in pairs in summer at our highest regions. Colorful breeding *Rocky Mountain* (*A. r. alticola*) subspecies is clean or slightly streaked pink and blue-gray. Congregating in winter foothills, earth-tone nonbreeding *Western* (*A. r. pacificus*) subspecies is olive-brown above, whitish or rich buff below, with distinctly streaked breast. Smaller than Horned Lark, pipit appears sparrow-like with warbler-like bill. Walks with bobbing head, pumping tail. Tertials uniquely long. Infrequently perches on wires. Almost exclusively terrestrial, camouflaged in earth-colored upper parts and coarsely streaked underparts, an appropriate pattern for *many* grass dwellers.

FLIGHT: Superb flier and far-ranging migrant. Eager to take wing; forms large, bounding flocks that spring simultaneously into flight. Often vocalizing, exposes white tail sides. Long winged, progresses with overly exaggerated bounding. Flies with curious head-down posture.

VOICE: Song, House Sparrow-like. A level, wet, burry series: *fittttz, fittttz, fitttz, few, fitttz, fitttz...* Flight call, high, strident two-note *tsit, siT*, with upward emphasis second note.

RANGE: Both slopes: *Rocky Mountain* rare local breeder in Alpine fell-fields, 10,000–12,000 feet, from south of Mount Whitney to Tahoe region. *Western* arrives from Alaska and western North America to Foothill grasslands up to Lower Conifer in October. Winters, then departs April.

SIMILAR SPECIES: Sparrows, conical bills, don't pump tails, most hop.

subdued

horns

white brow

bold face

speckled

white edges

FEMALE

MALE

JUVENILE

Horned Lark

Eremophila alpestris

Terrestrial songbirds, larks are represented with nearly one hundred species. Horned Lark has over forty subspecies across Northern Hemisphere.

THE BIRD: Huskier than pipits, larks have short legs and long hind claws. Creeping with halting steps, this gregarious ground-hugging "dirt worshiper" eludes detection. **Male** head devilishly embellished with erectile horn-like brow feathers. Colors diminished, **female** like subdued male. Confounding, **juvenile** unlike adult. Upper parts scaled, bill pinkish.

FLIGHT: Long winged, nimble, and exceptionally swift, flocks sweep frightfully close to the ground, cleaving the air just above it. Death defying, the breeding display is dramatic. Slipping Earth's embrace, male ascends to dizzying heights. Lost in the warm folds of summer's hazy sky, this lark is a challenge to spot. Teasing lift from thermals, it appears to float. Like a delicate waterfall pouring forth song, sweet tinkling notes sprinkle, cascade, and tumble to Earth. As the curtain closes on this airy performance, male folds his wings, bows earthward, and plummets stone-like. A hair's breadth before impact, he mercifully levels off, landing safely.

VOICE: Song, cadence of well-thrown skipping-stone. Each tinkling note followed quickly by next, until all run together. Call strident; downward emphasis on second note: *tsit-tseeK!*

RANGE: Foothill grasslands, plowed fields, alkali flats, Alpine meadows. **West Slope:** Locally common resident, Foothill winter visitor. Uncommon Alpine breeder. **East Slope:** Common low-elevation resident. Fairly common Alpine breeder.

SIMILAR SPECIES: **Sparrows**, **pipits**.

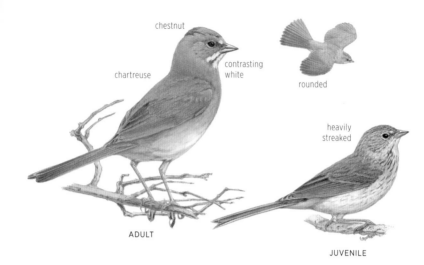

chestnut

chartreuse

contrasting white

rounded

heavily streaked

ADULT

JUVENILE

Green-tailed Towhee

Pipilo chlorurus

New World sparrows boast some 130 species, including towhees and sparrows.

THE BIRD: To come face-to-face with beauty, find yourself deep in chaparral. Stand chest high in an erupting fireworks display of spring wildflowers, or meander alone with your thoughts onto a fragrant stage of wide-open sage. If your inner conversation is interrupted by a song of mockingbird humor and Fox Sparrow jubilation, you are likely in the presence of this striking bird. Check brush near and twig far, as this songster could be perched anywhere. In a sweeping landscape big as all outdoors, this vocalist enthusiastically fills space with pleasing vibration. Slightly smaller than Fox Sparrow. **Adult**, beautiful. **Juvenile**, upper parts brownish, lacks reddish crown, extensively streaked.

FLIGHT: Moves covertly through brush appearing gray-green.

VOICE: Song, sweet, well defined, usually with trill. *Very* similar to Fox Sparrow, perhaps shorter, with emphasis on trills. Changes songs with thrasher-like quality. *Tsew, sweeeee, tsee? tsee? tsee? CHEW, tr-tr-tr-tr.* Call, frantic catlike *chi-YEAH!*, inflected second note rising.

RANGE: Both slopes: Arrives low elevations April; breeds May, June, depending on snow elevation; departs September. **West Slope:** Locally fairly common in chaparral from Lower to Upper Conifer. Breeds higher in scrub or post-fire areas, some to Subalpine, August. Winter, very rare Foothill. **East Slope:** Common, widespread, sage, mountain mahogany. Shuns high rocky, and dry lowlands.

SIMILAR SPECIES: Fox Sparrow song often indistinguishable.

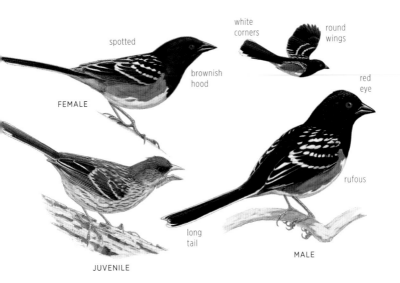

FEMALE

spotted

white corners

round wings

brownish hood

red eye

rufous

long tail

MALE

JUVENILE

Spotted Towhee

Pipilo maculatus

Predominantly ground dwelling, New World sparrows, which include towhees, have stocky bodies, short necks, conical bills, and relatively sturdy legs.

THE BIRD: Just smaller than California Towhee, Spotted bounds and hops through an underworld of brush and bramble. Frequenting seed feeders, a favorite of backyard nature lovers. With staring ruby eyes and smart tricolored outfit, it frequently flicks its long, white-cornered tail. Often located by noisy mulching from rake-like toenails; with rapid double kicks, it exposes morsels and sends leaf litter flying. Sexes are similar for nearly all sparrows and towhees, but this species is an exception. **Male** hood slightly blacker, and flanks marginally rustier than the **female**. Potentially confusing, **juvenile** unlike adult. Brown eyed, it lacks rufous flanks and has pale, heavily streaked underparts.

FLIGHT: With labored flapping interspersed with glides, flies low through cover, the long, white-cornered tail an identification key.

VOICE: Male clambers atop bushes to broadcast. Song, two sharp introductory notes followed by level trill, with tuning-fork quality: *tsit, chid-d-d-d-d-d-ddd*. Shy at heart, but exposes itself with nasal catlike *mewww* or questioning *shaw-wEEE*? Infrequently utters piercing notes on level pitch.

RANGE: **Both slopes:** Common resident. Breeds early April in foothills, later higher. Frequents Foothill to Upper Conifer chaparral and riparian, dominated by broadleaf shrubs. Uncommon Subalpine late summer, fall.

SIMILAR SPECIES: Potentially confusing; see **Black-headed Grosbeak**, **American Robin**, **Varied Thrush**.

rounded

streaks

JUVENILE

long,
dark

cinnamon

cinnamon

ADULT

California Towhee

Melozone crissalis

Not a bird of extremes, the "Golden State's Towhee" shuns California's hottest, snowiest, and soggiest locales but is common nearly everywhere else. Fidelity courses deeply through this humble, primarily sedentary, and down-to-earth bird. Nearly always in pairs, they go about their days next to, and with, each other. What they lack in arresting pattern, unusual form, or quality of voice is outweighed by a virtuous devotion and dedication to their mate. Comfortable around humans, birds frequently enter homes to forage on tracked-in birdseed. California Towhees defend territorial borders from neighboring California Towhees with noisy scrapes and gravel-kicking tussles.

THE BIRD: Slightly larger than Spotted Towhee. **Adult** earth brown, throat adorned by streaked necklace. Streaky **juvenile** appears like messy adult with whitish throat and coverts edged buff.

FLIGHT: Appears labored with vigorous flapping and short glides. Pairs move low, trailing rounded tails.

VOICE: Not vocally gifted. "Song" clear, ringing, run-together *tink...tink tink-tink-nk-nk kkkk*. Often at predawn, gives a repeated *TINK!* like striking an empty pop bottle with a knife. In interactions, gives hurried, jumbled, agitated descending *jrreep, jrreep, jreep, jrep, jrep jrp, jrp...*

RANGE: Resident. Begins breeding late winter. **West Slope:** Common widespread, chaparral, streamside thickets, Foothill gardens. Sparse above 2,000 feet. **East Slope:** Uncommon, very local breeder, Inyo and Kern Counties. Nonbreeding records, northwest side of Owens Valley.

SIMILAR SPECIES: **California Thrasher**, curved bill.

eye-ring

rufous eye line

black whisker

unstreaked

brownish

delicate streaks

ADULT

JUVENILE

Rufous-crowned Sparrow

Aimophila ruficeps

Reclusive sparrow of the arid West, fittingly camouflaged in somber hues. Scant in resources, it teases out an existence with few creature comforts. Sheltered within lichen-encrusted rock and tortured scrub, it reduces unwanted attention with its iron-rust, granite-gray, and brush-patterned ensemble. Feeds in cool of morning, seeks refuge from midday sun, and, beneath a blanket of stars, tucks itself in for the night. Brimming with spring's obligation for genetic renewal, male perches on the highest rock or gnarled branch to sing sweet, tinkling songs.

THE BIRD: Slightly smaller than White-crowned Sparrow. **Adult** crown and back streaks rufous. Face, underparts gray. Brow, eye-ring, throat white. **Juvenile** like unkempt adult, colors subdued, coverts edged pale.

FLIGHT: Often escapes threat fleeing uphill. Appearing rather dark, moves low from boulder to bush using sparse cover to its advantage.

VOICE: Sweet, tinkling trills composed of several elements. Fires off level, rapid *tsee, tsee, tsee, tsee, swEET! swEET! swee, swee, swee*. Often burry *jeet, jeet* at end. Call, an agitated, peeved, descending *JEER, Jeer, jeer, jeer...*

RANGE: Mostly sedentary to dry scrub, rocky hillsides, scattered oaks. Breeds February through May. **West Slope:** Fairly common. Patchily distributed in narrow band across lower foothills above Central Valley floor to about 2,500 feet, rarely higher post-breeding. **East Slope:** No documented records.

SIMILAR SPECIES: **Chipping Sparrow**, black eye line, gray rump. **White-crowned Sparrow immature** gregarious, central crown stripe.

dull
crown

streaks

JUVENILE

pinkish

white
eyebrow

black
eye line

black
bill

NONBREEDING

streaked

gray

FIRST WINTER

BREEDING

Chipping Sparrow

Spizella passerina

Sparrows feed primarily on seeds, fruits, and insects. Most are colored in earth tones, some with strongly marked heads.

THE BIRD: Small. Fractionally larger than Brewer's Sparrow. Chippings form smaller gatherings than most sparrows, especially in migration. Exciting to discover when winnowing through sparrow or junco flocks. Wayward sparrows frequently join Chippings; keep your eyes open for out-of-range species tagging along. Note streaked back, wingbars, clean underparts. **Breeding adult** crown bordered by bold brow, eye line. **Non-breeding adult** similar to breeding with pink lower mandible, tan brow and cheeks, dull-streaked crown with central stripe. **First winter** like subdued nonbreeding adult. **Juvenile** like first winter with streaked head, underparts. Unlike that of many sparrows, juvenile plumage is often kept into fall.

FLIGHT: Moves low from ground to bush or tree. Note gray rump and fairly long, narrow, slightly forked tail.

VOICE: At middle levels, often sings from forest edge. Song insect-like, similar to Dark-eyed Junco. Long, rapid series of level notes. Call, extremely high, thin *tsiT!*

RANGE: Except for deserts and Central Valley, widespread in California. Prefers scattered trees with shrub understory, nearby grass. **West Slope:** Locally fairly common breeder from oak savanna, Foothill woodland, to Upper Conifer, rare Subalpine. **East Slope:** Fairly common widespread breeder above low foothills to Subalpine.

SIMILAR SPECIES: Rufous-crowned Sparrow, rust eye line, black whisker. **Brewer's Sparrow** drab, no crown stripe, unmarked lores, brown rump.

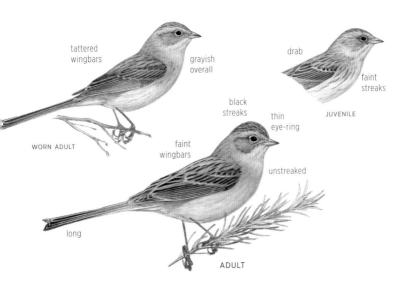

WORN ADULT tattered wingbars · grayish overall · black streaks · faint wingbars · long

JUVENILE drab · faint streaks

ADULT thin eye-ring · unstreaked

Brewer's Sparrow
Spizella breweri

Although small and understated, this sparrow has a big presence in swaths of the East Slope and Great Basin. Drifting on a breeze sweet with sage, its songs astonish. Carried far and wide, these mesmerizing vibrations knit the west together.

THE BIRD: Lacking rust, our smallest sparrow is a "riot" of subtlety. Come eye to beady eye with this wonder of understatement and behold the beauty of brown and genius of gray. Denizen of the desert, it all but vanishes when motionless or nestled in sage. In migration, often found with the slightly larger Chipping Sparrow. **Adult** has tiny pink bill, delicate face pattern, pale lores, streaked back, unmarked underparts. Trashed **worn adult** in late summer and fall appears like a tiny desiccated cow pie bleached in desert sun.

FLIGHT: Moving covertly through brush, appears overall gray-brown. Brown rump separates from Chipping.

VOICE: One of nature's exceptional sounds. Duration varies. Distinct, seemingly random buzzes, trills, accelerated staccatos, and ascending rolls: *jzee? jzee? jzee? t-t-t-t-t, zt! zt! zt! tri? tri? tri?*

RANGE: Breeds May through July, sagebrush, desert scrub, bitterbrush, pinyon-juniper, and conifers with understories. **West Slope:** Breeds commonly Kern Plateau, Tulare County. Local southern Kern, eastern Butte Counties. Birds likely move upslope after breeding. **East Slope:** Breeds commonly along length of Sierra.

SIMILAR SPECIES: Chipping Sparrow first winter, central crown stripe, black lores, gray rump.

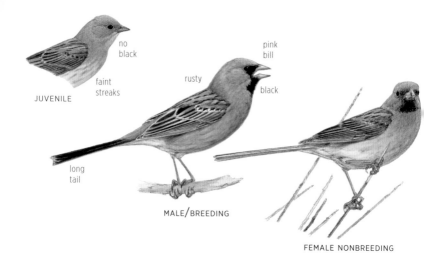

JUVENILE

no
black

faint
streaks

rusty

pink
bill

black

long
tail

MALE/BREEDING

FEMALE NONBREEDING

Black-chinned Sparrow
Spizella atrogularis

Reclusive. Locating, then observing, these dark, dainty sparrows can be a challenge. Viewing them demands effort, patience, and perhaps a bit of luck. Viewing them *well* demands sweat, as they prefer steep, hot, and rocky conditions. Listen for high, thin, tinkling songs cascading down sunbaked mountainsides. If confronted with impenetrable chaparral, quickly scan the tips of twisted manzanita or charred trees from previous fires, and you might be afforded views of this pewter-gray sparrow.

THE BIRD: Chipping Sparrow size, slate gray and rusty backed. Nearly black, the tail is quite long. **Male** shows black face and white wingbars. **Female** color and contrast subdued, black confined to throat, belly whitish. **Juvenile** shows dark upper mandible and pale throat and belly.

FLIGHT: Moving low through brushy habitat, appears small, dark, and long tailed.

VOICE: Cadence of song, a spinning coin coming to rest. Upward rotating spiral of high, thin notes smoothly increasing in tempo, coalescing into single ascending note that vanishes into the firmament: *swee, swee, swee, see, see, se, se, s, s, s, sssss.* Call, high-frequency, rising, Junco-like *tsit.*

RANGE: Post-fire chaparral with chamise. Arrives mid-April, departs August. Rare in migration. **West Slope:** Uncommon, highly localized breeder; rare north of Yosemite. **East Slope:** Rare, localized breeder south of Independence and west of Owens Valley.

SIMILAR SPECIES: **Rufous-crowned Sparrow** voice. **Dark-eyed Junco** gregarious, pinkish flanks, white tail feathers.

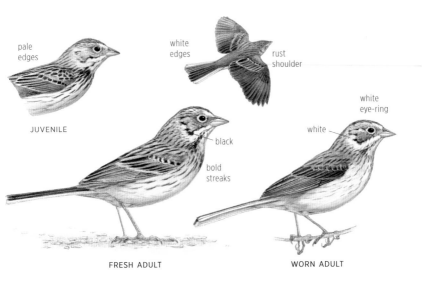

pale edges

white edges

rust shoulder

white eye-ring

JUVENILE

black

bold streaks

white

FRESH ADULT

WORN ADULT

Vesper Sparrow

Pooecetes gramineus

When first wandering into the world of sparrows, beginning naturalists might see Vesper as a bewilderment of browns. Put tormented thoughts to rest—this unique sparrow is our only streak-breasted friend with white outer tail feathers. Shunning most trees, this down-to-earth bird inhabits strata near ground, be it grass, low brush, or barbed-wire fence. Its native grassland habitat is disappearing because of degradation and fragmentation.

THE BIRD: Nearly Lark Sparrow size. Eye-ring imparts blank stare. White spot and black cheek "check" create unique pattern. **Fresh adult**, buff face and flanks, dark back streaks; breast streaks can form cluster-like spot. **Worn adult**, late summer, less buff, thin breast streaks. **Juvenile** upper parts scaled.

FLIGHT: Flies strongly. "Lopes" low; slight bounding. Rather large with diagnostic rusty shoulders and fairly long white-sided tail.

VOICE: Song, sweet—several introductory notes followed by defined, well-crafted elements: *tew, tew, tew, sweEE! cheeta, cheeta, sweeeee, chee, chee, chee...* Call, extremely high, thin *tsiT*.

RANGE: Two subspecies occur. **West Slope:** Winters uncommonly, Foothill grasslands. **East Slope:** Fairly common breeder April to July, grassy sagebrush with small trees in eastern Placer, Nevada, and Tulare Counties; Sierra Valley; Mono and Crowley Lakes. Most depart in winter.

SIMILAR SPECIES: **Savannah Sparrow** smaller. **Lincoln's Sparrow,** buff whisker. **Lark Sparrow** flees into sky. **Song Sparrow** heavily marked.

white corners

muted

ornate

brown

streaks

black spot

dusky spot

JUVENILE

long, rounded

ADULT

FIRST WINTER

Lark Sparrow

Chondestes grammacus

Aptly named, Lark Sparrows share several traits with Horned Larks. Both gregarious dirt-lovers, they're adept in flight, have harlequin faces, clay-colored upper parts, white tail sides, long legs, and sensational songs. Unique among sparrows, Larks stride rather than hop. Spring displays seem either an impressive advertisement or humorous performance. Like some animated wind-up toy, an excited male hops about near a prospective mate assuming the posture of a miniature grouse. Wings spread down, tail elevated wide, he proudly parades his posterior adornment.

THE BIRD: Roughly White-crowned Sparrow size. Fittingly illustrated in field guides for "Anatomy of a Bird." Each anatomical component delineated, **adult** head is boldly marked black, white, and chestnut. Upper parts, wings, and central tail feathers, clay. **First-winter** bird adult-like, but color saturation of head markings reduced. **Juvenile** breast streaked dusky, ghost of adult's pattern.

FLIGHT: Vocalizing, flocks flush, gain considerable altitude, and depart skyward, a unique trait among sparrows. Long winged with rounded black-and-white tails.

VOICE: Thrasher-like well-defined phrases, with comical quality. Rapid mechanical trills, static buzzes, sweet notes, and deep "back molar" grinding: *seeeeee, swee-ya, swee-ya, chuk, chuk, chuk, tsew, renK! renK! renK!* Call, a high, strident, repeated *tsiK!*

RANGE: Resident. **West Slope:** Common, Foothill oak savanna and woodland edges. **East Slope:** In low densities, an uncommon breeder at scattered locales in Sierra, Carson, and Owens Valleys.

SIMILAR SPECIES: **Vesper Sparrow** breast streaked.

white edges

white brow

black

fine streaks

ADULT

JUVENILE

Black-throated Sparrow

Amphispiza bilineata

With striking good looks, a dapper bird of desert wash and arid canyon. Few locations are too sultry for this seed eater, and the hotter the better. This sparrow forages deftly through thorny bushes and atop cactus spines, or coolly over scorching earth. On still mornings, often detected by beautiful song. Tinkling notes carry, as auditory sweetness sprinkles on rocky, Yucca-punctuated hillsides. Infrequently encountered in migration at random locales. Usually juveniles, these wanderers typically tag along with other sparrows.

THE BIRD: About Sagebrush Sparrow size. **Adult** head gunmetal gray bolstered by shadow-black throat. Brow and whiskers form bold white X on face. Black tail finely edged white. Lacking black on face, **juvenile** appears dingy and washed out, with delicate breast streaks.

FLIGHT: Dark gray-brown with black tail; white tail sides difficult to see.

VOICE: Similar to Bewick's Wren. Sweet notes: *swee, swee, swee, t-r-r-r-r-r-r*, or *grrrrr, tisss, swee, swee, swee...*, with grinding *grrr.* Call, a rapidly repeated, high, strident *sit, sit, sit...*

RANGE: Breeds April through August. Rocky hillsides with brush, yucca, pinyon-juniper, and Joshua. Rare fall and winter outside usual range. **West Slope:** Regular eastern Kern County, west of Walker Pass. Locally uncommon north to Tulare, Fresno, and Tuolumne Counties. **East Slope:** Locally fairly common arid canyons, Kern and Inyo Counties. Less predictable north to Alpine County.

SIMILAR SPECIES: **Bell's Sparrow** and **Sagebrush Sparrow** lack white brow.

dark gray

white spot

black whisker

tan flanks

flicks tail

ADULT

Bell's Sparrow
Artemisiospiza belli

With a limited range in the Sierra, this is a bird more typically associated with California's Coast Range, favoring dense hillsides of chaparral. Most easily located on cool spring mornings as birds sing from lofty perches in dense shrubby terrain. Wait too long in the day, and chances for detection diminish as temperatures rise, obliging birds to move deeper into cover or onto the ground. Bird hops and frequently flicks its dark elevated tail.

THE BIRD: Handsome. Slightly larger than Black-throated Sparrow. **Adult** strongly patterned; leaden-gray head contrasts with unmarked or lightly streaked brownish back and rich brown coverts. Malar area, throat, and underparts boldly white with black "stick-pin" in center of breast. Sides of the chest lightly streaked with pale cinnamon flanks. Late spring into summer, briefly held **juvenile** plumage appears like that of a drab, disheveled adult, extensively streaked on the crown, back, breast, and underparts. The wing coverts are crisply edged pale cream and warm brown.

FLIGHT: Dark brown with a thin, blackish, fairly long tail.

VOICE: Song nearly identical to Sagebrush Sparrow's. Perhaps more flowing, musical, and tinkling.

RANGE: Breeds northern California's Coast Range to central Baja and western Sierra. **West Slope:** Highly localized resident. Chemise chaparral, Placer and El Dorado Counties south to Mariposa County. **East Slope:** No documented records.

SIMILAR SPECIES: **Sagebrush Sparrow** East Slope only, head paler gray, back streaked.

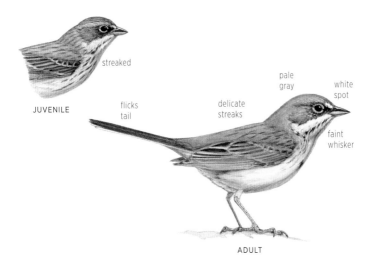

JUVENILE — streaked, flicks tail

ADULT — pale gray, white spot, delicate streaks, faint whisker

Sagebrush Sparrow
Artemisiospiza nevadensis

The true heart of the sage, a bird of wide horizons. Chest swollen, head back, this creature sprinkles sweet songs across fragrant landscapes. Investigating for insects in creosote or seeking seed below, this is a hardy bird. Instead of flying, it's just as likely to "offer" you an elevated flicking tail as it bounds off, leaving you in a miniature cloud of dust.

THE BIRD: **Adult** appears as a sun-bleached version of Bell's Sparrow. The eye-ring and the submalar are less distinct, and the back is marked by thin streaks. **Juvenile** appears disheveled, more streaked, less gray. Coverts pale edged.

FLIGHT: Moves low and quickly, appearing brownish gray with dark tail.

VOICE: Difficult to separate from Bell's Sparrow. Slightly thinner, buzzier. Sweet notes jumbled into a two-to-three-second *zee-diddle, de zee, zeee, diddle dee*. Rapidly repeated call, high, thin, Junco-like *tzit, tzit, tzit...* Also, agitated *jzzitt, jzzitt...*

RANGE: **East Slope** only, predominately sagebrush. Begins breeding March and April. North of Mono County, uncommon and highly local breeder. Fairly common northern Inyo County. **Note:** Bell's and Sagebrush Sparrows were considered one species, the Sage Sparrow. Differing in range, habitat, song, and, subtly, appearance, they were officially split in 2013. Some Sagebrush Sparrows are difficult to impossible to separate from some Bell's. There are ornithologists still unconvinced two species are involved.

SIMILAR SPECIES: **Bell's Sparrow** West Slope only.

streaky overall

JUVENILE

pink

streaks

yellow

short

pink

ADULT

Savannah Sparrow
Passerculus sandwichensis

Strolling through spring or winter grassland, notice the small brown birds flushing low before you. Across pastures they drop, usually disappearing once on the ground. Go to where they land; you will often discover that they have bounded elsewhere. Persistence pays off when this bird reveals its intricate beauty. This ground nester uses the tallest vegetation for singing. Named not for the savanna habitat it frequents but for its initial discovery in Savannah, Georgia.

THE BIRD: Variable and widely distributed, with numerous subspecies. Slightly smaller than Song Sparrow. **Adult**, elaborate face pattern. Separated from all streak-breasted sparrows by yellow brows. Gray-brown upper parts marked by fine streaks. Underparts generously streaked, with spot-like cluster in breast's center. Frequently flicks little tail. **Juvenile** more buffy than adult, with reduced yellow on brow. Coverts scaled. Tail tipped buff.

FLIGHT: Gregarious. Frequently calls when flushed. Short tailed.

VOICE: Song, high, thin *tsit, tsit, seeeeee, sit-iK!* or *seeeee sit-iK!* Call, high, thin, rising *tsit* or *sit*.

RANGE: Breeding populations augmented by northern and Great Basin migrants. Some move upslope in fall to Subalpine. **West Slope:** Common in Foothill in winter, often gregarious. **East Slope:** Fairly common breeder, lowlands to Subalpine. Uncommon or rare winter north of Inyo County, fairly common south.

SIMILAR SPECIES: **Vesper Sparrow**, white outer tail feathers. **Grasshopper Sparrow**, unstreaked breast. **Song Sparrow** heavily streaked. **Lincoln's Sparrow** delicately streaked, not gregarious.

delicate streaks

eye-ring

flat head

yellow

JUVENILE

blank face

unstreaked

tiny tail

ADULT

Grasshopper Sparrow

Ammodramus savannarum

Diminutive, secretive, cryptic, and extremely local. In grassland, mouse-like and adroit at evasion. Infrequently encountered, individuals that are discovered are nearly always singing males atop a bush or weed. The high, thin, buzzy song is for some extraordinarily difficult if not impossible to hear. To view this bird well, be diligent or dumb-lucky.

THE BIRD: Lincoln's Sparrow size, but far shorter tailed. **Adult** appears large headed with flat, dark crown bisected by white central stripe. Tail spine-like. Note the exquisite combination of mustard brow and bend of wing; blue-gray nape scrawled with rust; and face and unstreaked breast, blushed pumpkin. Coverts, tertials, and back feathers marked terminally by a dot, creating spotted appearance. **Juvenile** appears similar to adult, but shows delicate streaks at sides of breast. Fresh pale edges to upper parts and wing coverts create a scaled appearance.

FLIGHT: Usually silent in flight, evades threat by flying low, dropping, and creeping away. Note tiny spiked tail.

VOICE: Song, buzzy, insect-like. One upward and one downward note, followed by high-frequency trill: *tik? tsu, tssssssssssssssssss*.

RANGE: Because of difficulty in locating, status uncertain. **West Slope:** Highly localized uncommon breeder, Foothill grasslands March to September. Most records, Nevada County south. **East Slope:** Very rare. Possible breeding, Sierra Valley.

SIMILAR SPECIES: **Savannah Sparrow**, streaked underparts, intricate face.

smaller bill

"MONO"

contrasting wings

delicate spots

THICK-BILLED

faint wingbars

large spots

gray

SLATE-COLORED

yellow

dark spots

SOOTY

Fox Sparrow
Passerella iliaca

After towhees, our largest sparrow. Careful examination is required when attempting to differentiate between similar subspecies.

THE BIRD: A species with much variation; many consider it four subspecies, of which three occur in the Sierra. **Adult:** Sierra-breeding *Thick-billed* (*P. i. megarhyncha*) has grosbeak-like bill, gray face, white whisker, rusty wings and tail, and lightly spotted underparts. Its lower mandible turns yellow in winter. In Mono area, local *Thick-billed* averages smaller billed, inviting confusion with *Slate-colored* (*P. i. schistacea*), which has wingbars and more heavily spotted breast. Call notes noticeably different between subspecies. *Sooty* (*P. i. unalaschensis*), a winter visitor from the Pacific Northwest. Dark chocolate, heavily spotted below, orangey lower mandible.

FLIGHT: Large, dark, and rusty tailed. Doesn't form flocks.

VOICE: *Thick-billed* cheery, bright, somehow comical with Thrasher-like phrases, trills, and mimicked notes from local species. Calls vary. *Thick-billed* gives sharp California Towhee–like *TINK! Sooty* and *Slate-colored* similar to each other with inward-kissing *tcheP!* or Anna's Hummingbird–like "static snap."

RANGE: Chaparral, riparian, post-fire, shaded conifers, and neighborhoods. **West Slope:** *Thick-billed* breeds commonly, Lower Conifer to Alpine. *Sooty* winters in foothills after arriving from northern breeding grounds, late September. Departs spring. *Slate-colored* breeds Great Basin. Uncommon-to-rare winter visitor. **East Slope:** *Thick-billed* fairly common breeder. Very rare winter, mostly *Sooty* group.

SIMILAR SPECIES: **Green-tailed Towhee** song. **Song Sparrow** ornately patterned.

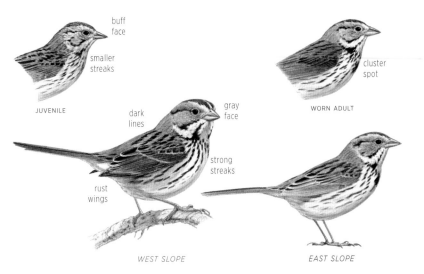

buff
face

smaller
streaks

cluster
spot

JUVENILE

dark
lines

gray
face

WORN ADULT

strong
streaks

rust
wings

WEST SLOPE

EAST SLOPE

Song Sparrow
Melospiza melodia

Are birds happy? Do they express elation? If jubilation is measured by frequency of song, then this must be a cheerful bird! Much of the year and at different hours of the day, this songster saturates wooded spaces with joyful refrain. Rare in sun-drenched land, infrequent in lofty canopy, this down-to-earth bird tends the domain of the low lying. In elaborate tangle, swaying cattail, or cool understory it melds. Typically doesn't form flocks, but any caucus of winter sparrows usually has one in attendance. Stroll through its living room, and from behind shadowed lattice, it observes and assesses. Inquisitive, rarely vexed, it offers soft calls until its castle's sanctity is restored by your departure.

THE BIRD: Smaller than Fox. **Adult** intricate brown, gray, rust, white, and chocolate. **Juvenile**, Lincoln's-like.

FLIGHT: Brown with fairly long tail that it curiously pumps upon landing.

VOICE: Rich song begins with three identical notes, followed by variable tumbling notes. Call, soft, sneezing *smew.*

RANGE: Subspecies difficult to differentiate away from breeding grounds. Averages darker in wetter regions, paler in drier. **West Slope:** *Heermann's* (*M. m. heermanni*) thought the primary subspecies. Common resident Foothill riparian marsh and meadow to Upper Conifer. **East Slope:** *Merrill's* (*M. m. merrilli*) likely most common subspecies. Paler gray, flank streaks thin and rusty. Fairly common at low elevations. Uncommon to rare, Subalpine.

SIMILAR SPECIES: **Savannah, Lincoln's,** and **Fox Sparrows.**

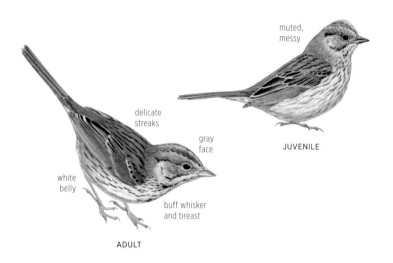

muted,
messy

delicate
streaks

gray
face

JUVENILE

white
belly

buff whisker
and breast

ADULT

Lincoln's Sparrow
Melospiza lincolnii

Often appears as a small rodent. First glances yield a grayish, mouse-like bird. A glimpse through dense cover and one might consider Song Sparrow, but clear views present differences. Fleeing low, Lincoln's is usually discovered when filtering through waves of "weedy" winter sparrows. Pay close attention to the smallest, most cryptic, and fewest of the assemblage sprinkled around the social fringes of "crowned sparrow" gatherings. Best located in spring by loud, upbeat songs.

THE BIRD: Slightly smaller than Song Sparrow. Inquisitive bird often raises a peaked crest. **Adult**, rusty crown bisected by gray. Delicately streaked breast, and flanks buffy. Throat and belly contrastingly white. Rust wings opposite olive back create unique appearance. **Juvenile** streaked overall, appearing disheveled.

FLIGHT: Dark gray-brown, flees low, weaving through dense foliage, grass, or brush.

VOICE: While Song and Fox Sparrows perform year-round, Lincoln's usually sings only in breeding season. Loud, rapid, robust, jubilant distinct phrases: *jewbella, jewbella, jee, jee, jeee seeeeeee-e-e, tee, tee, tee, juu, juu, too-buh-lah*. Calls include forceful Fox Sparrow–like *cheP!*, strident *tsit*, annoyed *raaah*, and quiet electronic *bzzzzt*.

RANGE: **West Slope:** Fairly common local breeder in Upper Conifer, uncommon to Subalpine. Fairly common winter visitor to wetland and riparian in lower foothills. **East Slope:** Similar status as West, but rare winter.

SIMILAR SPECIES: **Song Sparrow adult**, white malar. **Song Sparrow juvenile** disheveled, head buffy. **Savannah Sparrow**, yellow brow.

pale

streaked

orange

black

reddish

FIRST WINTER

FIRST WINTER

JUVENILE

GAMBEL'S

MOUNTAIN

White-crowned Sparrow

Zonotrichia leucophrys

Breeds, migrates, or winters throughout nearly all of Canada and the US.

THE BIRD: Composed of five subspecies; the Sierra has two occurring regularly: the breeding *Mountain* (*Z. l. oriantha*) and wintering *Gambel's* (*Z. l. gambelii*). Similar in appearance but with very different lives, *Mountain* breeds in the high Sierra spring and summer, and winters to Mexican highlands. *Gambel's* breeds Alaska and Canada, then arrives to winter in California's lowlands. In fall, one might encounter both subspecies. Filter through flocks for different subspecies of White-crowned and other sparrow species. Smaller than Golden-crowned Sparrow, White-crowns show gray faces, tan flanks, streaked upper parts, and brown wings, with white wingbars. **Adults**, black-and-white crowns. **First winter** reddish-brown and tan crowns. *Mountain* appears "swollen crowned," red billed, and dark lored. *Gambel's* shows bright orangey-pink bill and pale lores. **Juvenile** White-crowns are extensively streaked.

FLIGHT: Large winter flocks tend to fly low, straight, and without much meandering.

VOICE: Variable within subspecies. Song, sustained initial note, sweet jumbled notes, then short vibrating note: *surrrrrr, sweeee? seedle, twee, twee, twee, stttttt. Mountain* and *Gambel's* have similar songs, but *Gambel's* lacks final trill.

RANGE: **Both slopes:** *Mountain* breeds mid-May, departs mid-September. Fairly common, wet meadows with shrubby willows from Upper Conifer to Alpine. *Gambel's* common to locally abundant winter visitor in Foothill, mid-September through April.

SIMILAR SPECIES: **White-throated Sparrow** rare. **Golden-crowned Sparrow** darker, gold forehead.

extensive
black

dingy
crown

gray
bill

BREEDING

EARLY SPRING

overall
brown

FIRST WINTER

Golden-crowned Sparrow

Zonotrichia atricapilla

When days grow short, golden leaves fall, and first graders don oversize backpacks, a sustained crystal whistle, wistful in character, begins to permeate the subconscious. With a melancholy quality, the acclaimed song of the Golden-crowned predominates the autumn soundscape as Halloween pumpkin stands spring up on the edge of town. Lifting its voice in winter, this large sparrow mingles with White-crowned and cuts a formidable figure with its greater bulk. Breeding far to the north, it's about the last of the wintering sparrows to depart in late spring. Bring sparrows into view by kiss-squeaking the back of your hand.

THE BIRD: **Adult** molts into **breeding** plumage late spring, before migrating northward. The gold-and-white central crown stripe is bordered by black brows. **Nonbreeding adult** gold with reduced black. **First-winter** bird, crown varies in extent of brown and gold.

FLIGHT: With other sparrows, appears larger and grayish.

VOICE: Song, thin, clear, downward three-part whistle: *Ohhhhhhhhhh dear me.* Calls include angry chatters, *chew, chi, chew, chew*; contented babbling when feeding; strident *tsssssT!*; or California Towhee-like *chinK!*

RANGE: Breeds Canada and Alaska. **Both slopes:** Arrives to California mid-September at low elevations. Winters, then departs April. **West Slope:** Locally common Foothill to Lower Conifer. Mixes with White-crowned and other sparrows in chaparral, scrubby fields, or suburban gardens. **East Slope:** Fairly common fall through winter at lower elevations.

SIMILAR SPECIES: **White-crowned Sparrow**, colored bill.

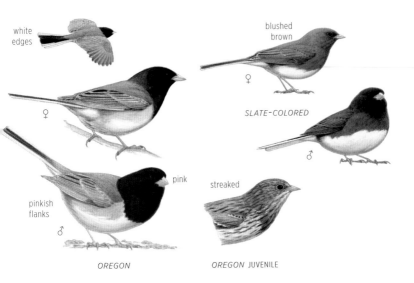

white
edges

♀

pinkish
flanks

pink

♂

OREGON

blushed
brown

♀

SLATE-COLORED

♂

streaked

OREGON JUVENILE

Dark-eyed Junco

Junco hyemalis

Familiar and common, this bird is widely distributed in the Sierra. Welcomed at backyard feeders and encountered on mountain trails. Observant naturalists filter through flocks for rare species. Dark-eyed Juncos are diverse in appearance. Differences may be age or sex related. Birds might be a rare subspecies, partially albino, or different by individual variation. Junco watching cultivates habit-forming skills for untangling variation and subtlety.

THE BIRD: Composed of over ten subspecies; the Sierra has two, the breeding *Oregon* (*J. h. thurberi*) and the infrequent winter visitor from the north and east, *Slate-colored* (*J. h. hyemalis*). Song Sparrow size, **male** *Oregon* shows black hood, brown upper parts, and pinkish flanks. **Female,** brown nape blends with back. **Juvenile** streaked overall with indistinct hood. **Male** *Slate-colored* dark gray with white belly. **Female,** brownish upper parts.

FLIGHT: Erupting into flight, flocks usually proceed to nearest cover. Bold white outer tail feathers are diagnostic.

VOICE: Song, sustained, level trill: *tr,tr,tr,tr,tr,tr,tr,tr...* Also, dry, insect-like *t,t,t,t,t,t,t,t,t,t...* Call, static snap-like *tchik!* In interactions, *tik-tik-tik...* and peevish *jer-jer-jer.*

RANGE: *Oregon* resident. *Slate-colored* rare winter visitor. **West Slope:** Common, most breed Lower Conifer to Alpine. Sometimes abundant in winter sparrow flocks Foothill to Lower Conifer. **East Slope:** Similar to West, but absent as breeders in dry canyons from southern Inyo to Kern County.

SIMILAR SPECIES: Black-chinned Sparrow, gray belly. **Chipping Sparrow** song drier.

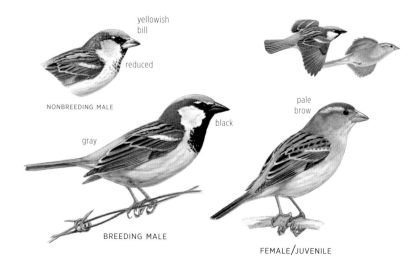

yellowish bill

reduced

NONBREEDING MALE

gray

black

pale brow

BREEDING MALE

FEMALE/JUVENILE

House Sparrow

Passer domesticus

The Sierra has one of about forty Old World sparrow species, the House Sparrow. Similar to New World sparrows, but small tailed, short legged. Whether snatching french fries from sticky fast-food tables, hopping between Holsteins at a foothill dairy, or nesting inside a traffic light enjoying periodic warmth, it's at home around our homes. Inhabiting urban areas, likely Earth's most frequently viewed bird. Introduced into North America in the mid-1800s, it's originally from the Middle East and has colonized swaths of the world flying or hopping alongside *Homo sapiens*. This invasive species has negative impacts on small, cavity-nesting birds by forcibly evicting occupants.

THE BIRD: White-crowned Sparrow size. Flicks tail. **Breeding male** clown-like. Bill black, crown gray, cheeks silver. Nape, back, wings chestnut. Lesser wing coverts white. **Nonbreeding male** like breeding, but colors and black throat diminished, bill yellowish. Brownish gray with buff brow and suspenders, **female** and **juvenile** are modest in conduct and attire.

FLIGHT: Powerfully barrels with shallow bounding. Note short tail, gray rump, white wingbar.

VOICE: Not a gifted songster; utters monotonous chirping *chee-ip, chee-ip... che-rip, che-ip... che-rip...* Also, wet *slipp, slipp, slipp...* and *chewp, chewp, che-dull-leep...*

RANGE: West Slope: Locally common resident towns, farms, stables, gas stations, Foothill to Lower Conifer. **East Slope:** Like West, but regular at higher elevations.

SIMILAR SPECIES: Some worn sparrows, buntings, and finches are similar to House Sparrow females.

JUVENILE

black

yellow

pink

BREEDING   WINTER

Gray-crowned Rosy-Finch
Leucosticte tephrocotis

Some two hundred Fringillidae occur worldwide. Bills vary. Feed primarily on seeds, insects. Stocky, small legged; some exhibit bold wing patterns. Most females gray, green, or yellow; most males red or yellow.

The "Crown Jewel" of the Sierra, this rosy gem is a diamond in rough terrain. To pay one's respects, venture to snowfields cradled by sweeping talus slopes and towers of wind-scoured rock. Whether thriving or clinging to life, this resilient bird chooses or tolerates this nearly inhospitable world of Alpine thunder, ice, and stone. Meals may consist of frozen insects, or grass and flower seeds.

THE BIRD: Slightly larger than Cassin's Finch. **Adult** brown blushed pink, crown gray and black. Sexes similar; **male** tends pinker. **Fall**, **winter** bill yellowish. **Spring**, **summer** bill black. **Juvenile** overall brownish, coverts and primaries edged buff, bill yellowish.

FLIGHT: Forms winter flocks. Powerful fliers, they bound dramatically. Wings long, silvery, translucent.

VOICE: Chattering *jrr, jrr, jrr...* House Sparrow–like *jewp, jewp, jew, jew...* Taking wing, forceful *Chew!*

RANGE: Sierra Nevada *Dawson's* (*L. t. dawsoni*) occurs almost entirely within Sierra at southern peaks from 10,000 feet to Mount Whitney's 14,500 feet. Easiest to locate on talus slopes of Tioga Pass. Rare north of Tahoe. **East Slope:** Mono and Inyo Counties, gathers in winter flocks, infrequently with rare, northern *Hepburn's* (*L. t. littoralis*) and, very rarely, Black Rosy-Finch (*Leucosticte atrata*).

SIMILAR SPECIES: None.

long
tail

blunt
bill

MALE

FEMALE

Pine Grosbeak
Pinicola enucleator

Pine Grosbeak, Great Gray Owl, and Black-backed Woodpecker share something in common. As polar caps receded at the end of the last Ice Age, regions of the Sierra Nevada remained ecologically comparable to boreal forest habitat, inclining these three to stay. Endemic, the "Sierra" Pine Grosbeak (*P. e. californica*) is isolated by hundreds of miles from its nearest Rocky Mountain neighbors and has adapted to become largely nonmigratory. Often difficult to locate; however, will allow close approach. Known to enter cabins, benefiting from "catastrophic" cereal spills. Consumes seeds and insects. Large, this nomadic finch mixes with other species at mineral springs.

THE BIRD: Evening Grosbeak size with longer tail. Round crowned, wing-bars bold. **Female** gray with head and rump greenish or ochre. **Male** rosy pink, scapulars and flanks gray. **Immature female**, adult female–like. **Immature male** female-like, with pinkish head and rump.

FLIGHT: Large, bull headed; long blackish tail; bold white wingbars.

VOICE: Song, beautiful ongoing Meadowlark and Black-headed Grosbeak mix. Call, repeated three to four level, Western Tanager–like notes: *che-de-dep...*

RANGE: Resident in high-elevation forests. Sparsely distributed, potential seasonal movements poorly understood. **West Slope:** Fairly common, lodgepole, whitebark pine forests near meadows and Subalpine streams. Uncommon down to red fir forests of Upper Conifer, rare lower. **East Slope:** Uncommon, localized Subalpine forests and meadows, Sierra County into Mono County.

SIMILAR SPECIES: **Red Crossbill male** smaller, no wingbars.

face pattern

thick bill

pinkish streaks

blurry streaks

MALE

FEMALE

Purple Finch
Haemorhous purpureus

Purple Finch intermediate between House and Cassin's. Occurs higher than House and lower than Cassin's. Crest is larger than House, smaller than Cassin's. Bill is less curved than House, more curved than Cassin's.

THE BIRD: Not purple. **Male** plumage blushed pinkish red. Crown red. Brow, malar, and coverts pink, flanks diffusely streaked. Shows white at bill's base. **Female**, dark ear patch framed by pale brow and whisker. Compared to Cassin's, Purple is darker grayish olive with extensive blurry flank streaks and unstreaked vent. Many birds are blushed, with greenish edges to upper parts. A bird appearing to be a female, but singing, is a **young male**.

FLIGHT: Likely giving telltale *PIK!* calls, moves strongly with deep bounds. Tail short and smartly forked.

VOICE: Difficult to separate; song *very* similar to Warbling Vireo. Notes chewy, garbled, sweet, fairly level tumbling *chee, chewy, chee, cheedle, cheeda chiddily chee...* Also, questioning *chee-dil-lik?*

RANGE: Resident, coniferous forests, moist canyons, meadow edge, and middle-elevation slopes. **West Slope:** Fairly common, Lower and Upper Conifer. Uncommon or rare, Subalpine. Uncommon in foothills, some winters rare. **East Slope:** Uncommon to rare, winter and fall. Potentially breeds north of Tahoe.

SIMILAR SPECIES: Cassin's Finch larger, eye-ring, straight culmen. **Male**, rose crest, pink plumage. **Female**, white underparts, vent streaked. **House Finch** crown rounded; thick flank streak. **Male**, red head, breast, rump. **Female**, no face pattern.

rose cap

crest

streaked

straight bill

thin streaks

white

MALE

FEMALE

Cassin's Finch

Haemorhous cassinii

It might seem Cassin's and Purple Finches pose identification challenges, but male or female Cassin's is at the lighter end of the color spectrum.

THE BIRD: Frosty and expressively crested. Just larger than Purple Finch, with distinct eye-ring and lores. Key feature is straight culmen, unlike Purple's curved. **Male's** rose cap contrasts. Nape and back, streaked tan and pink. Pure pink breast blends into white belly. Flanks faintly streaked, coverts edged pinkish. **Female** granite-gray and white. Underparts and vent with thin, dark Pine Siskin–like streaks. Face pattern bold. **Juvenile** female-like, but coverts edged pale.

FLIGHT: Strong, with longer distance between bounds than Purple. Covers ground more quickly. Elongated primaries impart long-winged look; Purple shorter. Fairly short tail distinctly forked.

VOICE: Song, rapid, variable, jubilant, tumbling notes. Similar to House Finch, but higher, sweeter, with House Wren quality. Calls, three-note *Chee-dull-ePP?*, repeated *Cha-wee-oh* or *chee-oh*, and conversational *fed-ree-oh, fed-ree-ched-dul-upp*.

RANGE: A bird of high-elevation western mountains. **West Slope:** Common breeders, lodgepole pine, red fir, mountain hemlock, Upper Conifer to Subalpine. Uncommon in Lower Conifer. Infrequent and sporadic in foothills. **East Slope:** Fairly common breeder in higher-elevation pine near tree line, and pinyon-juniper in winter.

SIMILAR SPECIES: Purple Finch male redder. **Female**, unstreaked vent. **House Finch**, low altitude. **Male**, red head, dark flank streaks. **Female**, no face pattern. **Pine Siskin** small, yellow in wings.

rounded

gray cheek

grayish brown

blank face

dark streaks

YELLOW MALE

MALE

FEMALE

House Finch
Haemorhous mexicanus

Ubiquitous at lower elevations, a bird for all seasons. The essence of jubilation, male sings for hours during warming days of spring, providing joy to any within earshot. In winter, swirling flocks lift off from foothill roadside and sprinkle back to Earth. In late summer, young follow worn-out parents as they learn to become "proper" finches. Frequenting bird feeders, this friendly bird mixes well with siskins, sparrows, grosbeaks. In wilder conditions, it forages for natural grain or small insects.

THE BIRD: Purple Finch size, bill blunt, tail longer. Most show wingbars and dark-streaked flanks. **Male**, red confined to head, breast, rump, and, infrequently, back; other red finches are blushed rose overall. Uncommon, **yellow male** is diet-deficient, unable to produce red pigment. **Female** drab, face lacks pattern. **Juvenile** female-like, but overall fresh, can show "ghost" of Purple Finch's pattern.

FLIGHT: Forms large winter flocks. Bounds dramatically. Sweet *tweet?* call. Appears bull headed, silvery winged, dark tailed. Shows longer, less forked tail than Purple and Cassin's. Landing, male exhibits red rump.

VOICE: Song, strong, sweet, rich, jumbled notes. Taking wing, cheerful *chweet* or *tweet*. Perched bird gives scratchy, questioning *jzzreep?*

RANGE: **Both slopes:** Locally abundant resident, Foothill farms, suburban gardens. Fairly common Lower Conifer. Uncommon to rare above middle elevations.

SIMILAR SPECIES: **Purple** and **Cassin's Finches**, shorter tails, different calls, habitats. Both **males** pinkish red; both **females** show face patterns.

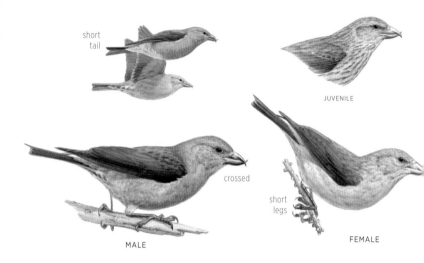

short
tail

JUVENILE

crossed

short
legs

MALE

FEMALE

Red Crossbill
Loxia curvirostra

With crossed bills, the perfect tools for extracting seeds from cones, the Red Crossbill is our only nonsymmetrical bird. Bird of mature conifers, it's sturdy in build and hardy in nature, and endures harsh conditions. Visits salt licks or mineral springs.

THE BIRD: Shorter than Western Tanager, but heavier. Wings, tail blackish. Note plumage variations. **Male** brick red, sometimes mixed orangey. Face grizzled. Some males lack red, appearing female-like—perhaps related to schedule of food sources, and forced to molt later or earlier than optimal period for growing red feathers. **Female** variable. Olive green, some grayish about head, back. **Juvenile** dull, streaked; lacks red or green. Molts into adult-like plumage within two months.

FLIGHT: Gregarious, irruptive, nomadic. Long winged, large headed; flies strongly, in a hurry, covers ground in long bounds.

VOICE: Song, long, unstructured, thin, clipped, lisping chips: *tsip, CHIP! TIP, chit, chit, tsip...* Flight call usually heard before bird is seen. Loud *KIP! KIP! KIP!* or *JIP, JIP...* Nearly similar calls vary among types of this crossbill.

RANGE: Resident, high mountains. **Both slopes:** Locally common, Subalpine to Upper Conifer, generally rare elsewhere. Numerous enigmatic populations are separated by bill structure and call types. Breeding in Sierra, type II has large bill. Four or five other types occur irregularly. Some populations may eventually receive full species status.

SIMILAR SPECIES: Pine Grosbeak, Purple Finch.

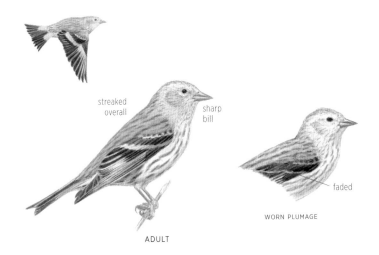

streaked overall

sharp bill

faded

WORN PLUMAGE

ADULT

Pine Siskin
Spinus pinus

First encountered, siskin is often "just another streaky-brown bird." Taking flight, however, it changes from somber to eye-catching. Familiar at backyard thistle feeders, this mighty-mite holds its own against any finch, red or gold, who dares compete for its nutritious fare. With wings and tail fully spread, it opens its tiny gray beak and aggressively jabs would-be diners.

THE BIRD: American Goldfinch size, sexes similar. Exhibits great variation related to age, seasonality, or status of molt. Some **worn adults** are less streaked, with yellow reduced. Others lack particular coverts, exposing normally concealed yellow wing patch. **Young** are heavily streaked below. After molting in fall, bird is fresh, with neatly edged feathers. **Juvenile** shows buff edges to coverts and tan blush to entire plumage.

FLIGHT: Flocks often sizable, form cohesive ball of high-pitched chattering finches. Individuals bounce dramatically with short stride. Yellow tail and wing stripe striking and diagnostic.

VOICE: Song, continuous jumbled conversational notes: *chee, dit, dit, chee, cheedle, chee, dittle, chit, chit.* Calls, buzzy, insect-like *bbbzzzzzZZZZZIP!* like running thumbnail up stiff comb. Also, down-slurred *cheeeez.* Feeding, utters *tit, tit, tit, uh, CHIP?*

RANGE: **Both slopes:** Widespread in coniferous forests. Locally abundant in Upper Conifer and Subalpine. Makes unpredictable winter movements to Lower Conifer and Foothill. Frequents farms, urban parks, ornamental trees, and suburban gardens.

SIMILAR SPECIES: **Cassin's** and **House Finch females**, no yellow, larger bills.

freckled black

JUVENILE MALE

green crown

green back

gray bill

white

yellow

MALE

FEMALE

Lesser Goldfinch
Spinus psaltria

Appropriately named, this diminutive bird is smallest of the finches. "Goldfinch of the West," it gets along well with others and is often encountered with siskins and various other finches. A lover of weedy places, especially with thistles.

THE BIRD: Warbler size. Note conical bill, thin voice. **Male** strikingly tricolored, mossy backed, lemon bellied, black winged. Tail spots and wings diagnostically marked by white. **Female** greenish, averages paler than male. Wings vary blackish to gray-green. **Young male** similar to adult, but crown freckled. **Young female** similar to drab female American, but tail shorter, plumage greener.

FLIGHT: Bounds dramatically with very short stride. Small, short tailed. Male shows diagnostic wing patch at base of primaries. Female subtle. Startled flocks vocalize and bound away in loose, rollicking "popcorn-popping" formation.

VOICE: Song, high, thin, sweet, rambling notes interspersed with accurate mimicking of resident species, one after another. This rapid mimicry rivals all others except for Lawrence's Goldfinch and perhaps Lark Sparrow. Call, high, strained, peevish, descending, melancholy *teeeeeee*.

RANGE: **West Slope:** Locally abundant residents of weedy fields, oak woodlands, riparian, chaparral, and residential gardens, Foothill to Lower Conifer. Fairly common to uncommon in Upper Conifer, rare higher. **East Slope:** Fairly common, same habitats as West. In winter, uncommon in lowlands except towns with bird feeders.

SIMILAR SPECIES: **American Goldfinch female** larger, white vent. **Warblers**, thin bills.

yellow rump

gray

pink bill

yellow wings

unmarked face

MALE

FEMALE

Lawrence's Goldfinch
Spinus lawrencei

"California's Goldfinch" breeds primarily within the Golden State and winters in the arid southwest. When it comes to goldfinches, nearly all birders cut their teeth on the widespread, luminous American. Western birders delight at the grass-green and lemon motif of the Lesser, yet frequently it's the beguiling Lawrence's that focuses the mind and controls the attention. With twinkling flight and tinkling call, Lawrence's appears sweet in disposition. The epitome of endearing, pairs refresh at shaded washes, seeking relief from spring heat in leafy cottonwoods. Here, males sing, stitching together an endless string of phrases. So deft at mimicking neighbors' songs, this "arid canary" can astonish.

THE BIRD: Fractionally larger than Lesser Goldfinch. **Male** gray, face black; breast, rump, and coverts golden. **Female** like a plain-faced, diffuse male. **Juvenile** female-like, lacks yellow breast, shows buffy-yellow wingbars.

FLIGHT: Bounds dramatically with short stride. Note white tail spots and yellowish rump.

VOICE: With high, intricate, and variable notes, male sings and mimics for prolonged periods. Call, pure, high, thin, repeated tinkling *tee-tul* or rising, questioning *fweeee?*

RANGE: Arrives mid-March, departs early August. Winters south. Rare, nonbreeding season. **West Slope:** Common breeder South Fork Kern River. Nomadic; present some years, absent others. Breeds Foothill oak woodlands near water. Uncommon Lower Conifer, rare higher. **East Slope:** Spring migrant, desert canyons, eastern Kern County; otherwise rare.

SIMILAR SPECIES: **Lesser Goldfinch** greenish.

FIRST WINTER   ADULT WINTER

gray bill

yellow

pink

greenish

yellow face

white

MALE BREEDING   FEMALE BREEDING

American Goldfinch

Spinus tristis

"America's Goldfinch." Flitting in gardens or pictured on "get well" cards, it's part of the American experience. Even non-birders likely recognize this ubiquitous creature. Annually transforms from summer yellow to winter drab, our only finch to do so. So if folk in spring say, "Look, those pretty yellow birds are back!" kindly inform them that they never really departed; they've just changed their wardrobe. Forages on seed, grass, thistle, and alder.

THE BIRD: Our largest goldfinch shows white rump and undertail coverts. Differentiating sex and age of nonbreeding birds often challenging. **Breeding male** unmistakable. **Breeding female**, pink bill, greenish crown, face. Underparts yellowish. Bold wingbars. **Nonbreeding male**, dark billed, muted tan, yellow on face, variable. Wings with buff or white wingbars. Tail tipped white. **Nonbreeding female** similar to nonbreeding male, dull wings and tail spots. **Immature, first winter** like winter adult, but wingbars and tertial edges buffy.

FLIGHT: Typically vocalizing, bounds dramatically with short stride. Male white underwings contrast; female and nonbreeding, less so.

VOICE: With jumbled notes, similar to high-pitched House Finch. Call, questioning *pit, tit-uh, chiP?*, like *potato chiP?* Also, wheezy *wizzz, wEEo.*

RANGE: **West Slope:** Fairly common resident, Foothill riparian, occasionally grasslands, oak woodland, chaparral. Uncommon Lower Conifer, rare higher. **East Slope:** Rare in breeding season. Visits feeders in nonbreeding season or sage in fall.

SIMILAR SPECIES: **Lesser Goldfinch female** smaller, greenish, yellowish vent.

massive bill

yellow spot

complex pattern

white patch

MALE

FEMALE

Evening Grosbeak
Coccothraustes vespertinus

"Striking" and "Wow!" are often the initial comments when discovering these large, boldly patterned finches. Flocks "loping" over forested mountains, lush meadows, or deep canyons are usually heard before materializing. At mineral springs, female's subtleties or male's smoky plumage can be better appreciated. Predominately forages in conifers. Also frequents deciduous trees for fruits and seeds.

THE BIRD: Heavier than other grosbeaks, short tailed and sexually so dissimilar, one might assume them separate species. Milky-greenish bill imparts top-heavy appearance. **Adult male** unmistakable. Grayish, **adult female** has smoky lores, a delicate whisker, a yellow blush to neck, and intricately marked wings and tail. Dark-billed **first-winter** bird, overall duller.

FLIGHT: Typically vocalizing, these powerful finches fly purposefully, covering distance with rollicking bounds. Male wing patches beacon-like. Female shows white "hand" spot.

VOICE: Song, monotonous frog-like up-slurred *greep? greep? greep?* Call, loud, piercing, far-carrying whistle: *TEW!* Flocks give rolling, querulous trill, *krrrrrree...* Evening Grosbeaks have at least four distinct call "types." Types I and II known from the Sierra.

RANGE: Irruptive, nomadic. **West Slope:** Locally abundant or absent depending on food availability. Breeds primarily mature Upper Conifer forests and Subalpine, late May until mid-August. Some move lower in nonbreeding season. Rare in severe winters to Foothill. **East Slope:** Locally fairly common, pine forests south through Mono County. Highest concentrations Tahoe Basin. Rare south.

SIMILAR SPECIES: None.

YOUNG MALE

silvery bill

lacks wingbars

MALE

FEMALE

Summer Tanager
Piranga rubra

Around fifty species of cardinalids are confined to the New World. Perhaps our most colorful birds, they include various tanagers, grosbeaks, and buntings. Skilled singers, males are flamboyant, even garish; females, somber. Largely fruit and seed eaters with conical or stout bills. Migratory. Winter as far as Central America.

THE BIRD: Formerly considered tanagers, Western and Summer Tanagers are cardinalids. When viewing North America's most extensively red bird, one is treated to a sort of natural shock-and-awe. Bulkier than Western Tanager, brilliant rose **male** glows among dark leaves. **Female** like female Western Tanager, but orangey green, without wingbars. With green-and-red "camo" pattern, **first-summer male** splotched, variable, and distinct. All **first-winter** birds female-like.

FLIGHT: Moves strongly and rapidly, with little bounding. Male unmistakable, female entirely greenish.

VOICE: Song reminiscent of an American Robin in need of practice. Repeats phrases *chee-dup, che-duh-lee? chee-up, chee-leep?* Call, first note rising, second descending, a two-to-three-note *pid-ucK!* or *piT-uh TUK!*

RANGE: **West Slope:** In the last few decades, Summers have begun breeding in forests along the South Fork Kern River. Whether they are pioneers colonizing new locales or an outlier population, the southern Sierra is the extreme northwestern limit of their range. Fairly common May to July, departs mid-September. Very rare elsewhere. **East Slope:** Very rare. A few breeding records, Inyo County. Rare migrants north to Mono County.

SIMILAR SPECIES: See **Western Tanager female.**

splotchy

NONBREEDING MALE

GRAYISH FEMALE

pale wingbars

MALE

FEMALE

Western Tanager
Piranga ludoviciana

From the tropics, this bouquet of feathers arrives to breed in the sweeping forests of the Sierra Nevada. Commanding attention, male appears escaped from an exotic pet store or like a vivid dream come to life. Furtive and understated, female is a challenge to spot feeding in green shadows or beneath sun-spangled boughs. Consumes mostly insects in breeding season, but trends toward fruit as they depart to winter as far as Central America.

THE BIRD: Slightly smaller than a grosbeak. **Breeding male** strikingly tricolored. Note yellow wingbar. Yellow neck and rump isolate black back. By fall, beguiling glow of male reduced. **Adult female** varies between bright apple green or dull grayish. **First winter**, both sexes female-like.

FLIGHT: Foraging high above the ground flycatcher-style, sallies for wasps and bees. Flying farther, moves directly without much bounding. Male bright, oriole-like. Female greenish with yellowish underwings.

VOICE: Song, with spaced phrases, like a burry American Robin. Call, a distinct repeated three-note *pea-dil-liK?*... Fall, infrequently gives Hooded Oriole–like questioning *weee?*

RANGE: Arrives late April, departs early October. **West Slope:** Breeds commonly, mature forests, riparian woodlands in Lower and Upper Conifer. After breeding, uncommon to Subalpine. **East Slope:** Breeds fairly commonly Jeffrey and ponderosa pines, fir forest. Pinyon-juniper in migration.

SIMILAR SPECIES: **Summer Tanager female**, no wingbars. **Hooded Oriole** slender, longer tail. **American Robin's** and **Black-headed Grosbeak's** songs sound "more practiced."

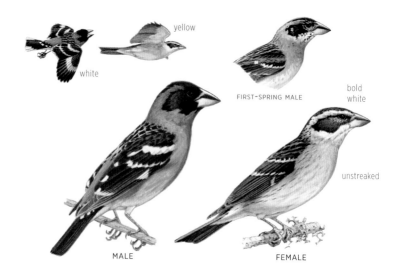

yellow

white

FIRST-SPRING MALE

bold
white

unstreaked

MALE

FEMALE

Black-headed Grosbeak
Pheucticus melanocephalus

Arriving as pastel swaths of wildflowers carpet spring foothills, this bold, large-headed finch moves upslope to nest. Male appears as a flash of orange, black, and white. Feeding low, sheepish females are sometimes anointed with staining on bill and face from ongoing "blackberry-eating competitions." Inquisitive, birds hop through spangled canopy and approach. Sizing you up with slow, head-turning stares, they will suddenly pivot, take wing, and depart for less crowded conditions.

THE BIRD: Slightly smaller than Evening Grosbeak. **Male** brow, body, rump burnt orange. Wings and tail marked white. Belly and underwings lemon. **Female** dark cheeked, body blushed orange, upper parts streaked. **First-summer male** appears as a mixture of both sexes. Bold eye line, streaked flanks, orangey underparts. **First-fall male** female-like.

FLIGHT: Singing on the wing, displaying male flaps with overexaggerated wingbeats. Flying farther, progresses with bounding stride. Male, bold wing patch, orangey rump. Female dull; lemon underwings.

VOICE: "Leader of the band!" Song, rousing and jubilant, with rich, lilting, American Robin–like phrases. Sweeter than Western Tanager. Call, sharp, strident, Downy Woodpecker–like *PEEK?*

RANGE: Winters Mexico. Arrives mid-April, breeds, departs late August. **West Slope:** Fairly common breeder, riparian, oak, conifer woodlands, Foothill to upper limits of Lower Conifer. After breeding, rare to Subalpine. **East Slope:** Breeds uncommonly in aspen, riparian. Rare to treeline through late August.

SIMILAR SPECIES: **Rose-breasted Grosbeak female** rare. **Varied Thrush. Spotted Towhee.**

splotchy

FIRST-SPRING MALE

slight
crest

chestnut

bluish

flicks
tail

MALE

FEMALE

Blue Grosbeak

Passerina caerulea

A more appropriate name for this grosbeak might be the Goliath Bunting. Big, blue, black, and chestnut, it shares the same genus with buntings. Similarities to its smaller kin include an understated crest; blue males, brown females; silvery bills; black faces; and a tail-flicking habit all but ingrained in buntings. Lastly, their preference for grassy habitat is more bunting-like than grosbeak.

THE BIRD: Larger than buntings, smaller than other grosbeaks. Glossy, **adult male** is deep blue with black face and wings. Rounded tail tipped white. Coverts and tertials boldly edged chestnut. Male often appears dark, sometimes blackish. Similar size and shape, **female** is warm brown with cinnamon wingbars, blue-gray shoulder and rump. **First-summer male** female-like, with emerging patches of adult male color.

FLIGHT: Moves low, straight and strongly. Male, dark blue. Female, warm brown with blue-gray rump.

VOICE: Song, Warbling Vireo–like dull conversational notes in up-down singsong cadence: *chee-we, chee-we, chee-duh-WEE-jull.* Call, a strident, wet *t-sliP!* with "crowned sparrow" quality.

RANGE: Uncommon breeder in Central Valley, barely reaches foothills. Arrives April, departs August. **West Slope:** Uncommon-to-rare highly localized breeder, typically in weedy lowland riparian. **East Slope:** Uncommon to rare, Mono and Inyo Counties. Very rare farther north.

SIMILAR SPECIES: **Indigo Bunting male** small, no wingbars; **female** lacks cinnamon. **Lazuli Bunting female**, wingbars whiter, lacks cinnamon. **Brown-headed Cowbird female**, no wingbars, no cinnamon.

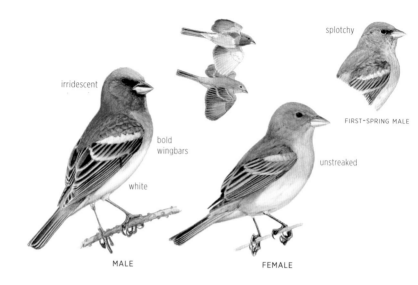

irridescent

splotchy

bold
wingbars

FIRST-SPRING MALE

white

unstreaked

MALE

FEMALE

Lazuli Bunting

Passerina amoena

Lazuli and Indigo Buntings are neatly divided by their western and eastern ranges. Sharing similarities of body size, shape, tail-flicking behavior, habitat preference, female plumage, and voice, they're clearly and closely related.

THE BIRD: Smaller than nearly all sparrows. Upper wingbar curiously thicker than lower. **Male** jade-like opalescent plumage unique among Sierra species. Distinct from Indigo male. **Female** furtive, often difficult to differentiate from Indigo. Understated brownish with pale wingbars, unstreaked peach breast, and bluish wings and rump. **First-summer male** female-like, with blue emerging. **Juvenile** female-like through fall, with fine dusky breast steaks.

FLIGHT: Hesitant to reveal itself. Small, quick on the wing. Male's white belly and flashing wingbars obvious. Rust and blue more difficult to discern. Female appears unmarked. Seen well, shows bluish rump, tail, and wingbars.

VOICE: Song, high, thin, sweet, tumbling, tinkling notes, similar to Black-chinned or Rufous-crowned Sparrow, birds of similar habitat. Call, buzzy *bzzziP!*

RANGE: Arrives mid-April, breeds, departs mid-September. **West Slope:** Fairly common breeder, Foothill chaparral, willow-lined meadows, riparian to Upper Conifer. Rare to Subalpine post-breeding. **East Slope:** Fairly common breeder in aspen, cottonwood, and willow riparian to Subalpine.

SIMILAR SPECIES: **Indigo Bunting female** darker, whisker, faint breast streaks. **Blue Grosbeak female** larger, larger bill, cinnamon wingbars. **Western Bluebird male** gregarious, thin bill.

splotchy

FIRST-SPRING MALE

silver

whitish
throat

faint
streaks

HYBRID MALE
LAZULI X INDIGO

MALE   FEMALE

Indigo Bunting
Passerina cyanea

One's first impression of the male of this mostly eastern species is that of a small, dark bird. However, if the Indigo is bathed in sunlight, the true-blue color of this tail-flicking beauty will be instantly realized.

THE BIRD: Lazuli size, smaller than most sparrows. **Adult male** entirely indigo. Saturation deepest about the face. **Female** upper parts brown, throat pale, often with thin whisker and faint breast streaks. Rump and tail, blushed blue-gray. **First-summer male** variable, female-like, with blue splotches emerging. Where ranges overlap, hybrids between the two species of buntings occur infrequently. Most individuals appear Indigo-like with a white belly or wingbars. Some touched by Lazuli's rusty breast or flanks.

FLIGHT: Small, male appears dark, even blackish; female dull brown. Usually flies toward nearest cover. Flying high, covers ground with jerky bounding progression.

VOICE: Song, sweet series of paired phrases: *cheat, cheat, sweet? sweet? chee, chee, chee*. Difficult to spot in flight, but once learned, the strident, buzzy *bzzziT!* increases your encounters.

RANGE: Primarily an eastern species, it has expanded westward since mid-1900s. Arrives early May, breeds, departs mid-September. **West Slope:** Uncommon regular breeder in South Fork Kern River riparian. Rare elsewhere. **East Slope:** Rare migrant, aspen groves, cottonwood riparian. Hybrids with Lazuli regularly observed at Kern River Preserve, infrequently elsewhere.

SIMILAR SPECIES: See **Lazuli Bunting female**, **Blue Grosbeak female**, **House Finch female**.

BICOLORED

NEVADA

Red-winged Blackbird
Agelaius phoeniceus

Icteridae is a New World family with around 110 species. Males larger, often with gaudy pattern; females smaller in earth tone. In nonbreeding season, most are gregarious in open habitat.

THE BIRD: From Alaska through lower forty-eight, North America has about two dozen subspecies, three regular to Sierra. Slightly smaller than Tricolored. *Nevada* (*A. p. nevadensis*) breeds middle to high altitudes. **Male** coverts edged yellow. Worn, yellow diminished. **Female** paler than *Bicolored*. Rust in back feathers. Underparts streaked. **First-summer male** variable. Dark individual adult-like, dull. Pale individual, female-like, streaked underparts. **Winter male** adult-like, red reduced. Body lightly scaled. **Juvenile** female-like, heavily streaked underparts, face washed orangey. *Bicolored* (*A. p. californicus*) breeds Central Valley, West Slope foothills. **Male**, entirely red coverts. **Female**, blackish belly, throat often pale peach. *Kern* (*A. p. aciculatus*) restricted to eastern Kern County hills. Like *Nevada*, but longer billed.

FLIGHT: Wheeling formations transform. Individuals progress with rapid, shallow bounding. Shorter tailed, rounder winged than other blackbirds.

VOICE: Song variable. *Nevada*, a grinding *konK gurrr REEE!* with piercing *Tieeer* notes. Male flight call, sharp *TINK!* Females, gruff *chek*. *Bicolored* song less defined than *Nevada's*.

RANGE: Both slopes: Locally abundant resident, marshes, wetlands, agricultural fields in foothills March through August. Some winter. Breeds colonially in meadows to Subalpine.

SIMILAR SPECIES: See **Tricolored Blackbird**.

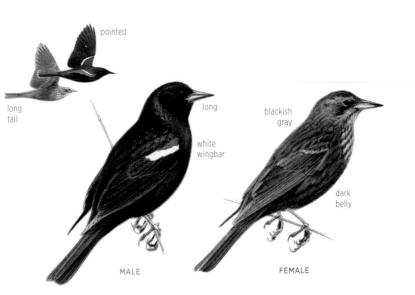

pointed

long
tail

long

white
wingbar

blackish
gray

dark
belly

MALE

FEMALE

Tricolored Blackbird

Agelaius tricolor

"California's Blackbird," this colonial breeder is declining rapidly due to loss of habitat. Tails at steep angles, dense flocks feed on foot for insects and grain. Progressing, Tricoloreds leapfrog over their flock, with rear birds continuously flying to the front.

THE BIRD: Fractionally longer winged, tailed, and billed than Red-winged, creating slightly different profile. **Male,** deep-red coverts, tipped white. Variable, **female** dark sooty with whitish brow, throat, and streaked breast. **Nonbreeding male** adult-like, often conceals red. Plumage scaled whitish overall.

FLIGHT: Compared to Red-winged, Tricolored slightly larger with more pointed wings, longer head, tail, bill. Covering distances, Tricolored flocks form wide horizontal "wing-shaped" mass with birds side by side and shallowly stacked, one above another. Consequently, all birds are vying for first place. Different from the ill-defined blob formation of Red-winged.

VOICE: Song, clamorous, strained, grinding, cat-in-heat-like *greeeeee-AGH!* Call less ringing than Red-winged. Gives conversational, guttural *grek, grik, krek, krek...*

RANGE: Vast majority of global population breeds in the Central Valley and western Sierra foothills. Moves extensively in breeding season, April to mid-June, as well as in winter. **West Slope:** Abundant near tule, cattail marshes, or Himalayan blackberry breeding colonies, Butte south to Kern County, below 1,000 feet. **East Slope:** Very rare. Breeding records, Honey Lake and Carson Valley. Declining populations and habitat losses; now state-listed **Threatened.**

SIMILAR SPECIES: Red-winged Blackbird, *Bicolored* male and female, *Nevada* male.

white

FIRST-YEAR MA

mottled

MALE

FEMALE

Yellow-headed Blackbird
Xanthocephalus xanthocephalus

Breeding or tending young, most birds seek seclusion and calm, correct? Perhaps. After swallows, marsh-nesting blackbirds are as gregarious as breeding songbirds get. And Yellow-headed? It reproduces in a state of utter commotion. Find yourself within a colony late spring, wild and clamorous. Scattered about with egos swollen, chests inflated, displaying males boast and swagger. Bobbing on arching cattails, wings flexed, they endorse their flawless wing spot with the subtlety of a boxer kissing his biceps. Bustling females come and go, bills packed with leggy groceries for perpetually famished chicks. With the single-minded purpose of genetic renewal, males create unearthly noises that startle and amaze.

THE BIRD: Larger than Tricolored Blackbird. **Breeding male** head orangey, vent yellow. **Female** marked by yellow head and breast, often scrawled white. **Immature male** female-like, but blacker with white coverts. **Juvenile**, some rich buff with bold wingbars, others yellow faced.

FLIGHT: Purposeful, strong with shallow loping. Male unmistakable. Female brownish, lacks white in wings. Face and chest yellow.

VOICE: Song, two to three clean introductory notes, followed by grinding "buzz saw" and strangled gulping. Call, husky *TREK!*

RANGE: Arrives mid-April, breeds, departs September. **West Slope:** Foothills, rare to uncommon. In north, breeds Lake Almanor. In south, South Fork Kern River. Rare elsewhere. **East Slope:** Locally abundant colonies in marshes from Sierra Valley south to Owens Valley. Very rare winter.

SIMILAR SPECIES: None.

white edges

flat crown

black

long bill

dull

BREEDING   NONBREEDING

Western Meadowlark
Sturnella neglecta

As winter gives way to spring, stroll curvaceous foothills past oak, weathered barn, and rusty windmill to fields where Holsteins stand, stare, and chew. If suddenly enveloped by auditory sweetness, scan for the vessel that pours forth these crystalline notes, a rotund songbird with long legs and outstanding chest.

THE BIRD: Slightly smaller than California Quail. **Male** larger than **female**, otherwise similar. Upper parts camouflaged by lacy mosaic of grass patterning. Breast sides, flanks streaked blackish brown. **Breeding adult's** brownish upper parts contrast with yellow throat and underparts. Breast with black V. **Nonbreeding adult** blushed by veil of winter feathering. By spring, wear to these feathers reveals full breeding plumage. **Juvenile** lacks breast band; colors muted.

FLIGHT: With stiff wingbeats and frequent glides, meadowlarks appear as if struggling to stay aloft. Winter flocks move fairly low in loosely knit groups. Reducing their speed, they descend with a hovering flutter, flashing their white-sided tails.

VOICE: Song, pure, clear tumbling liquid notes: *See-see, you REALLY SHOULD listen to me!* Flight call, questioning *fwEET?* Utters sharp *chreK!* while flashing white tail feathers. Also, wet, descending trills.

RANGE: Resident in foothill oak savanna, open shrub, tall grass with exposed perches. **West Slope:** Locally common fall to spring, uncommon to Lower Conifer. Post-breeding, sometimes moves to Alpine. **East Slope:** Fairly common sagebrush, agricultural pastures. Uncommon in fall to Alpine.

SIMILAR SPECIES: **Scott's Oriole** song.

light eye

purplish head

MALE

FEMALE

Brewer's Blackbird
Euphagus cyanocephalus

Although Brewer's might not have the bells and whistles of its color-ful cousins, displaying males are no less a wonder to behold. With pale eyes in a trance-like gaze, male perches prominently, bill skyward. Body feathers inflated, wings and tail spread, he gives a strong leg-bounce and emits an up-slurred *gush-SLIT!* Less gregarious than "cattail blackbirds," Brewer's often breeds in blackberry tangles and ornamental conifers. Unburdened by awareness? Venture near their nests, and a smart peck to your head will get your attention. Most encounter this species underfoot at the mall. In an asphalt refuge, nimble birds snatch morsels from crum-bled pastries or forage in the shade of SUVs.

THE BIRD: Larger than Red-winged Blackbird. With staring eyes, **male** is black, glossed green and purple. Brownish **female** has blackish wings and tail. Most have dark eyes, some pale. **Nonbreeding male** shows faint scaled appearance. Brow often pale gray, eyes yellow. **Juvenile** female-like, but wings and tail shorter.

FLIGHT: Winter Brewer's flocks fly in cohesive formations, but are not as adroit as European Starlings. Birds fly directly, with shallow bounding.

VOICE: Song, wet, slurred *gush-SLIT!* Utters slurping conversational sounds, interspersed with dry notes. *CHEK!* call lacks sharp ringing qual-ity of Red-winged.

RANGE: **Both slopes:** Locally abundant resident, foothill towns and farms. Fairly common in developed areas to Subalpine.

SIMILAR SPECIES: **Great-tailed Grackle, Brown-headed Cowbird, Euro-pean Starling**.

light eye · **pale brow** · **glossy**

FEMALE

MALE

Great-tailed Grackle
Quiscalus mexicanus

Appearing intently focused, female stares pale-eyed through smoky "mascara." The life of the party and ever the showman, male brims with self-esteem. With a swaggering stride and sashay of their prodigious tails, grackles appear noble if not a bit snobby, proudly carrying their prominent bills aloft. Displaying male points bill high and lets his oar-like tail hang. Vertical, he flattens his plumage as if squeezing the air from it. Properly slick, his high gloss is presented gift-like to the female, whether she's watching or not. Congregating each evening in communal roosts, marshes, or waterside parks, noisy birds gather, socialize, and, in the safety of numbers, rest.

THE BIRD: Three times a Brewer's Blackbird's weight. Tail keel shaped. **Male** glossed bluish purple. **Female** head and underparts ginger. Upper parts blackish brown. **Immature male** female-like. Glossy plumage emerges with maturity. **Immature female** like dark-eyed adult. **Juvenile,** tail length reduced.

FLIGHT: Level, steady, purposeful. Male's tail appears burdensome, female's smaller.

VOICE: Hard to ignore. Loud "video game" sounds with pure ascending whistle: *fweeeeeeeeeT?* followed by creative clicks, hard *CHEK*s, pristine tones, and a harsh, grating clamor. Roosting, gives repeated *chek*.

RANGE: Expanding from Mexico into western US. Local, colonizing agricultural and urban areas of Sierra foothills, spring–fall. **West Slope:** Mainly Nevada County to Kern County. **East Slope:** Colonies concentrated in Owens, Reno, and Carson Valleys.

SIMILAR SPECIES: **Brewer's Blackbird.**

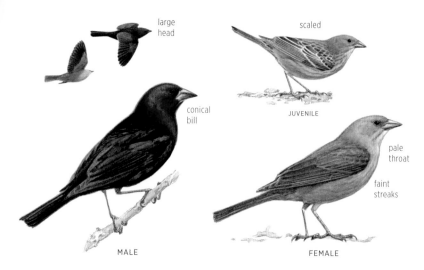

large head

scaled

conical bill

JUVENILE

pale throat

faint streaks

MALE

FEMALE

Brown-headed Cowbird
Molothrus ater

Brood parasites, females deposit their eggs into the clutches of unwitting hosts of over two hundred species. Once hatched, chicks usually outcompete the host's young. Feeding around cattle and pack horses, cowbirds are infrequently encountered in flocks. As livestock numbers increase, so do cowbirds, a reality with negative impacts for songbirds. Parasitism may seem harsh, but it's a part of nature that's been in balance for thousands of years. Before livestock, these birds benefited by associating with wild hooved animals.

THE BIRD: A small, stocky, bull-necked, short-tailed blackbird. **Males** gathering to display point bills high, cock their tails, and with a rowing motion from flared wings, pitch forward, expelling gurgling sounds. Smaller, **female** is somber gray-brown, with wings and tail vaguely darker. Early fall **first-year male** exhibits emerging black feathers. Scaled overall, **juvenile** plumage initially perplexing.

FLIGHT: Progresses hastily with slight bounding. Groups of "inky" males returning in early spring make their way north, typically before females.

VOICE: Song, a three-syllable liquid gurgle ending with high note: *clerk, ka-lurk, tseee?* Call, a strained, piercing *tseee?*

RANGE: Cowbirds first lodged in Yosemite Valley around 1934. Their range has expanded ever since. **Both slopes:** Locally common in Foothill. Fairly common to Subalpine, April through July. Foothill, uncommon fall–winter. Rare to Lower Conifer. Avoids dense stands.

SIMILAR SPECIES: **Brewer's Blackbird**, pale eyes, thinner bill. **House Finch female**, streaked underparts.

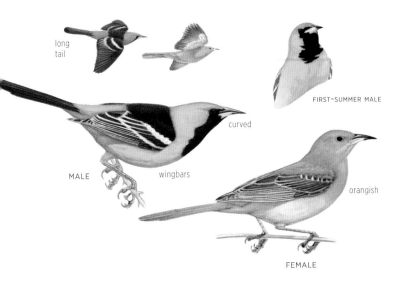

long tail

FIRST-SUMMER MALE

curved

MALE

wingbars

orangish

FEMALE

Hooded Oriole

Icterus cucullatus

The smallest Sierra blackbird. Active, this tail-flicking avian treat arrives from tropical locations. Wedded to fan palms for nesting, it uses the hair-like filaments to weave extraordinarily crafted basket nests to the frond's undersurface. This lofty locale offers shelter from rain and shade for growing offspring. As palms flourish farther north, so goes this bird. Feeding on insects, fruit, and nectar, it favors gardens and hummingbird feeders.

THE BIRD: Smaller, longer tailed than Western Tanager. Lower mandible, bluish based. Fresh **spring male** head, body, and rump orange. Face and bib black. Worn summer birds, yellower. **Female** delicate, slender, furtive, largely yellow-green. Breast orangey. Grayish backed, wingbars thin. **Immature male** female-like, throat black. **Juvenile** female-like, apple green with fleshy gape.

FLIGHT: Long tailed, flies rapidly with shallow bounding. Female dull green overall. Male's orangey-golden rump and black back are striking.

VOICE: Song carries on. Rich, comical phrases intermingled with chatters, *fweet?* notes, and imitations of other species. Call, clear questioning *fweet?* Gives machine-gun chatters: *ch-ch-ch-ch-ch...*

RANGE: Winters in west Mexico. Arrives March, breeds, departs September. Frequents areas with palms. **West Slope:** Locally uncommon in foothills, Nevada County to Kern County. **East Slope:** Uncommon-to-rare migrant, most from Mono and Inyo Counties.

SIMILAR SPECIES: **Bullock's Oriole immature male**, black eye line, narrow black throat. **Scott's Oriole female** larger, streaked back, peppered breast. **Western Tanager female**, thick bill, bold wingbars.

white

orange
tail

eye line

gray

FIRST-SUMMER MALE

pale
gray

MALE

FEMALE

Bullock's Oriole
Icterus bullockii

A bright, bold, beautiful male flashing from shadows into full sun can cause hearts to skip a beat. With a subtle combination of medium gray and orangey yellow, female seems a logical counterbalance to the unequivocally eye-catching male. Feeding, chooses from a wide array of insects, fruit, or nectar. Master of construction, weaves sack-like nest from hair-like fibers, plant cotton, or any delicate filaments.

THE BIRD: Larger than Hooded, about Scott's Oriole size. Orange-and-black **male** has distinct eye line and narrow throat patch. Note black T on orange tail. **Female** shows orangey hood and tail, gray back and wings with fairly bold wingbars. Flanks whitish gray. **Young male** female-like, but richer orange with narrow black throat. **Juvenile** female-like, but muted overall.

FLIGHT: Male obvious and striking. Note white wing patch. Female, orangey head and tail, gray upper parts, pale belly.

VOICE: Song, three to four distinct elements with comical flair and rapid chatters: *chiK, chi-diK, chi-dear, dear, dear.* Call, rapid chatter *chi-chi-chi-chi-chi...*

RANGE: Winters in Mexico. Arrives April, breeds, departs August. **West Slope:** Common Foothill breeder in open oak woodland and riparian forest. Fairly common in black oaks of Lower Conifer. After breeding in migration, uncommon to about 6,000 feet of Upper Conifer. **East Slope:** Fairly common in aspen, cottonwoods, deciduous trees near farms and ranches.

SIMILAR SPECIES: Hooded Oriole immature male small, extensive black throat, green flanks.

FIRST-SUMMER MALE

variable black

MALE

FEMALE

Scott's Oriole
Icterus parisorum

If you're wandering the southern Sierra along desert washes peppered by yucca or lined by Joshua and pinyon-juniper woodland, keep an eye out for a pair of large orioles, and an ear attuned for the male's rich, liquid song wafting across the landscape.

THE BIRD: Bullock's Oriole size. **Male** black hooded and backed with bold wingbars. Greenish-yellow shoulders, belly, rump, and tail base contrast. **Female** with streaked gray back, a unique feature among orioles. She is variably marked black on her face and breast. Greenish or orangey with white wingbars, female can resemble young male. Similarly patterned, **immature male** can breed in first year, so for some individuals, it's diffi-cult to discern sex or age. **Juvenile** appears like a dull female with white wingbars. The bill can show pinkish at the base.

FLIGHT: Often in pairs. Typically flies directly and fairly low. Adult male strikingly black with contrasting yellow-green wing coverts, rump, underparts, and base of outer tail feathers. Female largely greenish with gray back and head.

VOICE: Song, cheerful, meadowlark-like notes. Call, a strong repeated *chu! chu! chu!*

RANGE: Winters in Mexico. Arrives mid-March to mid-April, departs by late August. Uncommon to fairly common breeder. **West Slope:** South-ern and eastern Kern County deserts. **East Slope:** From southern edge of Inyo County, into eastern Kern County.

SIMILAR SPECIES: **Hooded Oriole female** small, greener.

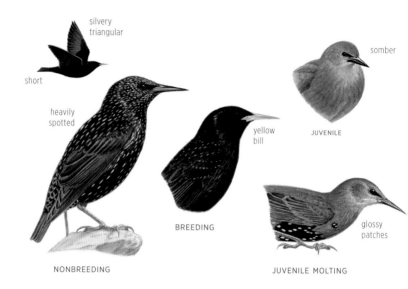

silvery
triangular

short

heavily
spotted

somber

yellow
bill

JUVENILE

BREEDING

glossy
patches

NONBREEDING

JUVENILE MOLTING

European Starling
Sturnus vulgaris

Starlings and mynas belong to an Old World family of over 110 species. European Starling is the sole New World representative. Introduced, it aggressively commandeers nesting cavities of many species. Feeds on insects, small invertebrates, and fruit. Although the name "starling" has nothing to do with the cosmos, winter adults appear blanketed by a galaxy of starry specks. Resembling blackbirds, it differs by having a seasonally yellow bill. Bird attains breeding plumage by losing winter spotting through the effects of wear, thereby revealing the underlying glossy feathering of high plumage.

THE BIRD: Shorter than Brewer's Blackbird, but far heavier. **Juvenile** dull with black bill. As bird matures, iridescent splotches peppered by white dots appear. By **fall**, young bird is largely spotted with a gray head. In **winter**, fresh bird is glossy and heavily spotted with rusty wing-feather edges. In **spring**, the bill turns yellow, **male** with a pale blue base, **female** pinkish. **Breeding adult** glossy blackish with little if any spotting.

FLIGHT: Powerful. Starlings move directly and rapidly. In tremendous numbers they dazzle, creating smoke-like swirling masses.

VOICE: With a wide repertoire, utters slurred notes, clicks, and electronic buzzes. Frequently imitates other species. Taking wing, often gives an annoyed, throaty rolling sound.

RANGE: **Both slopes:** Common resident in developed foothill, agricultural, urban, and suburban areas. Locally abundant in winter.

SIMILAR SPECIES: **Brewer's Blackbird male**, eye white.

APPENDIX A
RARE BIRDS

The following species are considered to be either rare or very rare in the Sierra region. The rare are birds seldom encountered and often highly localized; at least a few individuals occur in the region in all or most years. The very rare are birds not encountered in the region in most years, but a pattern of occurrence may exist over many years or decades.*

JUVENILE

Brant (*Branta bernicla*)

A "sea goose" found on large lakes and reservoirs. West Slope, very rare. East Slope, rare. Mostly spring and fall records from Mono County. Birds that frequent the highly saline and alkali waters of Mono Lake can be bleached light tan.

Eurasian Wigeon (*Mareca penelope*)

Uncommon to rare, this winter to early spring visitor from Siberia is typically found in foothill ponds and marshes on both slopes of the Sierra; nearly always in flocks with American Wigeon.

Greater Scaup (*Aythya marila*)

Visits large lakes and reservoirs from late fall to early spring. Rare on West Slope, more regular on East. Difficulty separating from Lesser Scaup may lead to overreporting.

Surf Scoter (*Melanitta perspicillata*)

Both slopes, fall, winter, and spring visitors to large lakes, reservoirs, and water treatment ponds.

White-winged Scoter (*Melanitta deglandi*)

Winters in low numbers down the California coast. Very rare in fall, winter, and spring, it strays inland slightly more often than Surf Scoter. Visits large lakes and reservoirs on both slopes.

Red-breasted Merganser (*Mergus serrator*)

Uncommon to rare in migration and winter on large lakes and reservoirs. Slightly more regular on East Slope.

BREEDING

NONBREEDING

Pacific Loon (*Gavia pacifica*)

Uncommon and irregular visitor fall, winter, and spring to large Foothill lakes and reservoirs on both slopes. Infrequent to Subalpine. Absent summer.

Horned Grebe (*Podiceps auritus*)

Uncommon fall, winter, or spring visitor to large Foothill lakes and reservoirs on both slopes.

Red-necked Grebe (*Podiceps grisegena*)

Most likely encountered on the East Slope, especially at Lake Tahoe. Most records from fall and winter, with a few in spring at large bodies of water.

Parasitic Jaeger (*Stercorarius parasiticus*)

These "lost" sea birds, primarily juveniles, usually occur in the fall but also in spring or early summer. Mostly found on the East Slope at large bodies of water, including Mono and Crowley Lakes, and Lake Tahoe.

Long-tailed Jaeger (*Stercorarius longicaudus*)

Status similar to Parasitic Jaeger. Found early summer and fall, on large bodies of water on East Slope, including Lake Tahoe, Mono and Crowley Lakes, and Bridgeport Reservoir.

Sabine's Gull (*Xema sabini*)

Rare spring and fall migrant on large lakes, reservoirs, or water treatment ponds primarily on East Slope.

Franklin's Gull (*Leucophaeus pipixcan*)

A long-distance migrant. A rare migrant in spring, summer, and fall, most records from large lakes and reservoirs on East Slope.

Mew Gull (*Larus canus*)

A rare, mostly winter visitor to large lakes and reservoirs on both slopes.

Western Gull (*Larus occidentalis*)

A few records from all seasons on both slopes. West Slope, one adult reported late June at Lake Almanor. More regular just west of the Sierra at Nimbus Dam, Sacramento County.

NONBREEDING

FIRST WINTER

Iceland Gull (*Larus glaucoides*)

Formerly called Thayer's Gull. As with other coastal gulls, inland sightings of Iceland Gull seem to be increasing in late fall and winter. Most Sierra records are from large bodies of water, especially on the East Slope.

NONBREEDING

FIRST WINTER

Glaucous-winged Gull (*Larus glaucescens*)

Like Iceland Gull, appears to be increasing in winter with isolated records from both slopes.

BREEDING

JUVENILE

Solitary Sandpiper (*Tringa solitaria*)

A spring and/or late summer, fall migrant. Frequents marshes and ponds with vegetative cover. Nearly annual East Slope, with most records late July through September.

BREEDING

JUVENILE

Lesser Yellowlegs (*Tringa flavipes*)

Late summer through early fall migrant, both slopes. Frequents wetlands, water treatment ponds, and pond edges, usually with Greater Yellowlegs.

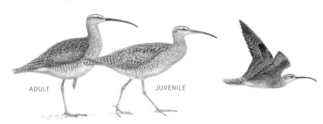

Whimbrel (*Numenius phaeopus*)

Rare in spring on East Slope, fewer from late summer to fall. A long-distance migrant, usually gregarious in dry grassland or shallow ponds.

Marbled Godwit (*Limosa fedoa*)

A rare spring or fall migrant on both slopes, often in flock. More regular on East Slope. Visits short grass, muddy river deltas, and lake edges.

Ruddy Turnstone (*Arenaria interpres*)

Very rare West Slope. Most sightings are from East Slope in May, July, and August.

Red Knot (*Calidris canutus*)

Most late summer, early fall. On East Slope, a few spring records, mostly Mono Basin and Owens Valley.

BREEDING

NONBREEDING

JUVENILE

Sanderling (*Calidris alba*)

Most records are East Slope spring and fall migrants. Found singularly or in small groups visiting muddy areas at creek deltas and lake margins.

BREEDING

JUVENILE

Semipalmated Sandpiper (*Calidris pusilla*)

Nearly all observations are from the East Slope in August, Owens Valley and Mono Basin.

BREEDING

JUVENILE

Baird's Sandpiper (*Calidris bairdii*)

Late summer to early fall migrants. Usually with other shorebirds on muddy edges of lakes and reservoirs. Most records East Slope, south Lake Tahoe to Owens Valley.

JUVENILE

Pectoral Sandpiper (*Calidris melanotos*)

Mainly fall migrant, with peak sightings in September. Prefers more vegetative cover than other *Calidris* sandpipers. Most records East Slope.

Short-billed Dowitcher (*Limnodromus griseus*)

Call, a soft *tew, tew, tew*. Rare away from coast, found only in migration. Most records, juveniles in late August to early September at muddy lakes or river deltas on East Slope. West Slope, very rare.

Red Phalarope (*Phalaropus fulicarius*)

Most records from East Slope in fall. Also, summer records from Honey and Mono Lakes. West Slope, few records.

Least Bittern (*Ixobrychus exilis*)

Historically East Slope marshes near Lake Tahoe, Mono Lake, likely Honey Lake. Most recent records May, June in Mono Basin, Owens Valley. West Slope, records from South Fork Kern River Valley. Secretive. Difficulty accessing suitable habitats makes status uncertain.

Cattle Egret (*Bubulcus ibis*)

Recorded on the East Slope, spring and fall. Occasional records from the South Fork Kern River Valley. Otherwise very rare on West Slope.

ADULT   JUVENILE

Yellow Rail (*Coturnicops noveboracensis*)

Documented breeding in marshlands, Mono Lake, and Bridgeport Reservoir in mid-1900s. Recent records of calling birds, Plumas County. Secretive. Difficulty accessing suitable habitats makes status uncertain.

Barred Owl (*Strix varia*)

Resident. While still rare, this species has recently expanded its range into the Sierra. Recorded as far south as Kings Canyon National Park, Tulare County.

♂   ♀

Broad-tailed Hummingbird (*Selasphorus platycercus*)

Breeds regularly in Great Basin up to eastern edge of Sierra. Aside from occasional breeding season reports from western Mono County, likely very rare. West Slope few, if any, confirmed records.

♂

Allen's Hummingbird (*Selasphorus sasin*)

Status uncertain. Difficult to separate from Rufous Hummingbird. Only safely identified in the hand by width of narrower outer tail feathers. Records on West Slope in Mariposa, Fresno, Tulare, and Kern Counties in spring, late summer, early fall.

ADULT JUVENILE

Cordilleran Flycatcher (*Empidonax occidentalis*)

Essentially identical to Pacific-slope Flycatcher, this species little known in the Sierra is identified by song. Some skeptical of species status consider them simply "Western" Flycatchers. East Slope only. Possible breeding in canyons west of Mono Lake and northern Inyo County.

Cassin's Kingbird (*Tyrannus vociferans*)

Occasional breeder and spring visitor. Has bred in Onyx, Kern County. Records mainly spring in Mono County and Owens Valley.

ADULT JUVENILE

Canada Jay (*Perisoreus canadensis*)

Winter visitor. This species' range barely crosses into the Sierra from the Cascades, but birds occasionally found near Lake Almanor on Christmas Bird Counts. Also fall and winter in Butte County above 5,800 feet.

ADULT FIRST WINTER

Northern Shrike (*Lanius borealis*)

West Slope, rare winter visitor. Recorded Kern River Valley and grasslands west of Yosemite. East Slope, uncommon but regular to flat lowlands north of Tahoe, rare south.

Bohemian Waxwing (*Bombycilla garrulus*)

Winter visitor. Flocks, sometimes large, occasionally winter as far south as Tulare County. Most records East Slope.

Red-eyed Vireo (*Vireo olivaceus*)

All records in late spring and early summer. Nearly all from the South Fork Kern River Valley, where it has bred. Recorded on East Slope at Butterbredt Spring and Mono Basin.

Northern Waterthrush (*Parkesia noveboracensis*)

More regular on East Slope than on West Slope. Late spring, early fall in leafy woodlands with streams in Mono and Kern Counties.

Black-and-White Warbler (*Mniotilta varia*)

Most frequently encountered on East Slope. Found in large deciduous trees and scrubby willows spring and fall in Mono Basin and Upper Owens River. West Slope, singing males recorded in May, Kings Canyon, Fresno County.

American Redstart (*Setophaga ruticilla*)

More regular on East Slope than on West Slope. Recorded in migration in late spring and early fall, usually at low-elevation riparian or desert oases.

Northern Parula (*Setophaga americana*)

A rare late-spring, early summer migrant. Most from mature cottonwoods and willows on East Slope, including Mono Basin.

Lapland Longspur (*Calcarius lapponicus*)

East Slope only, most winters near Honey Lake. Wide-open spaces with short, cropped grasslands, often with pipits, larks, and other longspurs.

Chestnut-collared Longspur (*Calcarius ornatus*)

Less frequent than Lapland Longspur. Most records East Slope. Winters near Honey Lake in wide open spaces with short, cropped grasslands, often with pipits, larks, and other longspurs.

American Tree Sparrow (*Spizella arborea*)

East Slope only. A winter visitor, mostly near Honey Lake and south to the Mono Basin. Found in areas with dense, shrubby vegetation.

FIRST WINTER

BREEDING

Swamp Sparrow (*Melospiza georgiana*)

West Slope, low foothills in winter. East Slope, few spring records in marshy wetlands and willows near Honey Lake, Mono Basin, and the Owens Valley.

WHITE-STRIPED

TAN-STRIPED

FIRST WINTER

White-throated Sparrow (*Zonotrichia albicollis*)

Uncommon or rare regular winter visitor to lowland and interior valleys on both slopes, mid-September through April. Fall migrants encountered mid-October to late November. Recorded to 10,000 feet.

NONBREEDING

FIRST WINTER

Harris's Sparrow (*Zonotrichia querula*)

East Slope, primarily in winter near Honey Lake and Mono Basin. Usually with flocks of "crowned" sparrows.

IMMATURE

Rose-breasted Grosbeak (*Pheucticus ludovicianus*)

Rare but regular migrant May and June, or September and October. Annual visitor to both slopes, mostly below 3,000 feet in the central Sierra, typically at bird feeders or in riparian habitat.

*For a list of "Accidental" species through 2011, please consult Beedy and Pandolfino, *Birds of the Sierra Nevada: Their Natural History, Status, and Distribution* (2013). Defined as: "Encountered in the region on one or a few occasions, and the species is well out of its normal range."

FULL CHECKLIST OF THE BIRDS IN THIS BOOK

Note: The order of the bird families on this list follows Howell, O'Brien, Sullivan, Wood, Lewington, and Crossley (2009). For a complete list of all bird species that have been documented in the Sierra region through 2011, please consult Beedy and Pandolfino (2013). This list includes accidentals that have been encountered on fewer than five occasions and are far outside their normal range.

SPECIAL-STATUS BIRD SPECIES IN THE SIERRA NEVADA (STATE AND FEDERAL LISTINGS)

State-listed Threatened (ST)
State-listed Endangered (SE)
Federally listed Threatened (FT)
Federally listed Endangered (FE)
California Bird Species of Special Concern (SSC)

Rare (R): Seldom encountered and often highly localized; at least a few individuals occur in the region in all or most years. This is not a formal state or federal designation for the species.

Very Rare (VR): Not encountered in the Sierra region in most years, but a pattern of occurrence may exist over many years or decades. This is not a formal state or federal designation for the species.

Bold indicates species that appear in Appendix A: Rare Birds and not in the main text of the book.

WATERBIRDS

SWIMMING WATERBIRDS

WATERFOWL (ANATIDAE)

- [ ] Greater White-fronted Goose
- [ ] Snow Goose
- [ ] Ross's Goose
- [ ] **Brant, SSC, VR**
- [ ] Cackling Goose
- [ ] Canada Goose
- [ ] Tundra Swan
- [ ] Wood Duck
- [ ] Blue-winged Teal
- [ ] Cinnamon Teal
- [ ] Northern Shoveler
- [ ] Gadwall
- [ ] **Eurasian Wigeon, R**
- [ ] American Wigeon
- [ ] Mallard
- [ ] Northern Pintail
- [ ] Green-winged Teal
- [ ] Canvasback
- [ ] Redhead, SSC
- [ ] Ring-necked Duck
- [ ] **Greater Scaup, R**
- [ ] Lesser Scaup
- [ ] Harlequin Duck, SSC
- [ ] **Surf Scoter, VR**
- [ ] **White-winged Scoter, VR**
- [ ] Bufflehead
- [ ] Common Goldeneye
- [ ] Barrow's Goldeneye
- [ ] Hooded Merganser
- [ ] Common Merganser
- [ ] **Red-breasted Merganser, R**
- [ ] Ruddy Duck

CORMORANT (PHALACROCORACIDAE)

- [ ] Double-crested Cormorant

LOONS (GAVIIDAE)

- [ ] **Pacific Loon, R**
- [ ] Common Loon

GREBES (PODICIPEDIDAE)

- [ ] Pied-billed Grebe
- [ ] **Horned Grebe R**
- [ ] **Red-necked Grebe, VR**
- [ ] Eared Grebe
- [ ] Western Grebe
- [ ] Clark's Grebe

FLYING WATERBIRDS

PELICAN (PELECANIDAE)

- [ ] American White Pelican, SSC

JAEGERS (STERCORARIIDAE)

- [ ] **Parasitic Jaeger, VR**
- [ ] **Long-tailed Jaeger, VR**

GULLS AND TERNS (LARIDAE)

- [ ] **Sabine's Gull, R**
- [ ] Bonaparte's Gull
- [ ] **Franklin's Gull, R**
- [ ] **Mew Gull, R**
- [ ] Ring-billed Gull
- [ ] **Western Gull, VR**
- [ ] California Gull
- [ ] Herring Gull
- [ ] **Iceland Gull, VR**
- [ ] **Glaucous-winged Gull, VR**
- [ ] Caspian Tern
- [ ] Black Tern
- [ ] Common Tern
- [ ] Forster's Tern

WALKING WATERBIRDS

PLOVERS (CHARADRIIDAE)

- [ ] Black-bellied Plover
- [ ] Snowy Plover, FT, SSC

- [ ] Semipalmated Plover
- [ ] Killdeer

STILT AND AVOCET (RECURVIROSTRIDAE)

- [ ] Black-necked Stilt
- [ ] American Avocet

SANDPIPERS (SCOLOPACIDAE)

- [ ] Spotted Sandpiper
- [ ] **Solitary Sandpiper, R**
- [ ] Greater Yellowlegs
- [ ] **Lesser Yellowlegs, R**
- [ ] Willet
- [ ] **Whimbrel, R**
- [ ] Long-billed Curlew
- [ ] **Marbled Godwit, R**
- [ ] **Ruddy Turnstone, VR**
- [ ] **Red Knot, VR**
- [ ] **Sanderling, VR**
- [ ] Western Sandpiper
- [ ] **Semipalmated Sandpiper, VR**
- [ ] Least Sandpiper
- [ ] **Baird's Sandpiper, R**
- [ ] **Pectoral Sandpiper, R**
- [ ] Dunlin
- [ ] **Short-billed Dowitcher, VR**
- [ ] Long-billed Dowitcher
- [ ] Wilson's Snipe
- [ ] Wilson's Phalarope
- [ ] Red-necked Phalarope
- [ ] **Red Phalarope, VR**

HERONS (ARDEIDAE)

- [ ] American Bittern
- [ ] **Least Bittern, SSC, VR**
- [ ] Great Blue Heron
- [ ] Great Egret
- [ ] Snowy Egret
- [ ] **Cattle Egret, VR**
- [ ] Green Heron

- [ ] Black-crowned Night-Heron

IBIS (THRESKIORNITHIDAE)

- [ ] White-faced Ibis

CRANE (GRUIDAE)

- [ ] Sandhill Crane

RAILS (RALLIDAE)

- [ ] Black Rail, ST
- [ ] **Yellow Rail, VR**
- [ ] Virginia Rail
- [ ] Sora
- [ ] Common Gallinule
- [ ] American Coot

LANDBIRDS

UPLAND GAMEBIRDS

QUAIL (ODONTOPHORIDAE)

- [ ] Mountain Quail
- [ ] California Quail

FOWL-LIKE BIRDS (PHASIANIDAE)

- [ ] Wild Turkey
- [ ] White-tailed Ptarmigan
- [ ] Greater Sage-Grouse, SSC
- [ ] Sooty Grouse
- [ ] Ring-necked Pheasant
- [ ] Chukar

RAPTORS

VULTURES (CATHARTIDAE)

- [ ] Turkey Vulture
- [ ] California Condor, SE, FE

OSPREY (PANDIONIDAE)

- [ ] Osprey

HAWKS (ACCIPITRIDAE)

- [ ] White-tailed Kite
- [ ] Bald Eagle, SE
- [ ] Northern Harrier, SSC
- [ ] Sharp-shinned Hawk
- [ ] Cooper's Hawk
- [ ] Northern Goshawk, SSC
- [ ] Red-shouldered Hawk
- [ ] Swainson's Hawk, ST
- [ ] Red-tailed Hawk
- [ ] Ferruginous Hawk
- [ ] Rough-legged Hawk
- [ ] Golden Eagle

FALCONS (FALCONIDAE)

- [ ] American Kestrel
- [ ] Merlin
- [ ] Peregrine Falcon
- [ ] Prairie Falcon

BARN OWL (TYTONIDAE)

- [ ] Barn Owl

TYPICAL OWLS (STRIGIDAE)

- [ ] Flammulated Owl
- [ ] Western Screech-Owl
- [ ] Great Horned Owl
- [ ] Northern Pygmy-Owl
- [ ] Burrowing Owl, SSC
- [ ] Spotted Owl, SSC
- [ ] **Barred Owl, VR**
- [ ] Great Gray Owl, SE
- [ ] Long-eared Owl, SSC
- [ ] Short-eared Owl, SSC
- [ ] Northern Saw-whet Owl

OTHER LARGER LANDBIRDS

NIGHTJARS (CAPRIMULGIDAE)

- [ ] Lesser Nighthawk
- [ ] Common Nighthawk
- [ ] Common Poorwill

PIGEONS AND DOVES (COLUMBIDAE)

- [ ] Rock Pigeon
- [ ] Band-tailed Pigeon
- [ ] Eurasian Collared-Dove
- [ ] Mourning Dove

CUCKOOS (CUCULIDAE)

- [ ] Yellow-billed Cuckoo, FT, SE
- [ ] Greater Roadrunner

KINGFISHER (ALCEDINIDAE)

- [ ] Belted Kingfisher

WOODPECKERS (PICIDAE)

- [ ] Lewis's Woodpecker
- [ ] Acorn Woodpecker
- [ ] Williamson's Sapsucker
- [ ] Red-naped Sapsucker
- [ ] Red-breasted Sapsucker
- [ ] Ladder-backed Woodpecker
- [ ] Nuttall's Woodpecker
- [ ] Downy Woodpecker
- [ ] Hairy Woodpecker
- [ ] White-headed Woodpecker
- [ ] Black-backed Woodpecker
- [ ] Northern Flicker
- [ ] Pileated Woodpecker

AERIAL LANDBIRDS

HUMMINGBIRDS (TROCHILIDAE)

- [ ] Black-chinned Hummingbird
- [ ] Anna's Hummingbird
- [ ] Costa's Hummingbird
- [ ] Calliope Hummingbird
- [ ] **Broad-tailed Hummingbird, R**

- [ ] Rufous Hummingbird
- [ ] **Allen's Hummingbird, VR**

SWIFTS (APODIDAE)

- [ ] Black Swift, SSC
- [ ] Vaux's Swift, SSC
- [ ] White-throated Swift

SWALLOWS (HIRUNDINIDAE)

- [ ] Purple Martin, SSC
- [ ] Tree Swallow
- [ ] Violet-green Swallow
- [ ] Northern Rough-winged Swallow
- [ ] Bank Swallow, ST
- [ ] Cliff Swallow
- [ ] Barn Swallow

SONGBIRDS

TYRANT-FLYCATCHERS (TYRANNIDAE)

- [ ] Olive-sided Flycatcher, SSC
- [ ] Western Wood-Pewee
- [ ] Willow Flycatcher, SE, FE
- [ ] Hammond's Flycatcher
- [ ] Gray Flycatcher
- [ ] Dusky Flycatcher
- [ ] Pacific-slope Flycatcher
- [ ] **Cordilleran Flycatcher, VR**
- [ ] Black Phoebe
- [ ] Say's Phoebe
- [ ] Vermilion Flycatcher, SSC
- [ ] Ash-throated Flycatcher
- [ ] Brown-crested Flycatcher
- [ ] **Cassin's Kingbird, R**
- [ ] Western Kingbird

CORVIDS (CORVIDAE)

- [ ] **Canada Jay, R**
- [ ] Pinyon Jay
- [ ] Steller's Jay
- [ ] California Scrub-Jay

- [ ] Woodhouse's Scrub-Jay
- [ ] Clark's Nutcracker
- [ ] Black-billed Magpie
- [ ] Yellow-billed Magpie
- [ ] American Crow
- [ ] Common Raven

SHRIKES (LANIIDAE)

- [ ] Loggerhead Shrike, SSC
- [ ] **Northern Shrike, R**

MIMIDS (MIMIDAE)

- [ ] Northern Mockingbird
- [ ] Sage Thrasher
- [ ] Bendire's Thrasher, SSC
- [ ] California Thrasher
- [ ] LeConte's Thrasher, SSC

THRUSHES (TURDIDAE)

- [ ] Western Bluebird
- [ ] Mountain Bluebird
- [ ] Townsend's Solitaire
- [ ] Swainson's Thrush
- [ ] Hermit Thrush
- [ ] American Robin
- [ ] Varied Thrush

DIPPER (CINCLIDAE)

- [ ] American Dipper

WAXWINGS (BOMBYCILLIDAE)

- [ ] **Bohemian Waxwing, R**
- [ ] Cedar Waxwing

PHAINOPEPLA (PTILOGONATIDAE)

- [ ] Phainopepla

PARIDS (PARIDAE)

- [ ] Mountain Chickadee
- [ ] Chestnut-backed Chickadee
- [ ] Oak Titmouse
- [ ] Juniper Titmouse

NUTHATCHES (SITTIDAE)

- [ ] Red-breasted Nuthatch
- [ ] White-breasted Nuthatch
- [ ] Pygmy Nuthatch

CREEPER (CERTHIIDAE)

- [ ] Brown Creeper

VERDIN (REMIZIDAE)

- [ ] Verdin

BUSHTIT (AEGITHALIDAE)

- [ ] Bushtit

WRENTIT (SYLVIIDAE)

- [ ] Wrentit

WRENS (TROGLODYTIDAE)

- [ ] Cactus Wren
- [ ] Rock Wren
- [ ] Canyon Wren
- [ ] Bewick's Wren
- [ ] House Wren
- [ ] Pacific Wren
- [ ] Marsh Wren

GNATCATCHER (POLIOPTILIDAE)

- [ ] Blue-gray Gnatcatcher

KINGLETS (REGULIDAE)

- [ ] Golden-crowned Kinglet
- [ ] Ruby-crowned Kinglet

VIREOS (VIREONIDAE)

- [ ] Bell's Vireo, SE, FE
- [ ] Plumbeous Vireo
- [ ] Cassin's Vireo
- [ ] Hutton's Vireo
- [ ] Warbling Vireo
- [ ] **Red-eyed Vireo, VR**

WOOD-WARBLERS (PARULIDAE)

- [ ] **Northern Waterthrush, VR**
- [ ] **Black-and-White Warbler, VR**
- [ ] Orange-crowned Warbler
- [ ] Nashville Warbler
- [ ] Virginia's Warbler
- [ ] MacGillivray's Warbler
- [ ] Common Yellowthroat
- [ ] Wilson's Warbler
- [ ] **American Redstart, VR**
- [ ] **Northern Parula, VR**
- [ ] Yellow Warbler
- [ ] Yellow-rumped Warbler
- [ ] Black-throated Gray Warbler
- [ ] Townsend's Warbler
- [ ] Hermit Warbler

CHAT (ICTERIIDAE)

- [ ] Yellow-breasted Chat, SSC

PIPIT (MOTACILLIDAE)

- [ ] American Pipit

LARK (ALAUDIDAE)

- [ ] Horned Lark

LONGSPURS (CALCARIIDAE)

- [ ] **Lapland Longspur, VR**
- [ ] **Chestnut-collared Longspur, VR**

NEW WORLD SPARROWS (PASSERELLIDAE)

- [ ] Green-tailed Towhee
- [ ] Spotted Towhee
- [ ] California Towhee
- [ ] Rufous-crowned Sparrow
- [ ] **American Tree Sparrow, VR**
- [ ] Chipping Sparrow
- [ ] Brewer's Sparrow
- [ ] Black-chinned Sparrow

Vesper Sparrow, SSC
Lark Sparrow
Black-throated Sparrow
Bell's Sparrow
Sagebrush Sparrow
Savannah Sparrow
Grasshopper Sparrow
Fox Sparrow
Song Sparrow
Lincoln's Sparrow
Swamp Sparrow, VR
White-throated Sparrow, R
Harris's Sparrow, VR
White-crowned Sparrow
Golden-crowned Sparrow
Dark-eyed Junco

OLD WORLD SPARROW (PASSERIDAE)

House Sparrow

FINCHES (FRINGILLIDAE)

Gray-crowned Rosy-Finch
Pine Grosbeak
Purple Finch
Cassin's Finch
House Finch
Red Crossbill
Pine Siskin
Lesser Goldfinch
Lawrence's Goldfinch
American Goldfinch
Evening Grosbeak

TANAGERS, GROSBEAKS, AND BUNTINGS (CARDINALIDAE)

Summer Tanager, SSC
Western Tanager
Rose-breasted Grosbeak, R
Black-headed Grosbeak
Blue Grosbeak
Lazuli Bunting
Indigo Bunting

NEW WORLD BLACKBIRDS, ORIOLES, AND ALLIES (ICTERIDAE)

Red-winged Blackbird
Tricolored Blackbird, ST
Yellow-headed Blackbird, SSC
Western Meadowlark
Brewer's Blackbird
Great-tailed Grackle
Brown-headed Cowbird
Hooded Oriole
Bullock's Oriole
Scott's Oriole

STARLING (STURNIDAE)

European Starling

Bibliography

PUBLICATIONS

Beedy, E. C., and E. R. Pandolfino. 2013. *Birds of the Sierra Nevada: Their Natural History, Status, and Distribution.* Illustrated by Keith Hansen. Berkeley and Los Angeles: University of California Press.

California Department of Fish and Wildlife, California Natural Diversity Database. 2019. *Special Animals List.* (Periodic publication).

Dawson, W. L. 1923. *The Birds of California.* 4 vols. San Francisco: South Moulton.

Dunn, J. L., and J. Alderfer. 2017. *Field Guide to the Birds of North America.* 7th ed. Washington, DC: National Geographic Society.

Dunn, J. L., and K. L. Garrett. 1997. *Peterson Field Guides: Warblers.* New York: Houghton Mifflin.

Farrand, J. 1983. *The Audubon Society Master Guide to Birding.* Vols. 1–3. New York: Knopf.

Gaines, D. 1992. *Birds of Yosemite and the East Slope*, 2nd printing revised and updated by Sally Gaines. Lee Vining, CA: Artemisia Press.

Grinnell, J., and A. H. Miller. 1944. *The Distribution of the Birds of California.* Pacific Coast Avifauna, No. 27. Berkeley, CA: Cooper Ornithological Club.

Grinnell, J., and T. I. Storer. 1924. *Animal Life in the Yosemite.* Berkeley: University of California Press.

Hoffmann, R. 1927. *Birds of the Pacific States.* Cambridge, MA: Riverside Press.

Howell, S.N.G. 2003. *Hummingbirds of North America: The Photographic Guide.* London: Academic Press.

Howell, S.N.G. 2010. *Peterson Reference Guides: Molt in North American Birds.* New York: Houghton Mifflin.

Howell, S.N.G., and J. L. Dunn. 2007. *Peterson Reference Guides: Gulls of the Americas.* New York: Houghton Mifflin.

Howell, S.N.G., M. O'Brien, B. L. Sullivan, C. L. Wood, I. Lewington, and R. Crossley. 2009. "The Purpose of Field Guides: Taxonomy vs. Utility?" *Birding* 41, no. 6: 44–49.

Howell, S.N.G., and B. Sullivan. 2018. *Peterson Guide to Bird Identification—in 12 Steps.* New York: Houghton Mifflin Harcourt.

Kaufman, K. 2000. *Birds of North America*. New York: Houghton Mifflin.

Laws, J. M. 2007. *The Laws Field Guide to the Sierra Nevada*. Berkeley, CA: Heyday.

Madge, S., and H. Burn. 1988. *Waterfowl: An Identification Guide to the Ducks, Geese and Swans of the World*. New York: Houghton Mifflin.

Pyle, P. 1997. *Identification Guide to North American Birds, Part I*. Bolinas, CA: Slate Creek Press.

Pyle, P. 2008. *Identification Guide to North American Birds, Part II*. Bolinas, CA: Slate Creek Press.

Shuford, W. D., and T. Gardali, eds. 2008. *California Bird Species of Special Concern: A Ranked Assessment of Species, Subspecies, and Distinct Populations of Birds of Immediate Conservation Concern in California*. Studies of Western Birds 1. Camarillo, CA: Western Field Ornithologists; Sacramento, CA: California Department of Fish and Game.

Sibley, D. A. 2003. *The Sibley Field Guide to Birds of Western North America*. New York: Knopf.

Sibley, D. A. 2014. *The Sibley Guide to Birds, Second Edition*. New York: Knopf.

Stokes, D., and L. Stokes. 2010. *The Stokes Field Guide to the Birds of North America*. New York: Little, Brown.

Quady, D. E., J. L. Dunn, K. L. Garrett, and B. E. Small. 2015. *Birds of Northern California*. Olympia, WA: R. W. Morse.

Wheeler, B. 2003. *Raptors of Western North America*. Princeton, NJ: Princeton University Press.

Williamson, S. L. 2013. *Peterson Field Guides: Hummingbirds of North America*. New York: Houghton Mifflin.

Winkler, D. W., S. M. Billerman, and I. J. Lovette. 2015. *Bird Families of the World*. Barcelona: Lynx Edicions; Ithaca, NY: Cornell Lab of Ornithology.

WEBSITES

eBird: ebird.org

Birds of the World: birdsoftheworld.org

Xeno Canto: xeno-canto.org

Index
INDEX OF COMMON NAMES

Main entries for a particular species appear in **bold**.

INDEX OF SCIENTIFIC NAMES

About the Authors

A barefoot kid exploring the woods of Maryland, KEITH HANSEN was happiest when outdoors. Captivated by birds, he began drawing them as a teenager. Life was a generous mix of art and travel as he illustrated numerous books, ornithological publications, and countless private commissions. In addition, he and several family members illustrated a 128-foot-long mural of the San Joaquin River. Keith counts himself fortunate to have birded the Galapagos Islands and worked aboard an NOAA vessel in the tropical Pacific. Gathering fundamental experience regarding bird anatomy, he studied and banded many hundreds over the years on California's Farallon Islands through the Point Reyes Bird Observatory. He has taken great pleasure exploring the Amazon, Scotland, the Andes, and the French Pyrenees. The New World tropics hold a special place in his heart; he has led tours to Guyana, Trinidad, Tobago, and Panama's Darien Gap. In addition, he and his wife, Patricia, have led tours to Costa Rica, Oaxaca, her native Yucatan, and extensively throughout Guatemala. They reside in Bolinas, California, where Keith has a gallery and studio.

EDWARD C. "TED" BEEDY has been birding in the Sierra for more than sixty years, ever since he was awarded his Bird Watching merit badge in the Cub Scouts in 1957. He received his BSc (zoology and English), MSc, and PhD (the latter both in zoology) from the University of California, Davis (UCD). His master's thesis concerned birds of the Donner Summit region, and his dissertation research focused on conifer forest bird communities of Yosemite. He taught ornithology and other biology classes at UCD and California State University, Sacramento, before starting his career in 1985 as an environmental consultant at Jones & Stokes (J&S) in

Sacramento. During the more than twenty years he worked at J&S, Ted conducted long-term studies of Tricolored Blackbirds, as well as sensitive bird species at Mono Lake, South Fork Kern River Valley, Sierra Valley, Sequoia National Park, and elsewhere in the Sierra. He coauthored *Birds of the Sierra Nevada: Their Natural History, Status, and Distribution* with Dr. Ed Pandolfino, illustrated by Keith Hansen. In 2006, he started his own firm, Beedy Environmental Consulting, at his home in Nevada City, where he lives with his wife, Susan Sanders, and a pond full of Mallards and Wood Ducks.

ADAM DONKIN grew up with a pair of binoculars around his neck, studying the birds and wildlife of Wolf Creek in the foothills of the Sierra under the tutelage of California birding legend Rich Stallcup. He has spent the last twenty years designing apps and games for major tech companies in Silicon Valley, volunteering as an advisor for Cornell's Lab of Ornithology, continuing to lead birding tours, and mentoring young birders. Adam is cofounder of Flock LLC, where he creates mobile app experiences that encourage people to fall in love with nature through birding. Adam and his wife, Devon, and son, Isaac, live in Forest Knolls, California, where they work together to restore the native ecology around their home, enjoying the birds and wildlife who have taken up residence there.

About Sierra College Press

The Sierra College Press endeavors to reach beyond the library, laboratory, and classroom to promote and examine the Sierra Nevada. For more information, please visit www.sierracollege.edu/press.

Board of Directors: Rebecca Bocchicchio, Sean Booth, Kerrie Cassidy, Dan DeFoe, David Dickson, Tom Fillebrown, Christine Freeman, Rebecca Gregg, Brian Haley, Rick Heide, Jay Hester, David Kuchera, Joe Medeiros (Editor-in-Chief), Lynn Medeiros, Sue Michaels, Gary Noy, Bart O'Brien, Sabrina Pape (Board Chair), Mike Price, Jennifer Skillen, Barbara Vineyard, Lynette Vrooman, and Randy White.

SIERRA COLLEGE PRESS